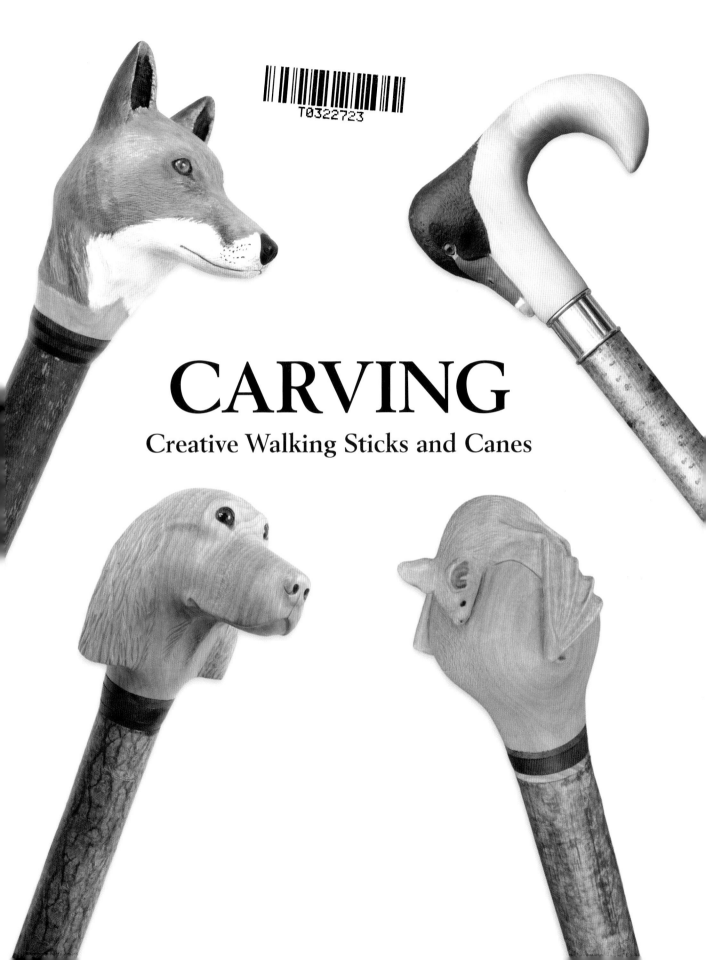

CARVING

Creative Walking Sticks and Canes

ISBN 978-1-4971-0011-4

Library of Congress Control Number:2019945988

To learn more about the other great books from Fox Chapel Publishing, or to find a retailer near you,
call toll-free 800-457-9112 or visit us at *www.FoxChapelPublishing.com*.

We are always looking for talented authors. To submit an idea, please send a brief inquiry to
acquisitions@foxchapelpublishing.com.

Printed in the United States of America
First printing

CARVING
Creative Walking Sticks and Canes

13 Projects to Carve in Wood

Paul Purnell

Fox Chapel
PUBLISHING
www.FoxChapelPublishing.com

Table of Contents

A Brief History

Walking sticks have been used since the dawn of time as walking supports, weapons of offense and defense, badges of honor, status symbols, and even tippling sticks, where a flask of alcohol was concealed within the stick. Shepherds of Britain were probably the first to adapt a stick with a crook for a specific purpose relating to their work.

Many famous historical figures have been collectors of sticks or canes. Dating back to 1358 BC, Tutankhamen had approximately 130 elaborately carved sticks (some with gold adornments) in his tomb to assist his travels in the afterlife. Other famous names include Henry VIII, Winston Churchill, Queen Victoria, Napoleon Bonaparte, and the first President of the United States, George Washington.

In the 1600s walking sticks became a fashion accessory, and their elaborate designs were an indication of wealth and social standing. At this time the shafts were made from reeds, rattan, bamboo, and cane. Hence, the term "canes" was born.

However, this may not be the true origin of the word *cane*. During the time of the Romans, savage packs of wild dogs roamed the cities and towns, scavenging for food. For protection, people carried a cudgel made of wood with spikes inserted in one end. The word *canis* was the Latin word for dog, and the plural of *canis* is *canes*. Today, the terminology of a walking stick or a cane is interchangeable.

Although in the United Kingdom a cane is still seen as a fairly short shank without a curved handle, the opposite is true in the United States. In the UK, traditional sticks are deemed to be functional, while the fancy sticks are for show or as collectors' items, and the original term used for making a traditional crook with a horn or wood handle is "stick dressing."

Over time, conventions have developed as to the size and shape of the traditional sticks when entering competitions, whereas sticks with more elaborate heads depicting animals, ducks, etc., have few restrictions other than the stick and head needing to look balanced. The range of decoration of these sticks is a testament to the artistic talent and ingenuity of their makers.

Paul Purnell

CHAPTER 1
Tools

Some carving traditionalists will say that only carving with hand tools is "real" carving and using any sort of power tools is not acceptable. Some will say that wood should never be painted. Everyone has an opinion. However, with the possible exception of when running a business, I believe that carving should be enjoyable, and any advice on tools, materials, and techniques should be helpful but not prescriptive.

You may try one of the many styles of carving, from the smallest netsuke through to chainsaw carving of a tree trunk. You will find what aspects of carving you enjoy and those that frustrate. After a few years of practice, you will develop your own individual style and discover what tools and materials you prefer and the techniques that suit you.

My style is a combination of power and hand tools, and I hope that the following information that I have discovered during my years of making walking sticks will help.

Band Saw

It was only after many years of carving that I treated myself to a band saw. If I could do it all over again, this would be first on my list of purchases. It is only when you have a band saw that you realize how much time is wasted when struggling to cut a blank with a handsaw, coping saw, or jigsaw.

You do not need a massive financial outlay to acquire a reasonable band saw. A small benchtop saw with an 8"–10" (20–25cm) throat is more than adequate for most woodcarving projects. The first thing to do when buying a band saw at the cheaper end of the market is to throw away the blade that it comes with, as it is likely to be of poor quality. The wobbly lines such a blade will make will make you wonder why you bothered buying the band saw.

Buy the best blade you can afford, even for a small hobby-rated machine.

The second most important thing to do is to learn how to set up the blade correctly, as without this you will have difficulty making straight cuts, no matter the quality of the blade. Check the blade manufacturer's website for instructions on setting up the blade properly. The blade width will depend on your projects. A ¼" (6mm) blade will cut a tighter radius; however, the ½" (13mm) blade will cater to most of your needs when making walking sticks.

One of the huge benefits of a band saw is the ability to cut the blank in two planes. You must start with a block that has 90-degree angles. The process for cutting out a hare head for a walking stick is provided on the following page.

A ½" (13mm) blade will accommodate most of your cutting needs when making walking sticks.

With a band saw, you can cut a blank in two planes.

Rotary Tool

A rotary machine is needed for power carving, and a flexi-shaft is an important addition, as it removes the weight and awkwardness of having to hold onto the machine. There are many makes of small handheld, hobby-rated tools. The type you choose depends on what you are carving and for what length of time the rotary tool will be operating.

I wasted time and money on buying different makes of the smaller type of rotary tools, as most burned out within a year. Then I purchased a Foredom® flexi-shaft with a hand controller. What a difference! The quality, reliability, and torque are impressive. The machine will deal with anything you throw at it, and with its ability to take a ¼" shank bit, roughing out is made easy. There are many different Foredom machines available in the US, but the choice is limited in the UK.

The general-purpose handpieces (see photo on page 8) comes with three collets for shank sizes: ³⁄₃₂", ⅛", and ¼". Quick-change handpieces shown below are available but only for the ³⁄₃₂" shank. Having a couple of handpieces each fitted with your favorite bit will reduce the need for frequent changes of collet.

Some carvers will have two or more machines to

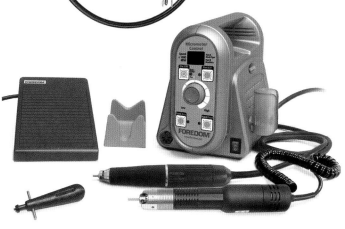

Foredom rotary tools are available with either hand controls (top) or foot controls (bottom).

CUTTING OUT A HEAD

1 Draw both the side and plan views on the wood block.

2 Use the band saw to cut one view. In this case, it is the plan view.

3 Secure the cut pieces back to the block with masking tape.

4 Cut out the side view. After removing the tape, all the cut pieces will fall away and you will be left with a blank that will reduce the amount of roughing out required.

The general-purpose handpiece accommodates ³⁄₃₂", ⅛", and ¼" shank sizes.

Two ends of the spectrum: compare this 1" by 1" (25 x 25mm) carbide-point bit (left) with this ¹⁄₆₄" (0.5mm) small dental carbide cutter (right).

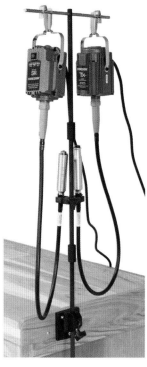

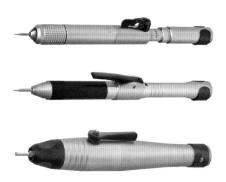

Quick-change handpieces are available only for ³⁄₃₂" shanks.

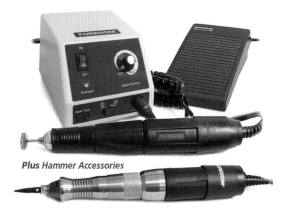

Plus Hammer Accessories

Micro-motors have smaller handpieces that are less tiring and useful for curving strokes with detailing stones.

A Foredom hanger is ideal for carvers using more than one rotary tool.

cover every eventuality. Foredom makes hangers (above right) in different styles and fixing brackets to cater for this.

If you intend to carve fine detail, a micro-motor (above center) is an invaluable addition to your main flexi-drive machine. While it does not have the torque of the Foredom machines, it has a smaller and more comfortable handpiece. This is less tiring on your hand and helps with the wrist movement required for curving the strokes when using the detailing stones.

When carving with a power tool, ensure that your sleeves are tucked out of reach of the bits, especially the carbide points. They love to snag on clothing, which could result in motor problems if you are holding the machine, or they will shear the inner cable of a flexi-shaft—a design feature to protect the motor.

Bits & Burrs

There is a bewildering quantity of burrs, bits, and buffers for a rotary machine. The photo above shows two ends of the spectrum of choice: a carbide-point bit at 1" by 1"

(25 x 25mm) with a ¼" shank and the smallest dental carbide cutter of ¹⁄₆₄" (0.5mm).

Fortunately, Saburrtooth® has every base covered with its extensive range of bits with razor-sharp, carbide cutting teeth in extra coarse (orange), coarse (green), and fine (yellow) for five shank sizes: ¼", ⅛", ³⁄₃₂", 6mm, and 3mm. (Other brands, such as Foredom and Kutzal®, also use color to distinguish courseness.)

The coarse bits (green) with the ¼" (6mm) shank are aggressive and extremely efficient at removing material during the roughing out stage. The ¼" (6mm) bits with fine cutting teeth (yellow) will effortlessly remove the marks left by the coarse bits and leave the wood ready for sanding.

With such a massive selection to choose from, where do you start? This will depend on your style of carving. There are some bits that you may use occasionally for a specific task, but there will always be a few personal favorites that you reach for most of the time. For carving the projects in this book, this is a selection of the carbide-point bits that I used. The choice is yours, but if you can, buy a couple of quality carbide-point bits, such as Saburrtooth, as they will last a lifetime.

 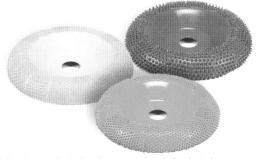

For even faster removal of wood, Saburrtooth has buzzouts (left) and donut wheels (right), but they need to be fitted to a separate angle-head grinding unit.

Types of Bits

For Roughing Out (First Stage)			For Roughing Out (Second Stage)		
¼" shank bull nose, ½" by 2" (coarse grit) 	¼" shank flame, ¾" (coarse grit) 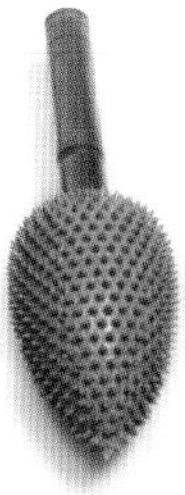	¼" shank bull nose, ¾" (coarse grit) 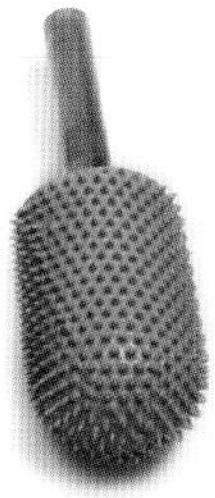	¼" shank ball (fine grit) 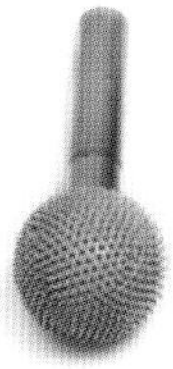	¼" shank bull nose, ½" (fine grit) 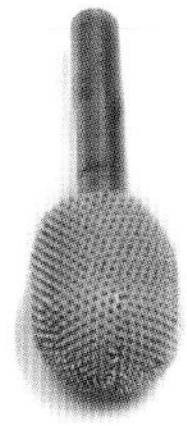	¼" shank cylinder, 1" (fine grit) 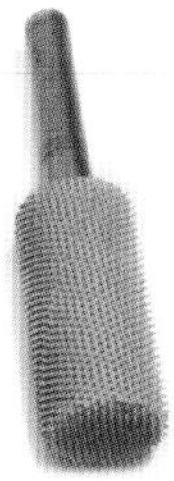

For Shaping			For Fine Detail		
⅛" shank cylinder (coarse grit) 	⅛" shank flame (coarse grit) 	⅛" shank bull nose (fine grit) 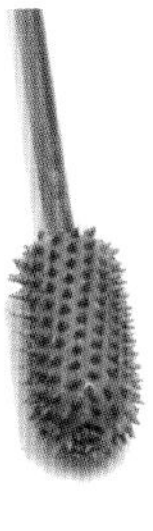	³⁄₃₂" shank diamond flame, ⁵⁄₃₂" 	³⁄₃₂" shank diamond flame, ⁵⁄₆₄" 	³⁄₃₂" shank ruby flame 

For Texturing			For Shaping with a Cleaner Cut	For Sanding	
³⁄₃₂" shank, inverted cone, blue Ceramcut stone large 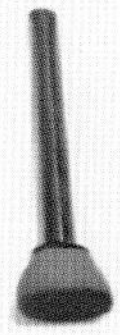	³⁄₃₂" shank, inverted cone, blue Ceramcut stone small 	³⁄₃₂" shank diamond cutting wheel 	⅛" shank, flame carbide cutter 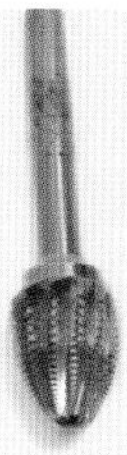	Cushioned-drum sanders with cloth-backed abrasive and Abradnet abrasive 	Split-mandrel sander with cloth-backed abrasive 

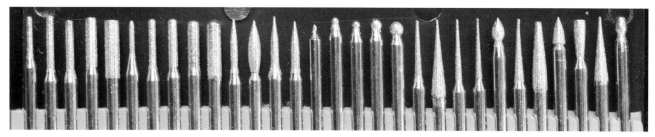

Diamond-coated bits are ideal for finer work and detailing.

A word of warning: when I say the ¼" (6mm) carbide-point bits are aggressive, I mean *aggressive*, and they love to run across your hands and fingers, leaving an attractive pattern! Naturally, with all the other health and safety advice, gloves would be considered essential when using these bits. However, if like me, you cannot carve with gloves, ensure you have a well-stocked tin of bandages handy in the workshop!

Carbide cutters will leave a smoother finish than the coarse carbide-point bits. However, these can dull fairly quickly compared to the carbide points.

Bits for finer work and detailing come coated with diamond, sapphires (which are slightly coarser than diamond), and ruby. Ruby is supposedly the coarsest of the three but is one of my favorite detailers.

Some small steel cutters are also available, and the ball bits can be useful for faster removal of material in the likes of eye sockets.

Very fine texturing (e.g., texturing of bird feathers and animal hair) can be achieved using tiny diamond discs, or what are commonly referred to as stones, stone burrs, or Arkansas stones. They come in different colors, representing assorted grits: red/pink are generally the coarsest, green is medium, and white is medium to fine. The white are normally natural Arkansas stone.

Ceramcut stones are colored blue and, in my opinion, the best. They have ceramic pieces bonded to the other materials they are made from, resulting in their holding a crisper edge and having a longer life.

Storage of Bits & Burrs

Storage becomes an issue once you have built up a collection of accessories. There are carousels from Foredom. A cheaper option is to make your own from scraps of wood or use a magnetic strip, which I have found does a brilliant job of stopping bits from rolling off the work surface into a pile of sawdust, never to see the light of day again!

Diamond cutoff discs are available for very fine texturing, but I find I don't use them often.

Ceramcut stones have a crisper edge and a longer life, and are in my opinion simply the best.

Carbide cutters dull quicker than carbide points, but they leave a smoother finish.

Ruby-coated bits are not quite as fine as sapphire- or diamond-coated ones.

Whether you buy a carousel or create your own type of container, proper storage of bits and burrs will save you and your tools in the long run.

Sanding

Saburrtooth also has sanding covered with the range of ½" and 1" (13 and 25mm) cushioned mandrels, with sleeves in extra-coarse, coarse, and fine.

Additional sanding products include: small and large sleeves coated with aluminum oxide grit; cushioned drums that need cloth-backed sandpaper to be fitted; and split mandrels that also need cloth-backed sandpaper. There are a few ways of wrapping the sandpaper around the split mandrels. The single wrap of abrasive is my favorite for detailed work such as feathering. Radial bristle discs are another alternative.

Sanding by hand will be required for all projects. Cheap abrasives will not last; cloth-backed sandpaper is essential for the cushioned-drum sanders and is ideal for general sanding by hand. For any hard-to-reach areas, apply some superglue to the backing to stiffen the abrasive. Abranet® sanding sheets and strips are made from a material that contains thousands of small holes. It will outperform and outlast other abrasive sheets, so these, in my opinion, cannot be beaten when sanding by hand.

Carving Knives

Carving knives are one of my favorite carving tools to use. As long as they are kept razor sharp at all times, they will be an asset to your carving equipment. Once again, there are many knives to choose from and it will depend on

your intended project. There are specialist knives for chip-carving, curved blades (for carving a bowl), and many different shapes of roughing and detailing knives in between. Flexcut® knives are supplied already sharpened, and this trio will deal with most tasks.

Each of these carving knives is specifically intended for (from left to right): detailing, cutting, and roughing.

Pyrograph

A pyrograph unit is not an essential piece of equipment even if you decide to feather and detail birds. The Ceramcut stones will do this adequately. However, the advantage of using a pyrograph is that it will give crisper lines when laying down feather barbs of the primaries and secondaries and defining the feather shaft. Some carvers will pyrograph all feathers of their carving, which requires plenty of patience!

In addition to the detailing work, a pyrograph unit is handy for cleaning up edges, undercutting feathers, and reaching into difficult places to burn away stubborn wood fibers. It is not essential for pyrographed feathers to be painted over. By using different heat settings and pressure, some excellent designs can be created that need only be finished with oil or varnish.

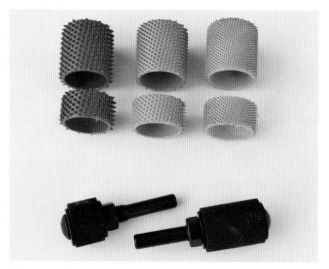

Saburrtooth sanding sleeves are incredibly efficient and will last a long time.

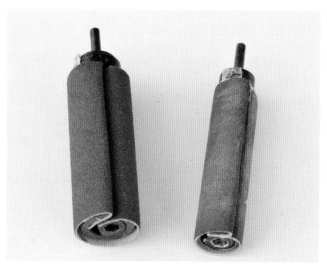

Cushioned-drum sanders come in various sizes and are used with cloth-backed abrasives.

These aluminium oxide sleeves are another sanding option, and, being smaller, they are ideal for tighter spaces.

Split-mandrel sanders can have sandpaper attached as a roll or just one wrap. These are great for tight spaces and are my favorite sanders for detailed work.

Radial bristles are useful sanders for finishing a piece and removing any fuzzy areas. Normally two or three discs are added to a mandrel.

Abradnet is a very efficient sanding cloth and, due to its design, does not clog. This is perfect if you are removing a surface that has previously been oiled.

Pyrography Tips

Rounded Skew

A good general purpose tip used for texturing fur and hair. Ideal for defining the quill of a feather, its edges, and the barbs on all stiff flight feathers (i.e., primary, secondary, and tail feathers). Will define the lamellae of a duck's beak.

Traditional Pointed Skew

Same as the rounded skew but will enable access into tight corners.

Ball Tip

On a light heat setting, can be used to burnish work ready for painting, and will get rid of the fuzziness often associated with lime/basswood after texturing. Gives an even burn and can also be used to write with.

Round Medium Writing Tip

Useful for heavy texturing and general burnishing.

Flattened Rounded Tip

Can be used for heavy texturing of fur and hair. Useful for undercutting feathers.

Round medium writing tip.

Useful for heavy texturing and general burnishing.

Large skew

Has a slightly rounded edge and can be used for shading and also heavy texturing and flattening of the wood on either side of a feather quill.

Scale-Making Tip

The ones shown here are "realistic keeled snake scale tips" especially used for rattlesnakes and others where the scales are keeled. Various shapes and sizes of scale tips include ones for fish.

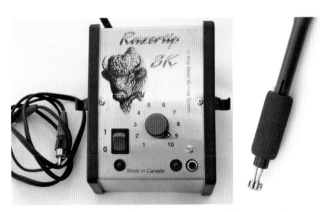

More than 900 tips are available for this Razertip pyrograph's interchangeable-tip pen.

Some pyrograph units have handpieces with fixed tips. In my opinion, this is limiting and costly. Razertip supplies a unit with handpieces that can take interchangeable tips. And there are more than 900 tips to choose from! There are special designs for creating scales of different species of snake, and creating the outline for small feathers. The two sharp tips shown at the bottom are the ones I use for the detailing in these projects. Wire is available for making your own tips if you wish.

Finishing

How you finish your projects also comes from personal experience. Experiment with the range of finishing oils and varnishes and you will find a product that suits you. Some carvers prefer a high gloss on a walking stick with a natural wood head and may use a yacht varnish. Others prefer a matte finish. If a stick is intended for hiking or game shooting, I prefer to finish with several coats of oil; this will soak into the head and shank, giving more protection. Additional coatings of oil can be applied over the original whenever needed; however, varnishes can fade and chip, and the only option is to strip away the original layers and re-varnish.

If the finished head is to be painted, your options will depend on whether you paint with oil or acrylic. I use acrylic exclusively. In this case, the wood can be sealed with a sanding sealer, painted, and then sealed with a finishing oil or polyester-based varnish.

Alternatively, the head can be sealed with a finishing oil, painted with acrylics, then be sealed with a final couple of coats of oil. Naturally, there are many personal opinions as to whether water-based acrylic paint can be finished with an oil-based product. Like everything when it comes to carving, experiment and find what works for you.

There are a couple of projects in this book that use this later method of finishing. Two things are important: firstly, test your intended process on a scrap of wood from your project. Secondly, if applying oil under or over acrylic paints, let the different mediums dry thoroughly for a week before applying the next.

HEALTH & SAFETY FOR WOODWORKERS

Most health and safety considerations in the workshop are common sense. However, following are a few reminders to ensure that your woodworking remains safe, enjoyable, and risk free.

- Wearing eye protection is one of the most important things when working with power tools, especially band saws, table saws, and routers. Sometimes bits can become loose from the rotary tool or they can break apart into small pieces if defective. You can guarantee that if this happens, they will aim straight for your eyes.
- Make sure you protect your ears when using noisy machines.
- Use a dust extractor/filtration system when using power tools.
- A good-quality dust mask is advisable. (The disposable painter and decorator masks are rarely good enough.) Firstly, it prevents dust particles entering the lungs. Secondly, even some of the more common woods are toxic to health, causing anything from a rash, headache, and eye problems through to cardiac issues. It could be argued that any wood could be toxic to a specific individual, but some are toxic to every wood worker. Always research the toxicity of the wood you are using if you are unsure.
- For a power or knife carver, a decent protective glove will prevent many injuries. A ¼" (6mm) coarse carbide-point bit loves to run across your hand, leaving marks like a pincushion. A sharp carving knife will give you a scar to remember. The standard of gloves is improving every year. They are lightweight with cut-resistant fibers incorporated into the design. Beware of cheap gloves, as they won't even save you from a thorn prick in the garden. And a pair of leather gloves will minimize injuries, but these are often too thick and stiff. They prevent you from holding the workpiece properly and feeling your work.
- Appropriate clothing should be worn at all times. Baggy sleeves will get tangled with a carbide-point bit if it comes within breathing distance. If you are using a flexi-shaft machine, it will cost you the price of a new inner cable, as they are designed with a shearing-point for such circumstances. Shirttails or loose jackets can become snagged in a band saw or table saw and result in serious injury. A leather apron, or other suitably reinforced material, is a must if you use a knife to carve your project while holding it in your hand.
- Remove any jewelry dangling from your neck or wrists.
- I have already mentioned that woodcarving should be fun, and I wouldn't want to go back on that sentiment; however, alcohol should be drunk only when you are admiring your finished article, not while carving it. The same goes for medication, so be aware of any side effects of the medication you are taking. Many types will make you drowsy and impair judgment.

 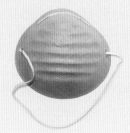  

Possible Reactions to Woods

Wood	Class (Irritant or Sensitizer)	Reaction Type	Potency	Source	Incidence
Alder	Irritant*	Respiratory, eye and skin	No info †	Dust	No info
Ash	Irritant	Respiratory	No info	Dust	No info
Avodire	Irritant	Respiratory, eye and skin	No info	Dust	No info
Baldcypress	Sensitizer**	Respiratory	Small	Dust	Rare
Beech	Sensitizer	Respiratory	Great	Dust	Rare
Birch	Sensitizer	Respiratory, nausea	Great	Dust	Rare
Black locust	Irritant	Nausea	Great	Dust	Rare
Bubinga	Irritant	Eye and skin	No info	Dust	No info
Red cedar, Eastern	Irritant	Respiratory, eye and skin	No info	Dust	Common
Red cedar, Western	Sensitizer	Respiratory	Great	Dust, leaves & bark	Common
Cocobolo	Irritant	Respiratory, eye and skin	Great	Dust & wood	Common
Ebony	Irritant & sensitizer	Respiratory, eye and skin	Great	Dust & wood	Common
Elm	Irritant	Eye and skin	Small	Dust	Rare
Goncalo alves	Sensitizer	Eye and skin	Small	Dust & wood	Rare
Greenheart	Sensitizer	Respiratory, eye and skin	Extreme	Dust & wood	Common
Ipe	Irritant	Respiratory, eye and skin	No info	No info	No info
Mahogany	Irritant	Respiratory, eye and skin	Small	Dust	Rare
Mapl (usually only spalted)	Sensitizer	Respiratory	Great	Dust	Rare
Oak, red	Irritant	Nasal	Great	Dust	Rare
Padauk	Irritant	Respiratory, eye, skin, and nausea	Extreme	Dust & wood	Common
Purpleheart	Sensitizer	Eye and skin, nausea	Small	Dust & wood	Rare
Rosewood	Irritant & sensitizer	Respiratory, eye and skin	Extreme	Dust & wood	Common
Sassafras	Sensitizer	Respiratory, nausea, and nasal cancer	Small	Dust & wood	Rare
Teak	Sensitizer	Eye and skin	Extreme	Dust	Common
Walnut, black	Sensitizer	Eye and skin	Great	Leaves & bark	Common
Willow	Sensitizer	Nasal cancer	Great	Dust	Common

* An irritant causes an almost immediate reaction each time the wood is used. ** A sensitizer does not necessarily irritate, but it makes a person more likely to be strongly affected by a wood classed as an irritant. If you are exposed to an irritant after being exposed to a sensitizer, you are more likely to have a more serious reaction to the irritant. † No info indicates that the information for this wood is still being developed.

- Ideally, the piece you are working on should be securely clamped in a workbench vice or one of the many carving holders available. This leaves both hands free. However, there are times when this is not possible, and most of the projects in this book cannot be carved using a carving clamp.
- Disconnect the power source before changing blades of band saws and table saws.
- Use drill bits that are sharp. Exerting undue pressure may cause the bit to wander and also put the user at risk of slipping.
- Keep your carving knife and gouges sharp. A sharp knife will do more damage than a blunt one if it slips, but a sharp knife reduces the chance of slipping. I carve with a thick carpet beneath my carving station. This minimizes damage to the blades if dropped. Also, it is natural instinct to try to catch a falling knife/gouge, but that can result in serious injury. With a rug or carpet beneath, you don't have to worry as much when dropping a tool.
- When using a table saw, always stand to one side to minimize injury should there be any kickback.

CHAPTER 2

Selection, Storage & Seasoning of Wood

Choice of Wood for the Heads

The genus *tilia* includes more than thirty species and hybrids of what is more commonly known as lime, linden, or basswood. If the head of the walking stick you are carving is to be detailed and/or painted, this is likely to be your first choice of wood along with tupelo (*nyssa*). Both of these woods are a plain creamy color but fine-grained and good at holding detail, as long as you purchase quality material free of defects. The downside of basswood is that using power tools can leave the wood with fuzz that is sometimes difficult to completely remove. Tupelo is a better option when using power. (Note to UK readers: this wood is difficult to source in the UK.) Both woods can be carved easily with a carving knife.

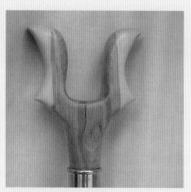

Thumb stick with brass collar.

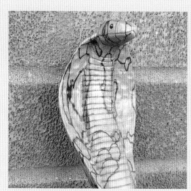

Cobra using spalting pattern of a piece of beech for effect.

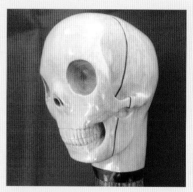

Skull.

Unicorn (commission for a psychic medium).

Caricature of a cowboy's head.

Natural wood carving of a cocker spaniel and duck.

If the head is not being painted nor detailed, you can choose any wood you have access to. Often this will depend on the country where you live, but any decent merchant should have a wide variety of wood species available. Throughout the world there are some exotic woods with stunning colors and grain detail. One of the joys of wood carving is that every piece of wood is different, and even a plain piece of basswood might hold a surprise if it has been attacked by a fungal growth, leaving patterns that can rival some of the exotics.

Selection of Wood for the Shank

There is nothing more satisfying than finding and cutting a shank to make your own walking stick. However, all land and every tree on it belongs to someone; you need the landowner's permission before cutting and removing any wood. In the UK, this also applies to common land where it is a criminal offense. Most landowners are approachable and amenable if you explain your purpose.

Almost any tree species is suitable for a walking stick shank. It is the country where you live that will often dictate which is available to you. The species you choose will also depend on your intentions: Will it be a stand-alone stick with no attachments? Will you need a straight or crooked shank? Will it have a head joined? Should the wood/bark be carved and/or stained/painted? Do you need a tall/short stick that is heavyweight/light? Will the stick be used as a walking aide, where strength is an issue?

Often, the wood will have several outer layers and can reveal some stunning patterns if the outer bark is sanded off. For straight sticks, look to the species that coppice well (e.g., hazel, ash, aspen, sweet chestnut.) Even within different species, there will be variations as to how the wood will behave. But this is all part of the enjoyment!

The most common species used in the UK are detailed in the table on page 18.

The length that you cut your stick will depend on whom it is for and the style preferred. If making a

Most bends in wood can be straightened with heat treatment, but an elbow joint like the one shown here, commonly known as a "dogleg," can be stubborn and often not worth the time and effort.

stick for someone else and you don't know his or her height, a rough guide for a hiking stick for a person 6' (1.8m) tall is 55" (1.4m). For a short walking stick, aim for 36" (0.9m). However, if you intend to make more than the one stick, cut any that you find, long or short, as they can all be put to good use when seasoned.

The diameter is also an individual preference. If in doubt, a standard diameter of a finished stick is around 1"–1³⁄₁₆" (25–30mm) at the top, tapering to a tip diameter of ⅝"–¾" (16–19mm). Don't ignore thicker shanks, as they can be used for carving wildlife and other features along their length.

Keep in mind when cutting that the shank will lose approximately 25 percent of its diameter during seasoning.

Common Species Used for Shanks in the UK

Hazel (*Corylus avellana*)

Hazel is very common in the UK and is the shank of choice for many handmade walking sticks.

It straightens easily and has attractive bark that ranges in color from silver to red brown with the many shades in between.

If you intend to attach a separate head to the shank, hazel is the most popular choice.

Blackthorn (*Prunus spinosa*)

Blackthorn has a rich cherry-red color. It often grows in dense clumps and has vicious thorns (and it is inevitable that the shank you are after will be in the *middle* of such a patch). A pair of gloves and eye protection are advisable.

Blackthorn is on the heavy side for a walking stick shank.

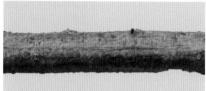

Hawthorn (*Crataegus monogyna*)

Another prickly character. A dense wood, like blackthorn, that makes an attractive shank with the bark left on.

Can be difficult to find a straight section long enough for a walking stick.

Ash (*Fraxinus excelsior*)

A tough wood that absorbs shocks (which is why it is used for cricket bats and the handles of many woodworking tools).

Identifiable in winter by its black, velvety leaf buds. Bark is a silver color.

Holly (*Ilex aquifolium*)

The bark can be fickle, in that it sometimes peels away easily when straightening. However, the bark is often stripped, as the wood can have a well-figured grain.

The inset photo shows a freshly cut, holly block-stick, demonstrating the vibrant color of its bark when green. It darkens with age.

Common Species Used for Shanks in the UK

Field Maple (*Acer campestre*)

This tree has wrinkly bark that may come loose during seasoning and will need to be removed.

Staining field maple may result in blotchy areas due to its high density.

English Yew (*Taxus baccata*)

Yew has an attractive reddish tinge to its bark.

Its thin stems are very flexible; it is better to cut slightly thicker branches for shanks.

It is rare to find a straight branch of yew that is long enough for a shank. A good place to look is an overgrown hedge.

Wild Cherry (*Prunus avium*)

The bark of a young wild cherry branch is of a similar color to blackthorn.

It is often hard to find shanks that are long enough for walking sticks.

Silver Birch (*Betula pendula*)

The young branches of a silver birch are an attractive russet brown with great patterns.

Can be a problem to find suitable shanks with a good taper.

Elder (*Sambucus nigra*)

Elder can be a tricky species to use for a shank. Small branches are hollow, and even larger stems can contain a degree of soft pith running through the center. However, it is worth the effort to search for this species, as the wood under the bark can be an attractive yellow-white with pink striations. The crinkly bark will need to be removed.

Interestingly, the name comes from the Anglo-Saxon *aeld*, meaning fire. The hollow stems were used to blow life into a fire like a pair of bellows.

Aspen (*Populus tremula/tremuloides*)

Also known as the quaking aspen due to how the single leaves flutter in the slightest breeze, aspen is native to both the UK and Northern America. It is a strong and lightweight wood that was used in the past for making oars and wagon bottoms.

Not commonly used for a walking stick, as it can be too flexible.

Rowan/Mountain Ash (*Sorbus aucuparia*)

A pale yellow-brown wood with a darker heart.

Easily identified by the abundance of scarlet berries.

English Elm

Elm will make a sturdy shaft, but due to the ravages of Dutch elm disease it is unfortunately hard to find in the UK.

Oak, sweet chestnut, apple, plum, sycamore, and beech are among other species suitable for walking stick shanks.

However, unless coppiced, it may be hard to find a suitable length of straight wood.

Hazel can come in a range of colors, from dark to light.

Not all North American tree species are suitable for straightening and attaching a head. However, the shape and grain of some (e.g., diamond willow) make extraordinarily attractive walking sticks. The table below has just a few of the species that are commonly used for making walking sticks.

Common Species Used for Shanks in North America

Hickory (*Carya species*)

A fantastic wood for a walking stick. It is one of the hardest and strongest woods and is shock resistant. Several species of hickory are found in North America.

Hickory has some of the best common names for tree species—water, shellbark, shagbark, pignut, nutmeg, bitternut, and mockernut.

Butternut (*Juglens cinerea*)

A member of the walnut family and often called white walnut.

Mature branches display the same well-figured grain as black walnut with a heartwood that often has a reddish tint.

Poplar (*Liriodendron tulipifera*)

A cream-colored, softish wood that carves easily and makes a good shank. The porous wood stains well.

Depending on mineral content in the soil where it is grown, the wood can be colored with purples, reds, and greens and is referred to as rainbow poplar.

Other common names for this wood include yellow poplar, American tulipwood, or tulip poplar.

Black Walnut (*Juglans nigra*)

Attractive bark, beautiful chocolate-colored heartwood. Abundant in eastern North America, and one of my favorite woods to carve.

The dark heartwood may not be evident in thin branches used for a walking stick.

Acer

The maples of the acer family, including the black, red, silver, bigleaf, striped, curly, and quilted, are abundant in North America. One of the most attractive is the birdseye maple.

This is not a distinct species but a pattern occasionally found within the sugar maple (*Acer saccharum*).

American Beech (*Fagus grandifolia*)

As with the European beech, it can be hard to find straight lengths of wood suitable for a walking stick.

Black Cherry (*Prunus serotina*)

Wood of the black cherry is fairly soft and easily damaged.

Dogwood (*Cornus florida*)

Dogwood has a sapwood with a pinkish tinge and a narrow band of dark brown heartwood. Makes a good stick.

Additional Species

Diamond Willow

This does not refer to a particular species of willow but rather is the description of an abnormal growth on fungus-infected willows. The tree grows diamond-shaped cankers as a reaction to the fungus attack, which forms amazing patterns beneath the bark. These are highly prized for both walking sticks and other carvings. There are six or seven species of willow (out of hundreds of species) that produce these diamond formations, the most common being Bebb's Willow (*Salix bebbiana*).

Cherrybark Oak (*Quercus pagoda*)

Has an attractive color, is very strong, and is a great wood for shanks. On the heavy side.

Black Ironwood (*Krugiodendron ferreum*)

As the name suggests, this is one of a couple of ironwoods that are extremely strong. Color can range from reds, violets, and oranges to browns.

Cutting

In the northern hemisphere, the best time to cut shanks is between the end of October and the end of February, when the sap is at its lowest. Shanks cut in the summer months are prone to excessive bending and cracking. Cut at least 2" (51mm) longer than is needed at each end for your project. Using a folding pruning saw, cut the bottom of the shank at an angle of 45 degrees to allow water runoff and to minimize damage to the tree.

When cutting a shank, cut at a 45-degree angle to allow rain runoff and prevent disease and dieback.

Check any fallen tree with its roots still attached, as they often sprout vertical branches along the fallen trunk. The fallen ash tree shown below will have several potential shanks in a few years.

Any species of tree that has a fallen limb will generate new growth that grows at around 90 degrees to the limb—a great place to look for shanks!

Use the saw or secateurs to cut any side branch to ½" (13mm) from the shank. Do not cut side shoots flush, as this can leave an ugly pockmark when dried. This especially applies to blackthorn, as the convention is to leave the side branches and thorns proud of the shank. When sanded, the small knobs give a distinctive look along the shank's length.

I would advise against using dead wood from a tree or picked up from the ground. It may appear sound, but woodworm may have set up home. Of course, if the stick is for you, then this will not be an issue. However, it certainly would be a problem, possibly even a legal problem, if the stick is for someone else and it breaks and results in injury.

Stripping the Bark

Removing the bark from your shanks will depend on its condition, the species of wood, and your personal preference. In the UK, when using hazel, blackthorn, and some of the other woods mentioned above, there is no need to remove the bark, as they have their own attractive patterns.

However, bark of other species from around the world will often wrinkle as it dries and is best removed. While this is easier to do when the shank is green, it will lose water faster than if the bark is left on and may result in splitting or cracking. This can be minimized

Removing bark from a shank is a personal choice. It may be that the bark is wrinkled and loose or you are looking for well-figured grain beneath that is common with some species. This twisty was stripped to allow the mouse to stand out more.

by allowing the shanks to dry for a few months before removing the bark. Other reasons to remove the bark is if you intend to decorate the shank, by either carving or using a pyrograph, or if you intend to stain the shank.

It is always worth considering stripping the bark, as it often reveals an attractive grain. You can experiment by applying different stains that will highlight this grain. Another good reason to cut your shanks longer than needed is because the small pieces you cut off are ideal for experimentation with stains and other colors to test their effectiveness and finish.

Styles of Natural Shanks

- For starters, there is the straight shank—tall or short—to which you attach a head. The choice of head is infinite and sometimes bizarre. Types of head include: dogs, animals, and birds carved from wood or horn; plain handle styles (e.g., regency, derby, crook, and market) in wood or horn; antler, horn, or wood "Y" thumb sticks and even combinations of the above (e.g., a crook with a small dog carved from the wood or horn). These shanks can even have items inserted into the shank or handle (e.g., compass, coin). There are many types of head precast from resin or metal, although as a woodworker I would not recommend these, as they cheapen the stick rather than enhance it.

- When wild honeysuckle grows around a branch in a spiral, it sometimes tightens, leaving a "twisty." Removing the honeysuckle will reveal deep or shallow grooves with oodles of character. The length of twist can vary from the entire shank or a short section. This stick gives a surprisingly comfortable grip. A twisty shank of the right thickness and height is difficult to find. Search in unmanaged woodland. If you find a perfect twisty, ignore the previous advice of when to cut; as long as you have permission, cut when you spot it—if you don't, someone else will! Some have tried to artificially fashion a twisty by spiraling a cord around a thin shank, waiting a few years, then checking the result. My understanding is that this has never produced much of a result and, more often than not, someone had stolen the shank! Nature is the best manufacturer of a twisted shank. All you need to do is keep searching.

A nice example of a spalting, in this case oak.

"Twisties" are caused by wild honeysuckle growing around and constricting the branch as both develop.

Sometimes the twist can be for the entire length of the shank or just parts of it.

- A short or tall one-piece stick cut with a section of root attached can be shaped into a knob or handle. The runners of blackthorn travel from the parent tree just under the surface of the soil. Scrape the soil from around the base of a straight section of blackthorn and check the root system to see if it is usable. Irish blackthorn and American iron wood are an excellent species for this. Short sticks with a piece of root make good cudgels or beating sticks for flushing game birds. They can even be carved, as with this dog handle (below) carved from a blackthorn root.

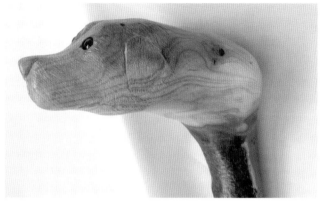

Blackthorn root utilized as a handle for a short walking stick and carved with a dog's head.

- If a twisted branch is not long enough for a shank, consider cutting just the twisted part, as this can be attached as a head to a straight shank.

This twisty attachment makes a surprisingly comfortably grip.

Blackthorn root finished with oil.

- A one-piece "Y" thumb stick.

One-piece thumb stick with buffalo horn caps.

- A crooked shank can have tons of character. Blackthorn and hawthorn are good candidates. The above photo is of a chunky, odd-shaped rowan stick, which, because of its shape and thickness, has many possibilities.

This crooked rowan stick offers many possibilities.

- An extra-thick shank, such as this wood spirit (top right), can provide material to carve or decorate.

This crooked rowan stick offers many possibilities.

- An ideally placed side branch coming from the shank can be decorated or carved. The photo below is of a Labrador on a twisty shank that had a thick side branch that I carved into the dog. I was also able to utilize a small knot at the end as the dog's nose.

When cutting a shank, if it has a chunky side branch, consider leaving a few inches attached, as you may be able to carve something from it, as with this Labrador head.

- If you cut the shank with a section of larger branch attached (a block-stick), the extra block of wood can be carved into a handle or many other designs. You need to be aware of what you are cutting when sourcing this style. Sometimes this may mean cutting down an entire young tree and, in this case, should be avoided. These are often more difficult to work on due to working access and having about four feet of shank waving around, knocking over everything in reach! Some amazing walking sticks can be fashioned from this style, especially one-piece crook handles. The hazel block-stick shown below was used to carve the shoveler duck at bottom.

Hazel block-stick used for the shoveler duck project.

Shoveler duck from hazel block-stick in previous photo.

- This unusual and rare rowan block-stick (below) provides several options. It could be used for making two walking sticks or a very special head on one stick.

Rare double-shank block-stick.

Storage

Moisture loss from a drying shank is highest through any of the exposed cuts. This may result in checking or cracking. The denser woods such as blackthorn, hawthorn, and yew are more prone to this. The problem can be eliminated if you have cut your shanks a few inches (centimeters) longer than needed so that any split end can be removed once seasoned.

Alternatively, the exposed end grain can be sealed. Paraffin wax is the best product for this. You can also try sealing with wood glue, beeswax, varnish, paint, or mineral oil.

Before sealing, remove excess moss and dirt and treat the shank with an anti-woodworm product. Write on one of the ends the date when you cut it and the variety of wood.

Store shanks in a cool, dark place with good air circulation. Attics of a dwelling are not suitable due to temperature extremes. Shanks can be stored upright

The extra piece of wood of a block-stick must always be sealed (wax was used to seal this field maple).

or flat, but not leaning against a wall. If single shanks are stored in the rafters of a garage, ensure that you place them on struts that are close together to stop excessive bowing.

Single shanks will have better air circulation and dry more evenly. To prevent too much movement on a special shank, consider securing to a board or rigid stick with plastic ties or even metal brackets. The photo below is an example of one way of doing this. The bark on this short holly shank was wrinkled, and the bark needed to be removed when green. It was secured to a straight piece of pallet wood with plastic ties. These can be tightened as the shank shrinks, as long as they don't cut into the shank. This was done for demonstration purposes only; the shank has little to offer in the way of being special.

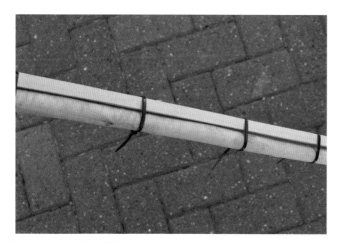

Secure any special one-off shank to a wooden board.

If you are drying only one or two shanks, tying them to a broomstick or piece of metal pipe will prevent excessive movement.

A couple of shanks can be tied to copper/metal tubing for seasoning.

Any movement caused by drying can be minimized by tying shanks in bundles of up to ten. Tie the bundles together at close intervals with a soft binding—strips of an old towel are ideal.

Storage of small bundles of sticks.

If you have a special shank, consider using a piece of hollow pipe to stop excessive movement. The photo below is of a field maple block-stick with the shank placed in a piece of PVC water pipe. This species is rare in the UK, and to find a straight shank with the block-stick configuration makes it deserving of such special treatment.

Seasoning

As the moisture level reduces during drying, a shank hardens and decreases in weight. Season a standard shank, of 1" (25mm) diameter, for a minimum of one year. Denser woods—blackthorn, yew, and hawthorn—may need longer. If the shank is thicker or has a block at one end or a knob, root, etc., it may need two years or more. The general accepted position is to season for one year per every inch (25mm) of diameter. Shanks left for more than three years tend to attract woodworm. If you are storing for this amount of time or longer, repeat the anti-woodworm treatment.

If your intended project will have a separate head attached, do not be tempted to use the shank before fully seasoned. There is the possibility of the shank continuing to shrink, which may loosen the joint.

Another way to season a special block-stick, using a length of PVC pipe.

CHAPTER 3
Straightening

No matter how straight your shank when cut, after seasoning it is likely to have a couple of bends. If the shank was stored correctly, it should not be too extreme. To straighten, there are two main methods, and each has advantages and disadvantages.

Paint-stripping tool

This method is adequate if you need to straighten one or two shanks at a time. Keep the hot-air gun moving over the bend and continually revolve the shank to prevent scorching the wood. A couple of minutes is enough, depending on the shank's thickness. Don't try to heat the entire shank; just concentrate on one area at a time. A downside to using this method is that it is very easy to scorch or lift the bark away from the shank. Also, it can be difficult to work on a second bend until the first has fully cooled.

Use of Steam for Bending Shanks

The use of steam to bend wood has been around for many years in the boat building and furniture making industries. Fortunately, this method can be adapted to help with the straightening of walking stick shanks.

Low-pressure steam introduced into a piece of aluminum ducting or a purpose-made steam box will soften the wood fibers of the shank and allow for it to be straightened in a jig.

If you need to straighten several sticks at a time, and on a regular basis, steam might be a better option than a heat gun. The duct or steam box will need to be slightly larger than the longest stick you intend to

Sometimes a bend near the top of an intended shank can be awkward to straighten. Consider utilizing this bend as part of the design, as with this carving of a gray partridge, where the bend complements the shape of the attached head.

straighten. Remember that the smaller the dimensions of the steamer, the faster it will heat. A length of 5' (1520mm) with a diameter or width of 4–6" (100–150mm) should suffice for most shanks.

Steaming will be necessary if you have shanks with difficult or stubborn bends. A chestnut shank can have one end steamed and bent into a crook-style handle. Holly can be particularly fickle if steamed, as the bark will frequently flake away, no matter how carefully it is handled.

Don't try to heat a shank until it has been properly seasoned, as the heat will likely cause the bark to soften. If it is then placed in a bending jig, the bark will peel away. Also, unseasoned shanks have a habit of creeping back to their original state when left overnight.

A simple steamer can be made from a length of aluminum ducting 4–6" (100–150mm) in diameter. Seal one end with a piece of wood or cap. Drill a hole the same size as the end of the steam outlet near to the sealed end of the pipe. Fix the steam outlet into the hole and seal with waterproof sealant.

While the shanks are steaming, a cover is needed to prevent steam escaping, but it needs to be loose, like a cloth, because the steam will build up a head of pressure! Decide how you are going to orient the tube, as a small hole needs to be drilled on the underside near to the sealed end to allow for accumulated water to escape. Resist the urge to use cheap plastic ducting; you might be fortunate to use it a couple of times, but it is likely to soften and become unusable. Of course, if you have access to professional-grade plastic rated for high temperatures, this would not be an issue.

WOODEN BOX STEAMER

A wooden box steamer is easy to make and will serve you for many years.

MATERIALS

- Marine-grade exterior ply of at least ¾" (20mm) thickness, sufficient to make four sides 5' (1520mm) by 4–6" (100 – 150mm) and two endpieces (Solid wood can be substituted for ply.)
- Wood to make two stands (This will depend on where you intend to install and use, either on a worktop of free standing on the ground. Ideally the steamer should be used outside.)
- Meat thermostat (optional)
- Hinges and latch to enable one end to open (Ideally, leather or similar should be used so there are no issues with rusting.)
- Sufficient wood screws for assembly
- A wallpaper-stripping machine (or other steam-generating equipment)
- A brass connector to attach the hose of the wallpaper-stripping machine (This will depend on the size of the machine's hose connector. If no connector is available, the hose can be inserted and sealed directly into the wood.)

ASSEMBLING

1. Cut the plywood to your chosen dimensions. Screw the four sides together with wood screws and butt joints. Glue is not needed.

2. Cut a piece of ply that will cover the outside dimensions of the end of the box. This will be used for the steam input. Drill a suitable hole for the brass connector to fit into this endpiece. The general size seems to be ⁹⁄₁₆" (14mm).

3. Cut another piece of ply the same dimensions for the other end. This will be the hinged door for access.

4. Fit the brass connector for the steam input hose into the endpiece. Screw this endpiece to the box.

5. Attach the hinges to the access endpiece, then secure to the box assembly. Attach a latch or other securing device.

6. If you intend to use a thermometer, drill a suitable hole in the top of the box to accommodate it.

7. In the bottom of the box, at the steam input end, drill a hole approximately ¼" (6mm) for condensation to escape.

8. In situ, the box needs to slope upward from where the steam enters. Make suitable legs to support the box.

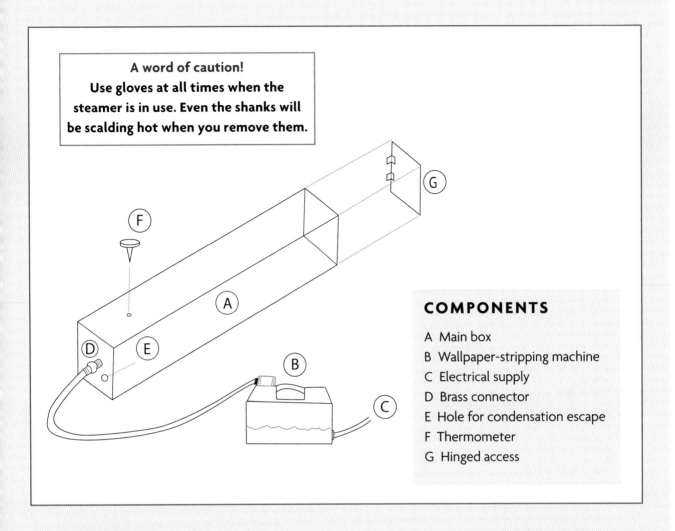

COMPONENTS

A Main box
B Wallpaper-stripping machine
C Electrical supply
D Brass connector
E Hole for condensation escape
F Thermometer
G Hinged access

OPERATION

Ensure that the wallpaper-stripping machine is not connected to the electrical supply. Fill the container with water to its maximum capacity. If you use hot water, the heating time will be reduced. Connect the hose between machine and box, and connect the wallpaper-stripping machine to the electrical supply. Check that the hole drilled for condensation to escape is working adequately when the unit is operating. Widen if necessary.

An approximate guide for steaming shanks is 30-45 minutes for a 1" (25mm) shank at the optimum working temperature of 212°F (100°C). It will take approximately an hour for the box to reach this temperature, but this depends on the size of the box and the thickness of the wood used in its construction. Initially, the steam will be used to heat the wood of the box (insulation could be added to the outside to reduce this time and help prevent excessive cooling), but the shanks can be placed into the box while waiting for it to fill with steam.

Work the shanks as soon as possible after removal from the steamer, as the shank will only remain workable for a few minutes. If you have multiple bends to work on, you may need to reheat the shank.

JIGS FOR STRAIGHTENING

You can straighten most bends over your knee, but bends at the extremities are difficult and a simple jig will help. The jig can be used to straighten the whole shank. There are several different designs of jigs and the following are some examples:

Jig 1: This jig is suitable for all straightening.

Jig 2: This second jig has a couple of advantages over jig one; it can take thicker shanks and deal with the more extreme bends. Also, I find having two jigs useful when having a shank-straightening session.

Jig 3: This design uses two round blocks of wood and can be secured either vertically or horizontally in a vice to adapt to your working conditions. It is assembled as follows:

a. Firstly, gather the components: two handmade wheels of oak, or similar hardwood, approximately 4" (102mm) diameter and 2" (51mm) thick; two ½" (13mm) bolts that are around 6" (152mm) long, together with at least 4 nuts; a block of oak, or similar wood, 16" long by 4½" wide by 2" thick (406 x 114 x 51mm); a block or oak, or similar, 4" by 4" by 4" (102 x 102 x 102mm).

b. Drill holes ½" (13mm) wide in the center of the wheels. Place a wheel toward one end of the base. Position the other wheel beside it, leaving a gap of approximately 1½" (38mm). This will then cater for a shank of this diameter or less. Mark their positions through the drilled holes. Drill the holes in the base. Attach the small block in the center of the underside of the base with five stout screws.

c. Use a coarse burr or rasp to make a concave shape around the edges of the wheels, then glue strips of leather around them.

d. Bolt the wheels to the base.

e. This shows the jig being used in a vertical plane and . . .

f. . . . a horizontal plane.

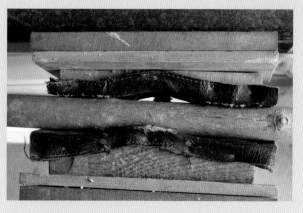

Jig 1.

Jig 2.

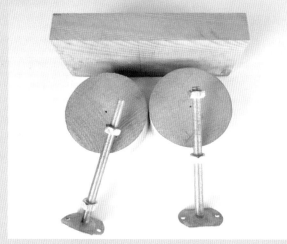

a) Materials needed for Jig 3.

b) Assembly.

c) Wrap wheels with leather.

d) Secure wheels to base.

e) Vertical.

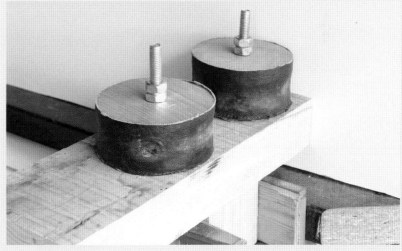

f) Horizontal.

To straighten a shank, methodically work from the top end and wait for a treated area to cool before attempting the next bend. An advantage of bending a shank over your knee is that you will feel the wood fibers stretch if heated sufficiently. Shanks when seasoned will still have around 15–20 percent moisture levels. When the shank is heated, it is the moisture that heats up, softening the wood tissue. You will get to know the smells given off from different species when they are "cooked," and this is also a good indication that it has been heated sufficiently. If you slightly overbend the shank, it will normally spring back straight. If the shank doesn't give, apply more heat but don't force, otherwise the shank may crack or snap. Some bends can be stubborn. This is not a task to rush; it can take up to an hour per stick. Once you have straightened the entire shank, place it flat on the ground, ideally in a cool place, to prevent the bends creeping back.

CHAPTER 4

Joining a Head to a Shank

The following are the two main methods considered when joining a head to a shank.

1. METAL ROD

The easiest, but not necessarily the best, method to connect a separate head to a shank is with a 5" (127mm) length of ⅝" (16mm) diameter, screwed metal rod. These rods are available with smaller or larger diameters, and if you have one of a different size you will have to alter the diameter of the holes you drill in the head and shank.

You need to decide from the outset if you are using a spacer, as this will affect the depth of holes to be drilled. Bone, horn, and antler spacers are available to buy, but it can be just as easy, and cheaper, to make your own from offcuts of wood. As shown in some of the projects in this book, a couple of spacers cut from contrasting woods can add an extra dimension.

The following are the steps for using this method:

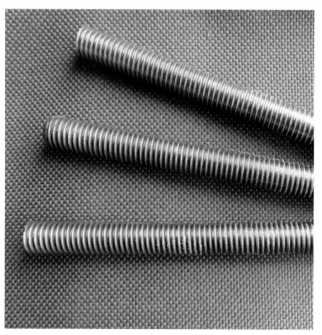

1 You will need a piece of precut metal rod of around 5" (127mm). Alternatively, you can buy a longer section and cut pieces as required. Half of the rod will fit into the shank and the other half into the head.

2 Place the shank in a vice or workbench. Protect it from damage by using a piece of foam copper pipe insulation or similar. With a two-way spirit level, ensure the shank is level in both planes. Find the center of the shank. A simple method is to use a metal washer about the same size as the shank and make a mark in the center.

3 Drill a ⅝" (16mm) diameter hole to a depth of 2⅝" (67mm). The additional ⅛" (3mm) over the 2½" (64mm) is needed to ensure the rod fits comfortably within the overall length of the hole that will be drilled in the head and shank. It will also provide a small area for glue to pool, which will increase the strength of the joint. If a spacer is included in the project, its thickness needs to be deducted from the depth of the holes drilled in the shank and head.

If you intend to use several spacers, you will need to consider using a rod longer than 5" (127mm). Make sure you have a drill that is sharp and in good condition, as this hole needs to be vertical and dead center. A worn drill will wander when starting, even if you have drilled a pilot hole. If the drill is in poor condition and needs to be forced, the effort will likely cause the drill to veer off center and create a wider and off-center hole.

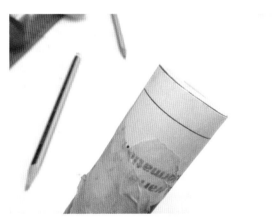

4 Check that the top of the shank is perfectly flat and smooth to ensure a snug fit with the head or spacer. You can wrap a piece of straightedge from a glossy magazine and secure with masking tape. This will show any irregularities that can be removed with a carving knife.

5 Slightly dish out the wood around the hole in the shank with a carving knife. This will help gather excess glue and ensure a better joint.

It is possible to use a belt sander to make this 90-degree angle, although it is not a method I would trust. A good way of flattening the two surfaces of a joint is with a small jig that I made. I normally use the next method of joining my heads to a shank, and this jig was made with this in mind. However, for this method of joining you will need only the half of the jig that fits into the shank. You will need to change the diameter of the piece that will fit into the hole to coincide with the diameter of the holes drilled in the head and shank. (Please see instructions for making this jig on page 43.)

6 Drill a hole of the same size as the metal rod in the center of the spacer.

7 Dry fit the shank, spacer, and head before gluing. This ensures everything fits snugly before a permanent fix.

Drill a hole in the head.

Mark all components where they align.

Once you are happy with the shank, you need to carry out the same process for the head. Secure the head in the vice or workbench and level out. Mark the center point, or the point where you intend to fit the shank, and drill a hole the same depth and in the same manner as you did for the shank above. This only applies to a head carved from wood.

When using antler as a head, sometimes the center is soft and needs to be scooped out and filled with epoxy resin prior to drilling. Obviously, when using hollow horn as a head, it also needs to be filled. If the hole is reasonably large, a piece of hardwood can be glued into it and the hole drilled into this piece of wood.

Check the flatness and angle of the bottom of the head in the same way as you did for the top of the shank. Now, test fit the head, shank, and spacer together. Keep adjusting all three components until you achieve the best fit. Normally, there will always be one place where everything is aligned. Mark all components where you achieve this fit for future reference. If the head and shank do not come together flush, small adjustments are possible. Put some protection around the shank, then clamp it in a vice or workbench. Tap the metal rod with a lightweight hammer in the direction that will remove the gap. Only tiny adjustments are possible; if this is overdone, the shank can split. Joining the head and the shank at an angle is possible—between 20 and 30 degrees is the usual.

There are conventions in competitions when fitting the head of a market stick, cardigan, crook, and similar designs. The neck of the head must be in alignment with the taper of the shank, parallel to the shank or with a slight backward flare of the head, but never with the head leaning forward. If the head is of a carved subject, such as dog or bird, the only criteria is that the stick should look balanced.

When using a metal rod, it is your choice to either glue the rod into the shank and glue the head onto the rod after it has been finished or to the rod into both head and shank in one go, then finish the bottom of the head once the glue has dried. Use plenty of epoxy glue around the threads of the rod, whichever method you choose. Use a cloth dampened with mineral spirits to remove any excess glue around the joint before it dries. Sometimes an air pocket can force the joint apart. Hold the pieces in place until the epoxy is set.

2. DOWEL

The second method involves carving the end of the shank to form a dowel that fits into a hole drilled into the bottom of the head. This is the traditional method used by early walking stick makers. In my opinion, it is the strongest and best way to join a head to a shank, as drilling the hole into the shank could weaken it.

The following are the steps for this method:

1 Secure the head in a vice or workbench and ensure it is level in both planes. With a sharp ½" (13mm) wood drill, bore a hole to a depth of around 1½" (38mm). This is sufficient depth for a decorative head that will not be used as a handle nor any pressure exerted on it. If the head is a handle (e.g., cardigan, market, thumb stick), then this depth needs to be approximately 2½" (64mm).

2 Find the center of the shank. Take a ½" (13mm) metal washer and place it over this point. Draw a circle around the washer.

3 Measure the depth of the hole drilled in the bottom of the head. Although you know you have drilled to a depth of 1½" (38mm) in step 1, it is still advisable to double-check. Remember to include the spacer(s) if you are using any. A flat-bottom pencil is ideal for this. Insert the flat end into the hole and mark with a fingernail on the pencil at the correct depth.

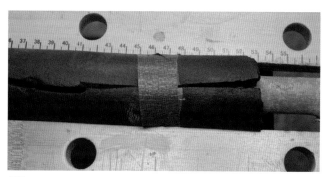

4 Transfer this measurement over to the shank and mark the distance down from the top. Wrap an edge of a glossy magazine around the shank at this point. Wrap the magazine below the mark, not above. Secure with masking tape. Remove some of the stickiness from the tape—dab on a dusty surface—to avoid pulling away the bark when removed.

5 Clamp the shank in a vice or workbench. Protect the shank with pipe insulation or similar.

6 Use a junior hacksaw to cut around the circumference of the shank at the straight edge. Cut with care.

Guide for Cutting around the Circumference of a Shank

The junior hacksaw blade is ¼" (6mm) in depth. If using a shank with a 1" (25mm) diameter, cut to the depth of the blade around the shank's circumference. This will leave you with an internal measurement at the bottom end of the dowel of ½" (13mm)—the size you need to carve. Adjust the cut according to whether the shank is smaller or larger than 1" (25mm). The blade depth can still be used if the shank is smaller in diameter; just cut until the top portion of the blade is showing. If using another fine-toothed saw, you can mark the blade or place a piece of masking tape at the required depth.

7 Use a carving knife to take a wedge out above the hacksaw line.

8 If you take the wedge down to the bottom of the hacksaw cut line, it will act as guide when whittling the dowel. It will also prevent the knife slipping and damaging the shank in the next step.

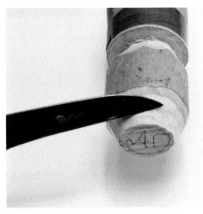

9 Use a knife to whittle a dowel that will fit into the hole drilled in the head at step 1. Start at the tip and shave away material down to the line drawn around the washer in step 2.

10 Start removing the outer section of wood between the tip and the base to form a dowel.

11 Next, concentrate on whittling the tip of the dowel until it just fits into the hole of the head. Twist the head a few times and this will give the exact size needed at the top of the dowel.

12 Using this and the hacksaw cut at the other end, you have a guide as to what wood needs to be removed to make the perfect dowel. Continue to shave away wood so that the head slides on further.

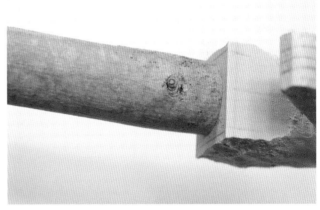

13 You are aiming for a squeaky-tight fit of the head. Don't force the head, as it may split. Keep checking the fit as you carve, as you do not want it to become too sloppy.

14 If you are using a spacer(s), the head will stop short of the shoulder. Continue to carve the dowel until the spacer(s) also fits on the dowel.

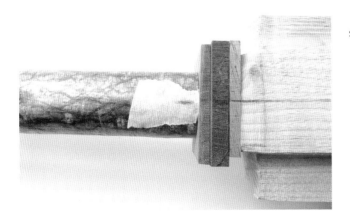

15 With the knife, cut a dish shape around the hole in the head. This will help the head seat better on the shoulder of the shank.

16 If you are using a spacer, cut this dish shape on the surface of the spacer that will abut the shank.

17 If the two surfaces do not fit flush, small adjustments are possible by paring away tiny amounts of wood from the shank or head. Alternatively, you can use a small jig to smooth and square the surfaces of the dowel shoulder and the bottom of the head. This is the half of the jig used for the shank and . . .

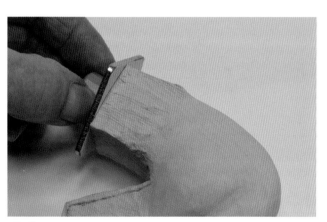

18 . . . this is the other half used for the head.

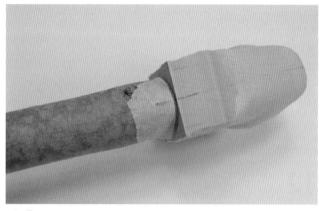

19 Where you achieve the best fit between the head and the shank, mark this position on all of the components.

As with the metal rod, it is a matter of personal choice as to whether the head is glued to the shank before it is finished or after. This applies to a simple handle or thumb stick only. With a decorative head, it is usual to finish the carving, detailing, and painting before attaching to the shank. However, there will still

be the choice as to whether the extreme bottom of the head carving, where it joins the shank, is finished before or after gluing. These slight variations are further explained in the following projects.

Creating the joint at an angle is also possible as mentioned in method 1 above.

3. VARIATION OF METHODS 1 & 2 ABOVE

A collar can be fitted over the joint between the shank and the head. This is decorative but also strengthens the joint. Collars of brass, copper, silver-nickel, and silver can be bought either plain or rolled-top. Others can be self-made from horn or antler.

The following is a method for fitting a collar when using the dowel method of joining:

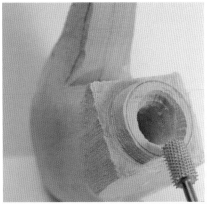

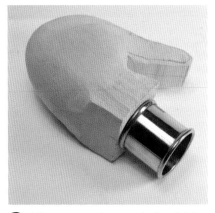

1 Drill the hole in the head as described above. This rolled-top collar is 1" (25mm) long and just under 1" (25mm) in diameter. Place the collar being used centrally over the hole in the head. Draw around the outside and inside the diameter of the collar onto the head blank.

2 Use a fine, safe-ended, cylinder carbide-point to remove the wood around the head under the line drawn and down to the inner diameter of the collar.

3 When you are almost at the line, finish and clean up with a carving knife until the collar fits snuggly over the lip and up against the bottom of the head.

For this project, I am placing ¼" (6mm) of the collar on the head and the remaining ¾" (19mm) over the shank. The positioning of the collar is a personal choice and, on most occasions, would be placed half on the shank and half on the head. Draw a line around the head ¼" (6mm) up from the bottom.

4 Place the head on the shank without the collar. You will be able to see how much of the shank needs to be removed to match with the lip carved on the head.

5 Approximately ¾" (19mm) needs to be removed from the shank to match with the ¼" (6mm) lip of the head. However, to be on the safe side, measure ¹¹⁄₁₆" (17.5mm) down from the top of the shank and wrap a straight edge of glossy magazine on the lower side of this mark. Secure with masking tape. This will give some wriggle room at the bottom of the collar. You don't want to remove too much, as the bare wood will show below the bottom ridge of the collar.

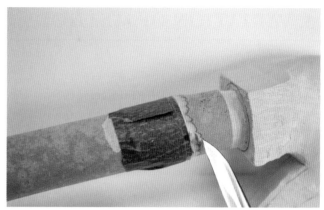

6 Use a carving knife to run a stop-cut around the straight edge. Remove a thin wedge of wood from the upper side of the stop-cut.

7 Remove the head and carve away the wood from the shank above the stop-cut to match the profile of the lip carved on the head. The collar needs to fit snuggly over the shank, so carve the wood away gradually while checking the fit.

8 Ensure that the collar fits flush up against the stop-cut on the shank. Remove the collar and place the head back on the shank. Place the collar alongside the sections you have carved to check that it exactly matches the section of wood removed. If it doesn't, the top of the collar will push up the head and there will be a gap left resulting in weakness of the joint. You won't see this, as it will be hidden under the collar. If necessary, nibble away a touch more wood from the shank until you achieve a perfect fit.

9 Put the collar on the head and draw around the outside diameter. This will give you a guide as to how much wood needs to be removed from the head to match the profile of the top of the collar.

Carving Creative Walking Sticks and Canes

Other Less Common Joining Methods

The following are some of the less common methods of joining a head to a shank:

- Double-ended wood screw
- Threaded rod and nut (enables the use of interchangeable heads)
- Long/short hardwood dowel in place of the metal rod
- Plug and anchor

4. JIG

The following is how to make a simple jig for flattening the surfaces of shank and head as mentioned at steps 17 and 18 on page 40. The components can also be made from wood.

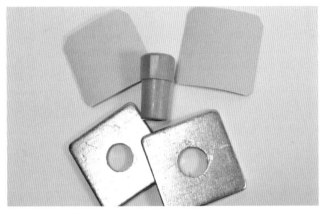

1 I have used two square, heavy-duty metal washers that are 1½" (38mm) square, a plastic screw finder that is just under ½" (13mm) at its widest, and two squares of 240-grit sandpaper. Enlarge one washer hole to ½" (13mm) and the other until the screw finder fits tightly.

2 Fit the screw finder into its respective washer. This can be glued if it is not a tight fit. Super glue the sandpaper to the appropriate faces of the washers as shown.

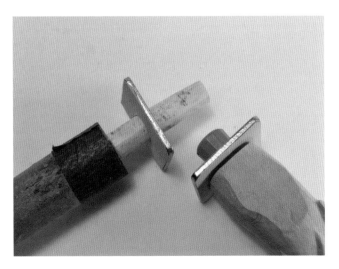

3 The washer with the screw finder will fit into the hole drilled into a head, twisted to obtain a flat and smooth surface. The screw finder fits snuggly into the hole. The other plain washer will fit over the dowel whittled from a shank. The square washers give a better grip than round ones.

PROJECTS

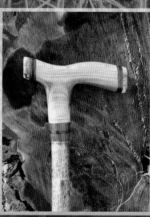

(See page 217 for pattern)

PROJECT 1

Multi-Wood, Lyre-Shaped Thumb Stick

Anyone making their first walking stick where a separate head is joined to the shank is likely to make a basic thumb stick. However, basic does not mean it has to be boring. There are some beautifully grained woods that are more than suitable for a one-piece handle. Nevertheless, for this project, I have laminated three contrasting species to give some added interest. A planer is not required, since the pieces can be prepared using a band saw (or another type of saw) and a belt sander. The pieces are fairly thin, and if clamped thoroughly they will flex and take up any discrepancy in their flatness. While this may seem more trouble than using one piece of wood, the delineation between the layers can be utilized to assist with accuracy and symmetry of your carving.

MATERIALS

- Wood: two pieces of American black walnut 5" x 3½" x ¼" (127 x 89 x 6mm); two pieces of cedar of Lebanon 5" x 3½" x ¼" (127 x 89 x 6mm); and one piece of sapele 5" x 3½" x 1⁄16" (127 x 89 x 1.5mm)
- Cardboard for template
- Hazel shank
- Glue: two-part epoxy and a wood glue

- Brass ferrule
- Buffalo horn spacer, ½" (13mm) thick
- Sandpaper: 120- to 400-grits
- Mineral spirits
- Finishing oil

PREPARATION

The diameter of the shank I am using for this project is 1" (25mm). The thicknesses of the wood used for the head is designed to accommodate this measurement. If the diameter of the shank you are using is significantly different, you will need to adjust the width of the neck in the plan and the thicknesses of the wood you have chosen to use.

1 The thickness of the wood listed in the materials section is the finished measurement. If you are cutting your own pieces by handsaw or band saw, cut them slightly thicker to enable sanding of the faces down to their finished dimensions. The grain needs to run vertically along its 5" (127mm) length. The combined final thickness of these five pieces before lamination is just over 1" (25mm), giving a small margin for sanding.

Tip

As an example, say you have a block of American black walnut, 5" x 3½" x 2" (127 x 89 x 51mm), that has been purchased from a merchant. It is likely that the two outside faces will be flat, having been prepared by machine. Instead of cutting two consecutive slices from the block, cut a slice from each of the two prepared faces. Then, when making up the laminated block, position these two faces, which will not need sanding, on the inside up against the pieces of cedar of Lebanon. If you repeat this for all five pieces, you will reduce the faces that need sanding and leveling by half.

Once you have cut the pieces, bearing in mind the tip above, they need to be sanded to their final thickness. If you have a planer, this will be simple. If you do not, as I don't, cut the pieces oversize with a handsaw or band saw. Sand by hand on a flat sheet of sandpaper or on a medium-grit sanding belt. When you have all of the inside faces flat and smooth, glue them together with wood glue. It can be easier to manage if the middle three pieces are glued first, allowed to dry, and then the outside pieces glued to the block of three. Clamp thoroughly with as many clamps as you can fit and leave overnight to dry.

CUTTING THE BLANK

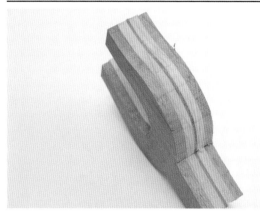

2 Use the plan to make a cardboard template, then draw around the template on your block of wood. Cut out the shape of the blank using a band saw or coping saw.

3 Clamp the blank upside down in a vice or workbench and use a two-way spirit level to ensure the face is level in both planes. Mark the center of the bottom, and at this point use a wood drill to bore a ½" (13mm) hole. Drill to a depth of 1¾" (44mm). Drill a hole in the center of the buffalo horn spacer with the same drill.

4 The blank and horn spacer with holes drilled.

Tip 🖉

When using a round piece of horn that has been prepared by the seller, a washer can be used to find the center point. Lay a washer, slightly smaller than the spacer, on top of the spacer. Position the outer edge evenly around the spacer and this will help you locate the center point.

ROUGHING OUT

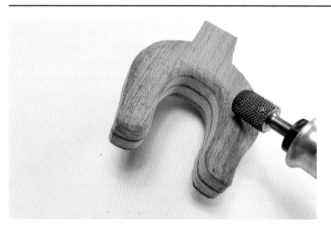

5 Use a coarse, cylinder carbide-point bit in your rotary tool and gradually taper both sides of the two arms of the blank. This is where the lamination is helpful, as you can taper down to just before the start of the cedar of Lebanon slices and thereby ensure that both arms are of equal thickness. Round over the four edges of each arm. Do not take any material from the neck at this stage.

6 Give the head a rough sanding with a 120-grit sandpaper in a cushioned-drum sander. Check the shape and symmetry of the carving so far. Adjust if necessary.

7 Wrap the shank with a protective sheath. Water pipe lagging is ideal. Find the center point at the top of the shank and mark with a bradawl. Place a metal washer with an external diameter of just over half an inch (13mm) on this center point and draw around it. This will give you a guide as to the diameter of the dowel at the top of the shank.

8 Use a flat-ended pencil to find the combined depth of the hole in the head and the spacer. Although you know this is 2" (51mm) (1½" [38mm] deep hole in the shank plus spacer of ½" [13mm]), it is still advisable to double-check using this method. Mark this measurement by pressing in your fingernail.

9 Transfer this measurement over to the top of the shank. Wrap a piece of straightedge from a glossy magazine page around the shank at this mark and secure with masking tape.

When joining the head using the method of cutting a dowel from the shank, there are many ways in which to achieve a neatly cut shoulder on which the head will sit. A fine-toothed saw is essential. I found by trial and error that a junior hacksaw with a blade depth of ¼" (6mm) worked well with the one-inch (25mm) diameter of most shanks used for a walking stick. If you cut around the shoulder with the hacksaw to the depth of its blade, this will leave an internal diameter (which will form the base of the dowel) of ½" (13mm)—the diameter of the hole drilled in the head. You can adjust how far you cut down with the hacksaw to accommodate a different diameter of shank. Always err on the side of undercutting; otherwise, if the saw cuts into the base of the dowel, it will be weakened. Any other saw could be marked with a permanent marker at the ¼" (6mm) depth to achieve the same result.

10 Cut around the shank until the top of the hacksaw blade is slightly above the surface of the shank.

11 Use the carving knife to cut a groove around the upper side of this cut.

12 Next, cut down the top end of the shank to roughly equal with the circle drawn earlier with the washer. You will now have a guide at the top and bottom of this section equaling the diameter of the dowel that needs to be carved.

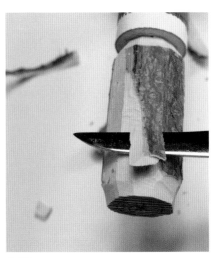

13 Remove the waste with a carving knife.

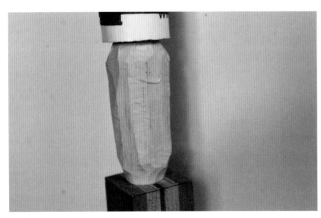

14 At the start, concentrate on the top of the shank until the dowel being whittled fits into the hole in the head.

15 Continue to remove wood with the knife until the head slides on. You are aiming for a squeaky-tight fit. If the dowel is too thin, it will result in a weakened joint. On the other hand, do not try to force on the head, as the wood may split.

Eventually, the head will slide down the dowel, leaving a gap where the spacer will sit. Remove the head and continue to carve away the wood of the dowel until the spacer fits snuggly.

16 Chamfer the bottom inside edge of the horn spacer. This will help it to seat better and give a place where excess glue can pool.

SHAPING THE NECK

17 Place the spacer and head on the shank. Turn all components until the best fit is achieved and mark them at this place.

18 Wrap a few rounds of masking tape around the top of the shank. Use the course, carbide-point bit to shape the bottom of the head, and the horn spacer to match the shape at the shoulder of the shank. If the head or spacer is loose, wrap some tape around the dowel.

> When shaping the neck of such a thumb stick, crook, or other similar handle, the convention is to have the sides of the neck parallel with the shank or for them to correspond to the slight taper of the shank. However, this is mainly for competitions and the finish of the head is your choice.

19 Use the medium flame to tidy up the angle between the neck and the arms and to round over the edges of the neck to conform to the shape of the arms.

SANDING

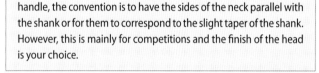

20 With the head still on the shank, sand the neck and spacer with the cushioned-drum sander and 120-grit paper.

21 Remove the wrapping of masking tape from the top of the shank. Now sand with 240-grit sandpaper to take the bottom of the horn spacer flush with the top of the shank. Sand the remainder of the neck and head with 240-grit paper. Lastly, one final check that you are happy with the symmetry and shape of the head, then sand by hand with 320- and 400-grit paper. A wipe with a cloth and mineral spirits over the head and holding it up to the light will show up any tiny blemishes. If there are any, mark their location with a pencil and sand again.

GLUING

22 Use two-part epoxy glue to attach the spacer and head to the shank. It can be easier to do this in two stages. Wipe away any excess glue, before it has dried, with a lint-free cloth and mineral spirits. Check the joint is neat once the glue has dried. By using epoxy glue instead of wood glue, you will still have the option to do any minor sanding of the joints if needed.

(b) Use the knife to remove wood from the tip of the shank to accommodate the shape of the ferrule. Keep testing the fit as you carve. The inside of the ferrule will have a residue of machine oil, and this can be used to indicate where the high spots need to be removed.

FINISHING

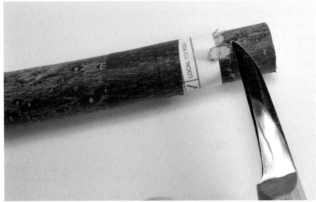

23 **(a)** Prepare the shank to receive the brass ferrule. Measure the height of the ferrule and transfer this measurement to the shank. At this point, wrap around an edge of magazine as was done when the dowel was cut from the shank. Use a carving knife to place a stop-cut around the edge of the magazine and remove a sliver of wood from the bottom side.

(c) Continue to pare wood from the tip of the shank until the ferrule is approximately 2-3mm from the stop-cut. Leaving this gap enables the ferrule to be tapped up to the stop, ensuring a tight fit.

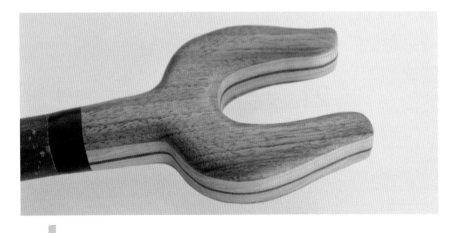

24 Ensure the shank is smooth, then wipe with mineral spirits to remove dust and, when dry, apply your choice of finishing oil. Applying the oil around where the ferrule will be fitted gives extra protection to the work-end of the walking stick. When the oil has dried, glue the ferrule with two-part epoxy glue.

(See page 217 for pattern)

PROJECT 2

Barley Twist Thumb Stick

The shape known as barley-sugar twist, or more commonly referred to as barley twist, is thought to have derived from the oral account of the helix-shaped structural pillars for the roof of Solomon's Temple, circa 6th century BC.

The design arrived in the UK with Katherine of Braganza of Portugal in 1661 when she married Charles II. Furniture makers and master carvers found that the twist gave additional strength to heavy tables and other furniture. Originally, it had to be carved by hand, until woodworkers learned how to create the shape using a lathe. This opened up their opportunity to create more intricate designs, such as double and open helix.

Revivals of the design over the centuries has seen the barley twist used as an ornamental feature rather than one of structure.

The head for this walking stick is a stylized version of a closed, double helix barley twist.

MATERIALS

- Wood: piece of olive ash (or other patterned hardwood) 7½" along the grain by 3" wide and 1¼" thick (191 x 76 x 32mm); piece of oak 1³⁄₁₆" square by ¾" thick (30mm square x 19mm thick)
- Cardboard for template
- Metal screwed rod: 5" long by ⁵⁄₁₆" thick (127 x 8mm)
- Hazel shank

- Dowel, ⁵⁄₁₆" wide by 1" long (8 x 25mm)
- Two-part epoxy glue
- Sandpaper: 120- to 400-grits
- Mineral spirits
- Finishing oil

PREPARATION

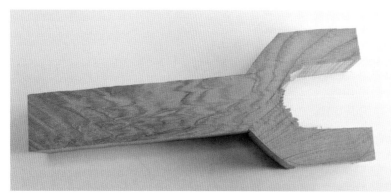

1 Make a cardboard template from the drawing and use it to cut out the blank with a band saw.

DID YOU KNOW?

The term *olive ash* does not refer to any specific species of ash (Fraxinus genus), but instead refers to the darker, streaked heartwood found in some ash trees that resembles the beautiful grain of olive wood.

2 Ensure that the top of the shank and the bottom of the head are smooth, flat, and at right angles to each other. Drill a ⅛" (3mm) pilot hole in the center of the shank and the center of the bottom of the head.

This walking stick head is an example of how to join the head to the shank with a screwed, metal rod instead of the carved, wooden dowel in the previous project. The metal rod I am using is around ⁵⁄₁₆" (8mm) thick and 5" (127mm) long. These can be purchased as a long rod from which a piece can be cut or as short lengths of around 5" (127mm). If what is available to you is shorter or of a different diameter, change the drill size used in the following step.

3 Clamp the head in a vice or workbench. With a sharp wood drill, bore a hole to a depth of 2 ½" (64mm). Use a sharp drill to prevent wander, as there is little margin for error when drilling the hole. Do the same for the shank. If you mark your drill with masking tape for the depth required, give the drill an extra rotation when you reach this depth. This will ensure that the head and shank will be flush when the metal rod is inserted. If you drill the two holes just under 2 ½"(64mm), the two rod surfaces will not meet and you will have to drill one of the holes deeper.

SHAPING THE BARLEY TWIST

Remove the head from the shank. Use the template on page 218 to map out the spiral on the head. Start from the top of the neck where it joins the arms, and measure segments down the neck in ¾" (19mm) increments. You should have five segments and around an inch (25mm) left bare at the bottom of the neck. Draw a line through the center of each of the four sides of the neck, which will aide symmetry and reference.

4 Insert the rod into the shank and place the head on top. Twist the components until a good fit is achieved. There should always be one position where all align in the vertical plane and the two surfaces fit flush without any gaps. Refer to the section on joining if you need to tweak the components to achieve the perfect fit. Draw a mark on the head and shank at this point for later reference.

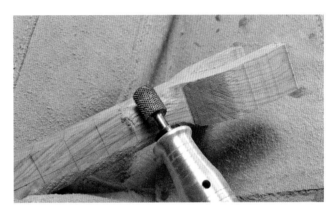

5 Use a coarse cylinder carbide-point bit to round over the four edges of the neck. Take them close to the drawn centerlines but not beyond, as this will enable you to still see the segment marks.

6 Use 120-grit sandpaper in a cushioned-drum sander to roughly sand out the coarse bit marks. Redraw the segment marks at the center of the sides if erased. This time, use those marks to draw the spirals around the neck. There are four. They will intersect at the crossover of the segment marks and the centerlines drawn along the sides, as shown in the photo.

7 Run a coarse flame carbide-point bit around the four spiral lines to define the pattern.

8 With the same bit, gradually deepen these grooves. Try to keep them an equal distance apart. Aim for a groove that will be 5/16" (8mm) wide and deep.

9 Use the coarse cylinder carbide bit to reduce the thickness of the two arms.

10 Define the crossover of the two arms. Make sure that you follow the twist leading to them, as they will be on opposite sides. Don't make the crossover too deep, as comfort is the first priority. Round over the top of the arms. These can be finished in any way you chose.

11 Use the medium, flame carbide point to round over the edges of the spirals.

SANDING

12 Wrap a few turns of 120-grit sandpaper around a split mandrel to obtain a thickness that will fit into the grooves of the spirals. Sand the grooves.

13 Use the cushioned-drum sander with 120-grit abrasive and the above split-mandrel sander to round over the edges of the spirals. Don't go near the extreme bottom of the neck, as there is danger of this ruining the joint between head and shank.

14 Sand the two arms with the cushioned drum and 120-grit sandpaper.

GLUING THE HEAD TO THE SHANK

When you are happy with the shape and symmetry of the barley twist head, other than final sanding, you can fix it to the shank with two-part epoxy glue. It is better to do this in one step; in that way you can ensure the head and shank are aligned to the marks made in step 4 and seated properly. Wipe away any excess glue with a lint-free cloth and mineral spirits. If you allow the glue to dry, it will be difficult to remove without damaging the shank.

15 The neck of the barley twist should still be overhanging the joint with the shank at this stage.

Tip

Never take any material from the top of the shank to match with the shape of the head whenever you are using wood. It should always be the other way around—the head should be shaped to that of the shank. Shanks, especially holly, can have an oval profile, and this is when a spacer is handy, as it allows you to use the spacer to take up the different shape of both head and shank. Antler can sometimes be oval and offer a good match to a holly shank.

If you are using antler with an oval profile, sometimes it is necessary to remove material from the antler for it to fit onto the shank. However, this can look ugly, and often a spacer will save you from having to do this. The top of the spacer can be shaped to the oval profile of the antler, and the bottom can be shaped to the profile of the shank.

16 Use a medium cylinder carbide-point bit to shape the bottom of the neck to match the profile of the shank. Sand with 120-grit on the cushioned-drum sander, but leave enough wood for final sanding.

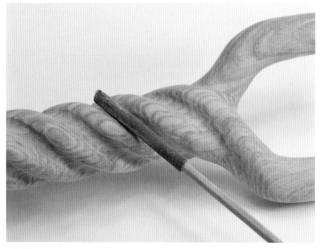

17 Finish sanding the head with 240-, 320-, and 400-grit sandpaper. Sand by hand or split mandrel, and if you wrap and glue sandpaper to a ⅛" (3mm) dowel, it will be perfect to access the grooves.

19 Use epoxy glue to glue the oak tip on to the shank, using the dowel. When dry, round over the tip with the medium flame and sand with 120-grit abrasive.

> I have used this tip for demonstration purposes and as an option should nothing else be available. I would consider it a temporary solution and would never rely on this method if the walking stick was being made for somebody else.

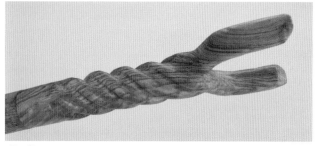

20 Apply several coats of the finishing oil of your choice to the stick. I have used a matte oil.

FITTING THE TIP

18 This is the stage that a ferrule would be fitted. However, the following process will see you through in circumstances where you do not have available a brass ferrule or other suitable material for the tip. I have fashioned a tip from a hard oak. You will need a piece about 1 ³⁄₁₆" square x ¾" thick (30 x 19mm).

Drill a ⁵⁄₁₆" (8mm) hole in the shank and piece of oak to accommodate the length of the dowel, but drill no more than approximately ⁵⁄₁₆" (8mm) into the piece of oak.

(See page 219 for pattern)

PROJECT *3*

Lady's Half-Crook Walking Stick

In the seventeenth and eighteenth centuries, lady's wooden canes incorporated materials such as ivory, whalebone, and rhinoceros' horn, and were also decorated with jewels and gemstones. This was a way to parade their wealth to others when out for a stroll.

This project is a lady's half-crook walking stick with the handle carved from cedar of Lebanon. While this project is devoid of expensive metals or gemstones, the nose of the handle has been cut away and replaced with a piece of American black walnut to add contrast and decoration. In addition, it includes three spacers of purpleheart and African blackwood. The head is attached to a hazel "twisty" shank using the metal rod method.

MATERIALS

- Wood for the handle: cedar of Lebanon (*Cedrus libani*) 5½" (140mm) along the grain x 4" (102mm) x 1¼" (32mm) thick

- Wood for the end cap: American black walnut (*Juglans nigra*) 1¼" (32mm) along the grain x 1" (25mm) x ¾" (19mm)

- Wood for the spacers: two pieces of African blackwood (*Dalbergia melanoxylon*) and one piece of purpleheart (*Peltogyne pubescens*) 1¼" (32mm) square x ¼" (6mm) thick

- Cardboard for template

- Screwed metal rod, 5¾" (146mm) long and ⁵⁄₁₆" (8mm) diameter

- Hazel shank

- Two-part epoxy glue

- Wood glue

- Brass ferrule

- Sandpaper: 120- to 400-grit

- Mineral spirits

- Finishing oil

- Dowel, two pieces ¼" (6mm) diameter and 1" (25mm) long

PREPARATION

1 The dimensions of this handle are to fit onto a shank with a diameter of approximately 1" (25mm). If the shank you are using is significantly different, you will need to alter the drawing to accommodate. Make a cardboard template from the drawing on page 219 and use it to cut out the blank with a band saw. The template also comes in handy for reference during roughing out of the blank.

2 Next, ensure that the bottom of the handle is flat and at 90 degrees to the neck. Find the center at the bottom. Clamp the head in a vice or workbench. Use a sharp, ⁵⁄₁₆" (8mm) wood drill to bore a hole to a depth of 2 ½" (64mm). Use a sharp drill to prevent wander.

3 Use a metal washer to help find the center of the top of the shank.

4 Make sure the top surface of the shank is flat and smooth. Test fit the handle to ascertain there are no gaps. Drill a hole in the shank using the same method as used above for the handle.

You can start by drilling a pilot hole if you wish. If you mark your drill with masking tape for the required depth, give the drill bit an extra rotation when you reach it. Alternatively, you can set the masking tape to a depth of just over 2½" (645mm). If you drill the two holes at exactly or just under 2½" (64mm), the head and shank will not fit flush when placed on the metal rod. As this is a handle intended for support, these depths should not be less than those stated or there will be insufficient strength at the joint.

Tip

Refer to the section on joining (Chapter 4) for some tips on freehand drilling of these vertical holes.

CUTTING THE NOSE

Having the nose capped with a different wood is an optional step. The size of the cap and the wood species is also one of personal choice. I have used a piece of American black walnut. Cut a small block to approximately 1¼" by 1" by ¾" (32 x 25 x 19mm). Cut the block to match the orientation of the grain of the piece of cedar removed.

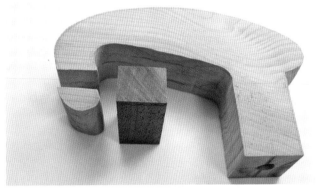

5 Cut two spacers from African blackwood and one from purpleheart at approximately 1¼" (32mm) square and ¼" (6mm) thick.

Find the center of the spacers and drill a ⁵⁄₁₆" (8mm) diameter hole through them. You can do these one at a time or all three together. Either way, when drilling, place them on a scrap of wood to prevent any tear-out. Also, when cutting thinner sections than these for spacers or decoration, they may split if drilled without any backing.

> If you trust your band saw setup to produce perfect cuts, you can use it to cut the spacers to the exact thickness. If not, cut them slightly thicker and use a belt sander, or similar, to reduce them to ¼" (6mm). This thickness is not critical, as the holes drilled in the head and shank can be altered to accommodate any variation of thickness. You can, if you wish, replace the three spacers with one of ¾" (19mm). This is good practice for the next project, where several different sections of wood are joined.

6 Use the band saw to cut a slice from the nose of the handle of approximately ¾" (19mm). Cut horizontally to match the orientation at the bottom of the neck of the handle.

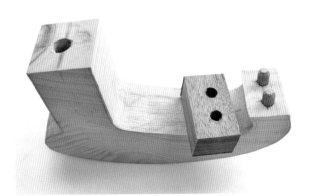

7 Drill holes for the dowels, to secure the cap, in both the handle and the piece of walnut. Use dowel pins to ensure the hole positions match. The piece of walnut is slightly larger than needed to allow for small errors. Drill no more than ⅜" (10mm) deep into the walnut block.

8 Before gluing the dowels, make sure the two surfaces where the cap will meet the handle are at 90 degrees to the neck and are flat and smooth. Test fit the cap, and when you are happy with the joint, glue the end cap onto the handle using epoxy glue or a wood glue suitable for exterior use.

SHAPING THE HANDLE

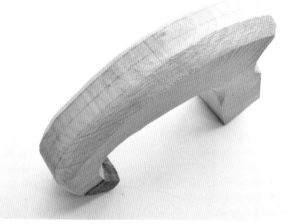

9 Allow the glue to set overnight. Use a coarse, cylinder, carbide-point bit to shape the block of walnut to the original shape of the handle. This is where the cardboard template will help.

10 Draw the centerline around the handle. The finished width of the handle will be approximately 1 ⅛" (29mm). Divide the top of the handle into quarters from the centerline outward. Each will be approximately ⁵⁄₁₆" (8mm). Use the coarse cylinder bit to flatten the corners of two outside quarters of the upper and lower edges of the handle. Carve down the handle to approximately the same distance as the top surface. Stop short of the nose of the handle as shown in the photograph.

SANDING THE HANDLE

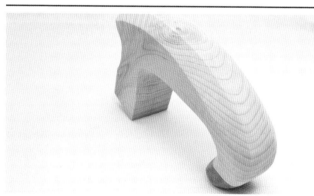

12 Sand the head with 120-grit sandpaper on the cushioned-drum sander. Do not touch the extreme bottom of the neck. When sanding, keep the edge faces flat, as carved in step 10. Of course, this is optional and can be rounded over if you prefer.

11 With the same bit, taper the nose of the handle, starting approximately 2½" (64mm) from the tip. Taper to just outside the first quarter drawn from the centerline in the previous step (approximately ⁵⁄₁₆" [8mm]).

DID YOU KNOW?

It is believed that the earliest canes used by women were in France during the 11th century. These lightweight apple canes carried a decorative head, a bird being one of their favorites. In the late 18th century, Marie Antoinette, Queen of France, was known to use a shepherd's crook.

FIXING THE SPACERS

I mentioned in the section on joining that the decision to glue the head and shank when using the metal rod method is a matter of personal choice as to whether it is done in one or two steps. This project will show how to join in two steps. Dry fit the head and shank to double-check that the faces to be joined are flush. Twist the components until the best fit is achieved. Often, there is one position where all align in the vertical plane and the two surfaces fit flush without any gaps. Refer to the section on joining if you need to tweak the components to achieve this perfect fit.

SHAPING THE NECK OF THE HANDLE

14 Place the head back onto the metal rod and use the coarse cylinder to shape the sides of the handle and spacers to the shape of the shank. Leave plenty of wood for sanding.

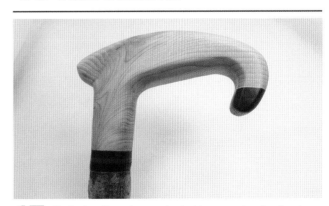

16 Lastly, sand by hand with 240-, 320-, and 400-grit sandpaper. Cedar of Lebanon gives a beautiful finish the finer you sand. If available, continue sanding with 600- and 800-grit paper. Lightly round over the hard corners but keep the distinct shape of the edges.

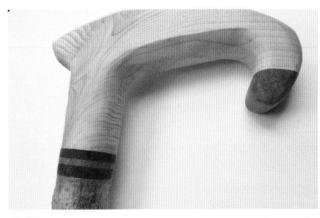

13 Draw a mark on the head, spacers, and shank at this point for later reference. Glue the spacers and the metal rod into the shank with plenty of two-part epoxy glue. Wipe away any excess around the joint and above the spacers with a cloth and mineral spirits. This is very important, otherwise the head will not seat properly.

15 Use 120-grit abrasive on the cushioned-drum sander to sand the neck and the spacers. If there is any movement of the head while doing this, wrap a couple of rounds of masking tape around the metal rod. Remember to remove before gluing.

FIXING THE HANDLE TO THE SHANK

17 Fix the handle to the metal rod with epoxy glue, fit a ferrule, and apply several coats of your choice of finishing oil. This is the finished walking stick.

(See page 218 for pattern)

PROJECT 4
Gentleman's Dress Stick

This next project is for a comfortable walking stick that is suitable for leisure purposes or as a walking aide. This design is sometimes referred to as an escort stick, a fritz, or even a pistol grip. Therefore, it would seem that unless the handle has a recognized name (e.g., crook, derby), you can refer to a shape in almost any way you wish.

To take the walking stick design a step further, this handle has the addition of end caps and accent pieces, which add a touch of refinement and color and complement the English walnut handle.

MATERIALS

- Wood for handle: piece of English walnut (*Juglans regia*) 6¾" along the grain x 4" high x 1³⁄₁₆" wide (171 x 102 x 30mm)

- Wood for accent pieces: four pieces of purpleheart (*Peltogyne pubescens*), two at 1⅗" x 1⅗" (41 x 41mm) and two at 2" x 1⅗" (51 x 41mm), and all ⅛" (3mm) thick; two pieces of African blackwood (*Dalbergia melanoxylon*), one at 1⅗" x 1⅗" (41 x 41mm) and one at 2" x 1⅗" (51mm x 41mm), both ⅛" (3mm) thick

- Wood for caps: two pieces of spalted beech (*Fagus sylvatica*), one at 1⅗" x 1⅗" x ¼" (41 x 41 x 6mm) and the other 2" x 1⅗" x ⁷⁄₁₆" (51 x 41 x 11mm)

- Wood for spacers: one piece of African black wood 1⅗" x 1⅗" x ⁵⁄₁₆" (41 x 41 x 8mm); two pieces of purpleheart 1⅗" x 1⅗" x ½" (41 x 41 x 13mm)

- Cardboard for template

- Hazel shank

- ¼" (6mm)–diameter dowel, approximately 5" (127mm) long

- Cloth-backed sandpaper 120- to 400-grits

- Brass ferrule

- Epoxy glue

- Finishing oil

- Mineral spirits

PREPARATION

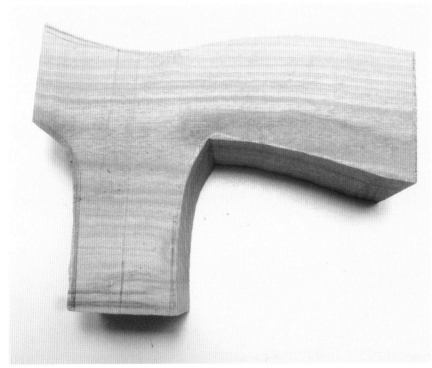

1 Make a side template from the drawing (see page 219) and use the band saw to cut out the blank. The shank I am using is about 1⅛" (29mm). This plan allows for ¹⁄₁₆" (1.5mm) margin for error. If the shank you are using significantly differs, adjust the diagram and template accordingly.

2 Find the center point at the bottom of the handle. Clamp the head into a vice or workbench. Use a two-way spirit level to ensure the blank is level in both planes. Drill to a depth of 2½" (64mm) with a ½" (13mm) wood drill. Ensure you use a sharp drill to prevent wander.

3 This project incorporates three spacers between the head and the shank: two purpleheart and one African blackwood. Use any wood of your choice. Drill the three spacers with the ½" (13mm) wood drill. Remember to drill them on a backing board to prevent any tear-out.

CUTTING THE DOWEL FROM THE SHANK

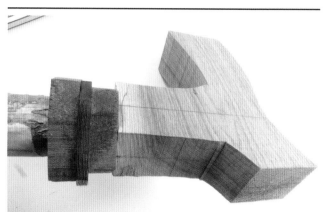

4 Use a carving knife to prepare the dowel from the top section of the shank. It must be long enough to fit into the head and through the spacers. Dry fit the three spacers and head. Wherever you achieve the best fit, use that alignment to mark all the pieces. (Please refer to the chapter on joining for this process.)

PREPARING AND FIXING THE ACCENTS AND CAPS

5 As a variation of this joining process, to show it is a matter of personal choice, glue the spacers to the shank. Normally I prefer to glue the spacers and head when all carving is finished. However, as this handle only needs to be rounded over and does not involve detailed carving, it can be glued separately to the spacers.

6 Use a band saw to cut out the end caps and accent pieces for the front and rear of the handle. Aim for a new blade and correct setup when cutting their thickness, as any gaps between these pieces will spoil the appearance. In total, you will need four purpleheart at ⅛" (3mm); two spalted beech, one ¼" (6mm) and the other ⁷⁄₁₆" (11mm); two African blackwood at ⅛" (3mm). Cut the front pieces to approximately 1⅗" (41mm) square and those for the rear 2" x 1⅗" (51 x 41mm). As with the spacers, use any wood and design of your choice.

7 Once you have cut the slices for the accents and end caps, arrange them until they fit together snugly and leave no gaps. Number the pieces in the order and orientation that you have decided upon.

8 The accent pieces and the end caps need to be drilled for fixing with a dowel. The end caps are not drilled completely through. Double-check the layout before drilling.

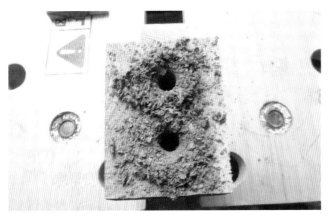

9 Drill two ¼" (6mm) holes, about ½" (13mm) deep and ⅜" (10mm) apart, in the rear end of the handle (largest end) for the dowels.

10 Place two dowel pins in the holes.

11 Take the first piece of purpleheart that will adjoin the handle at the rear, ensure you have the correct orientation, and lightly press onto the pins. Ensure you have wood overhanging the blank on all sides.

DID YOU KNOW?

It became fashionable for men to carry a walking stick as part of their daily attire during the 17th century. Rules of etiquette were established and any deviation from those codes was considered extremely poor manners. From the early 18th century, this was taken even further in London. It was deemed a privilege for a man to carry a stick, and he was required to obtain a license.

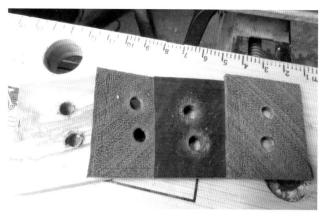

12 Place the piece of purpleheart, with the two marks on the top of the other two accent pieces that adjoin it, on the rear of the handle. Secure on a workbench with clamps, ensuring you keep their alignment. Drill ¼" (6mm)–diameter holes through the three pieces, using each of the two marks as your center. Then take the spalted beech cap for the rear and, using one of the accent pieces as your template, drill into the side that will abut the accent pieces. Drill approximately ¼" (6mm), or not more than halfway through. Mark the depth on your drill with masking tape to ensure you do not break out of the other side.

13 Repeat this process for the accents and cap for the front end of the handle. Now you have all of the accents and caps ready for gluing to the handle.

14 Cut four pieces of ¼" (6mm)–diameter dowel long enough to fit into the handle, through the accent pieces, and into the end cap. This will be approximately 1" (25mm) for the front and 1⅛" (29mm) at the rear. Start by cutting two pieces of dowel oversize for the front part of the handle, insert them into the handle, then load the three accent pieces onto the dowels. Ensure they fit flush. Now you will be able to see how much dowel is needed for the spalted beech end cap. Trim the dowel at this length and dry fit the end cap. When you are happy that everything is in its correct place and the joints are neat, carry out the same process with the rear end of the handle. Ensure all accents and caps overhang the handle blank for shaping.

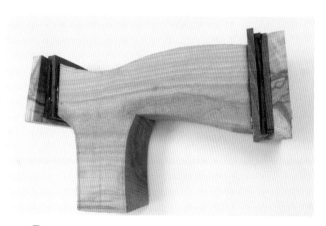

15 Glue the accents and caps onto the handle with two-part epoxy glue. You can do this in one or more steps. I found it best to glue all the pieces at the front and, when dry, do the same for the other end.

SHAPING SPACERS & NECK

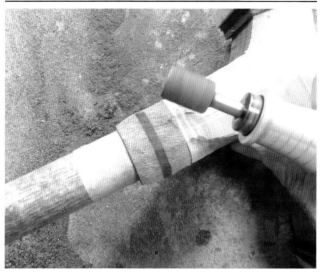

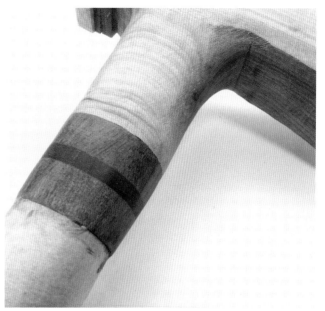

16 Put the head back onto the shank temporarily and line up with your marks. Wrap masking tape around the shank a couple of times where it meets the spacers for protection when using the rotary tool. With a coarse, cylinder, carbide-point bit, shape the neck of the handle and the spacers to the desired shape.

17 Sand the spacers and the neck with 120-grit paper on a cushioned-drum sander. Leave sufficient wood for fine sanding later on. Good quality 120-grit sandpaper is usually capable of removing deep burr marks. However, you can use a medium burr before sanding if you wish.

SHAPING THE HANDLE

18 Remove the handle from the shank. Use the coarse, cylinder, carbide-point bit to match the rectangular shape of the accents and caps to their respective ends of the handle. Be mindful that the wood of the accents and caps may be of different densities if you have used different species of wood. On this handle the spalted beech I have used is much softer and more care is needed, especially when using a ¼" (6mm) shaft carbide point.

Tip ✏️

Never shape the spacers or the neck without their being joined together. No matter how careful you are, there is always the tendency to round over the edges, which will spoil the joint.

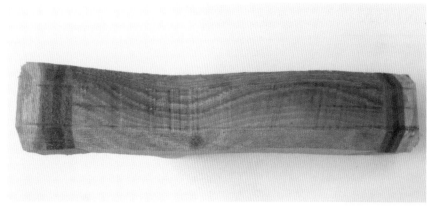

19 Draw a centerline around the handle, then divide each side in half. Use the coarse cylinder bit to knock off the corners at the top and bottom of the handle down to the first quarter.

20 A view of an end cap showing the outline of the previous step.

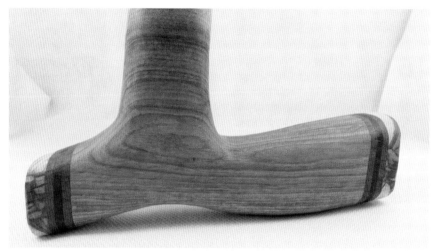

21 Use the cushioned-drum sander with 120-grit abrasive to round over the hard edges. Do not round over the handle, just the edges to leave the profile as shown in this photo.

22 Sand the entire handle by hand for the final sanding. Use 240-, 320-, and 400-grit sandpaper.

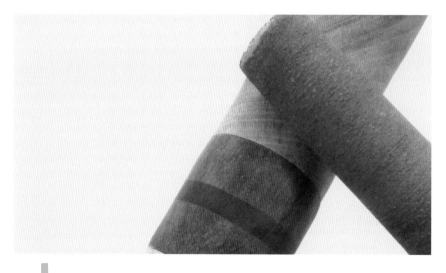

23 Refit the handle onto the shank. Sand the spacers and neck with the cushion-drum sander, and finally by hand.

GLUING HEAD TO THE SHANK & FINISHING

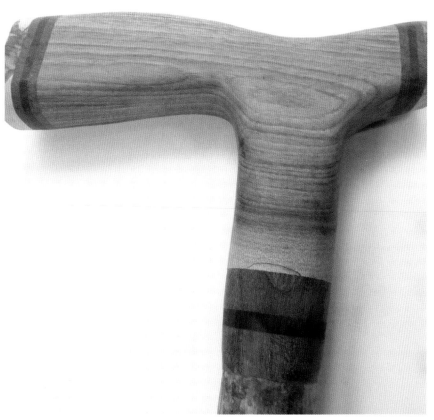

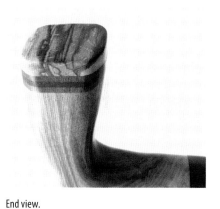

25 Wipe the stick and head with mineral spirits on a lint-free cloth. Apply at least four coats of the finishing oil of your choice. This stick has been finished with matte oil. Fix a ferrule to the end.

24 Use epoxy glue to fix the head to the shank once you are happy that all sanding is finished.

End view.

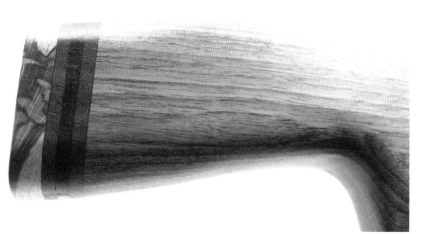

Close-up of handle.

(See page 220 for pattern)

PROJECT 5
English Cocker Spaniel Head Walking Stick

The projects until now have been of functional walking sticks that could be accomplished using basic woodworking tools such as a saw, rasp, and sandpaper. They have involved shaping more than carving of the blank.

This project is of a stylized cocker spaniel head and introduces some basic carving and detailing techniques.

Although this is a stylized carving of the cocker spaniel, it is advisable to gather as much reference material as you can. When attempting to create a realistic look, reference is essential. You cannot have too much. Sometimes trying to source, for example, a photo of the underneath of a dog's muzzle is impossible; in that case, stop and chat with someone walking their dog and surreptitiously check out the features of its head.

Carving Creative Walking Sticks and Canes

MATERIALS

- Wood for head: cedar of Lebanon 3¼" (83mm) with the grain (top to bottom) x 3½" (89mm) wide (back of head to nose) x 2½" (64mm), measuring from ear to ear
- Wood for spacers: two pieces of American black walnut 1¼" x 1¼" x ⅛" (32 x 32 x 3mm); one piece of purpleheart 1¼" x 1¼" x ¼" (32 x 32 x 6mm)
- Cardboard for template
- ¼" (6mm) glass eyes, brown or hazel

- Cloth sandpaper 120- to 800-grit
- Hazel shank
- Brass ferrule
- Epoxy glue
- Epoxy putty
- Finishing oil
- Mineral spirits

CUTTING THE BLANK

1 Use the drawings on page 220 to create side and top templates from cardboard. Use them to draw both views onto your piece of cedar. This project introduces the method of cutting a blank in both side and top views with a band saw. The sides of the block of wood being used need to be at 90 degrees to carry out the next three steps. Also, your band saw needs to be set up correctly.

2 Use a band saw to cut out the side view.

3 Replace the pieces of wood that you have cut away and secure with masking tape. A hot glue gun can also be used instead to reattach the offcuts. Ensure that the pieces are secure and that everything lines up.

> ### DID YOU KNOW?
>
> The sturdy cocker spaniel was mainly bred for hunting woodcock, and hence its name.

English Cocker Spaniel Head Walking Stick | 73

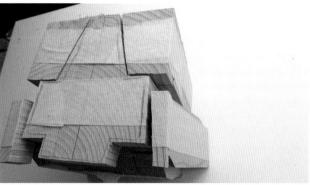

4 Use the band saw to cut the top view. Grip the block firmly and check that it is holding together. You will end up with a jigsaw of pieces.

5 Remove the masking tape and you will end up with a blank looking like the one shown in the photo. This method will save time on the initial rroughing out. However, it is not how I normally cut out my blanks, as it wastes plenty of wood.

DRILLING A HOLE IN THE HEAD

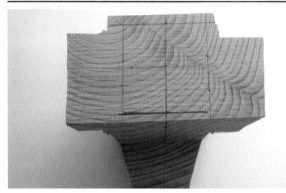

6 Draw a centerline around the head. This drawing is for a 1" (25mm) diameter shank plus a ⅛" (3mm) safety margin. If your shank differs, adjust accordingly. Find the center point of the bottom of the head. Mark a 1⅛" (29mm) square around that point.

7 Secure the head in your workbench or vice. Use a two-way spirit level to check for levelness in both planes. With a ½" (13mm) wood drill, bore a hole to a depth of 1¾" (44mm) at the center point. Use a sharp drill to prevent any wander.

PREPARING THE SPACERS

DID YOU KNOW?

The cocker spaniel originates from Spain—as the name suggests. They have been around as hunting dogs since the 1400s. In the early years, one litter could produce both cocker and springer spaniels. It wasn't until 1892 that the British Kennel Club acknowledged they were different breeds.

Cocker spaniels are affectionate, lively, and often noisy. With their amazing sense of smell, they make excellent gundogs.

8 Cut the spacers. For this project I have used three spacers, as outlined in the material section above, that measure a total of ½" (13mm). Use any wood of your choice or just one spacer of a ½" (13mm) thickness.

9 Drill ½" (13mm) holes in the center of the spacers. The purpleheart is brittle and the walnut is thin; both are liable to crack. Clamp them down with a backing board to prevent this from happening.

10 Drilled spacers.

If you use a different colored wood for the backing piece, that color sawdust will rise to the surface as you drill to confirm you have drilled all the way through the spacers.

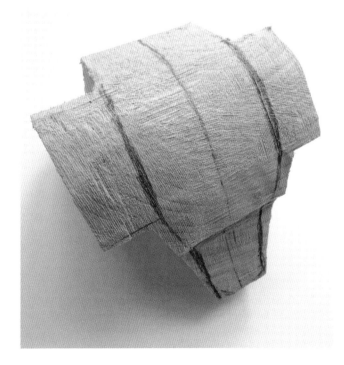

SHAPING THE HEAD

11 Depending on the width of the blade you used on the band saw, you may have to clean up the side profile. As I used a ½" (13mm) band saw blade, I had some tidying up to do. If necessary, use the template to redraw the head, and tidy with a coarse, cylinder, carbide-point bit.

12 Redraw the centerline around the head if it has been erased by the previous step. Use the top template to redraw this view, and use the same coarse bit to bring the blank down to the template's dimensions.

PREPARE SHANK

13 Prepare the shank to fit into the head before any more carving of the head is carried out. Carve a dowel from the top of the shank to fit the head and spacers. Mark all pieces where you achieve the best alignment.

SHAPING THE SPACERS

14 Put a couple of wraps of masking tape around the top of the shank beneath the spacers for protection. Use the coarse cylinder bit to reduce the size of the spacers. Carve the bottom of the spacers to match the profile of the shank. Next, carve the spacers to match the square bottom of the head. Then round over the corners at the bottom of the neck. This is only the initial shaping, and you will come back later to refine. Redraw the alignment marks of head, spacers, and shank any time they are erased.

CONTINUE SHAPING THE HEAD

15 Use the template to block in the ears with the coarse bit. Err on the generous side at this stage, as they can be further reduced as you continue to shape the head.

16 Further define the shape of the ears with the same bit. Reduce the thickness of the ears from the top, where they are almost level with the head, down to the middle. Don't remove wood from the bottom of the ears.

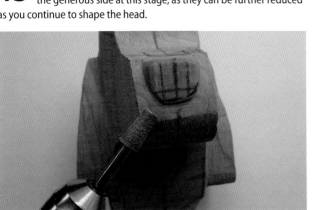

17 Draw the shape of the nose. It is approximately ⁹⁄₁₆" (14mm) wide and ⁷⁄₁₆" (11mm) from top to bottom. Use a blunt-ended, truncated-cone diamond bit to outline the shape. Lightly round over the edges and tip.

18 Use a medium flame bit to round over the top of the snout, and feather the sides into the nose.

19 With the coarse bit, round over the crown and occiput (Latin for "back of the head").

20 With a cushioned-drum sander and 120-grit paper, give the head a rough sand. You don't have to be fussy with this sanding, as it is to help give a better view of the piece to enable a shape and symmetry check. Once done, make any adjustment if necessary.

21 Draw some reference lines at ¼" (6mm) intervals from each side of the centerline to assist with symmetry. Use the same sander with 240-grit paper to remove material from the top of the muzzle to make it a touch narrower.

Identify the position of the eyes. The center of each eye is approximately ⅜" (10mm) from the centerline. They sit at an angle of approximately 20 degrees back from a line drawn through the inside edge of both eyes. Flatten out the plane of the eyes and mark the center. Taking different measurements with a pair of dividers is a useful way to confirm your calculations.

DID YOU KNOW?

Dog folklore down the ages believed that the size of the occipital bone on the top back of a dog's head was a measure of their sense of smell or intelligence. These areas are prominent in hunting dogs, such as Labradors and spaniels, and is probably how the association came about. However, there is no science to support this myth.

In fact, the occiput's main function is to protect the brain and facilitate the articulation of spine and head. It does contain many nerve endings and is massaged during canine therapy to calm a dog. The occiput has been called the following: knowledge bump, brain bump, wisdom bump, and smart bump.

FACIAL FEATURES

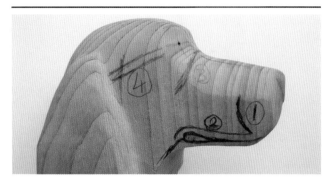

22 Now to add some definition to the muzzle. First, identify and draw the following features:

(1) The fleshy mound at the front of each side that is the nerve bed for the whiskers and sometimes called the cushion when the area is pronounced.

(2) The upper lip or flews at the bottom sides of the mouth created by the underlying orbicularis oris muscle.

(3) The concave area of the muzzle in front of the eyes.

(4) The bone of the zygomatic arch.

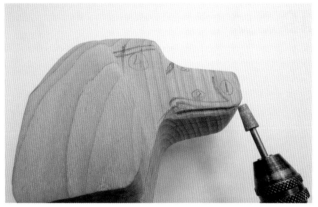

23 Before starting on these features, use the truncated-cone bit to take up the sides of the mouth from beneath the top lip by about ⅛" (3mm), as shown.

24 Use a ⁵⁄₃₂" (4mm) diamond ball to outline the features 1–4 from step 22.

25 Blend them into the surrounding area with the same bit.

26 Sand with the split-mandrel sander and 240-grit paper.

DOG'S HEAD ANATOMY

The dog's head consists of four parts: the occipital bone, skull, stop, and muzzle. The occipital bone is mentioned above. The skull is the top of the head and protects the brain; the skull ends and the muzzle starts at the "stop." This is the sloping area between where the brows, or frontal bones (*supercillary arches*), surround the eyes, at the start of the muzzle. The stop is this area of depression that slopes between the eyes, rather than a single point. In some dogs, such as the cocker spaniel, this is more pronounced and extends upward along the skull in a furrow. The muzzle is the whole of the upper area from the eyes to the nose, including the lips, and is often referred to as the face. The bony part on the top of the muzzle is called the bridge of the nose.

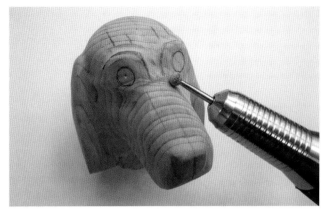

27 Use the diamond ball to outline the arch over the eyes and the stop running between the eyes up onto the forehead. Sand with 240-grit paper.

THE EYES

When a carving will be painted, the almond shape of a dog's eyes can be achieved with epoxy putty or plastic wood. If the carving is to be left natural wood, the situation is more difficult. You have three alternatives: (1) drill out a round hole just big enough for a glass eye to fit snuggly; (2) carve the eye shape and eyeball and paint; and (3) carve the oval eye shape and carve into the socket above and below the outer limit to enable the eye to be slipped up into this void and then pushed back down into place. The following is a method of achieving the latter.

28 The eyes for this project are ¼" (6mm) and glass. I have used hazel to complement the wood. Draw the almond shape of the eyes.

29 Locate the eye centers. Drill a pilot hole at the center of each eye with a ¹⁄₁₆" (1.5mm) drill bit. Drill to a depth of ½" (13mm), as these holes will come in handy—to be explained later. Drill out the socket to a depth of at least ⁷⁄₁₆" (11mm) with a ⅛" (3mm) diamond ball. Use a combination of a ³⁄₆₄", ⁵⁄₆₄", and ⅛" (1, 2, and 3mm) ball to shape the eye sockets. Aim for an opening in the center of no more than ⁷⁄₃₂" (6mm). Now, undercut the sockets above and below their upper and lower limits. Check the eye will fit by inserting backward.

When you come to fitting the eye, you will need to put the eye into the bottom recess and then push it up until in place. The difficulty with this method is that you cannot test the eye fit with it facing forward, as it would be nigh impossible to retrieve the eye. Also, when it comes to fitting them, you will only have one chance to place them in the sockets correctly.

30 Add the tear ducts at the inner margin of the sockets as shown.

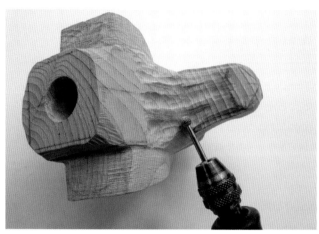

31 Finish the eyes by rounding the edges of the sockets and the tear ducts with a rolled-up piece of 240-grit paper.

THE LOWER MANDIBLE

32 Draw the mouth shape of the lower mandible and position of the dewlaps.

33 Using a ⁵⁄₃₂" (4mm) diamond ball, carve out the indentation that runs through the center of the bottom of the lower mandible. Then carve the dewlaps. Round over the inside edge of the lower mandible so that it meets the line of the mouth carved in step 24. Make sure you do not take any material away from the bottom of the neck where it joins the shank.

34 Sand the lower mandible with 120- and 240-grit paper on the split-mandrel sander.

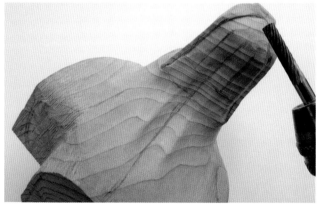

35 Draw the position of the inner edge of the upper mandible's flews or lips. Using a ⅛" (3mm) cylinder carbide cutter, carve along the inside of this line. Cut at an angle to give the appearance of the lower mandible disappearing into the upper.

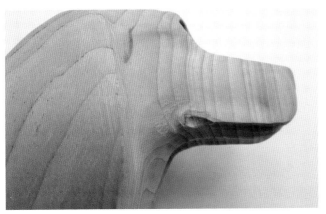

36 Use the ⅛" (3mm) diamond ball to define the indentation where the upper and lower mandibles meet at the mouth commissure as shown. A muscle (orbicularis oris) loops around the commissure, causing a depression behind. Use the ⅛" (3mm) ball to define.

37 With 240-grit paper on the split mandrel, sand the features carved on the lower mandible and lightly round over the edges of the top lips.

NOSTRILS

38 Make sure you are happy with the shape of the nose before carving the nostrils. Draw the nostrils—they should be shaped like a comma. It will help if you draw some reference lines.

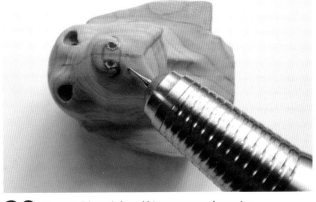

39 Use a ³⁄₆₄" (1mm) dental bit to open up the cavity.

40 Once you have the main shape, use a scalpel to open up the slit that runs to the outside edge and along the side of the nose. This constitutes the alar fold and opens when the dog is running or scenting to increase the airflow.

Use the scalpel to define the philtrum. This is the thin indentation that runs from halfway up the middle of the nose, down to the top of the mouth.

> ### DID YOU KNOW?
>
> The first cocker to enter the United States sailed on the Mayflower in 1620.

SHAPING THE EARS

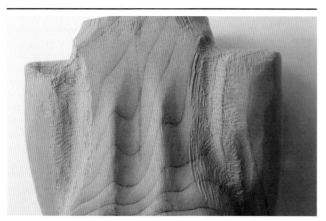

41 With a medium flame bit, shape the ears by rounding over the edges to meet the head. Give an impression of the separation of the bottom of the ear from the head by carving an indentation with the medium flame. Sand with 240-grit paper on the split mandrel.

TEXTURING THE EARS

Even though this is only a stylized carving of the cocker spaniel, some basic texture on the ears will add character. Fine texture can be achieved in several ways, including a diamond wheel/cutter, pyrograph, and ceramic stones, which come in various colors denoting their grit. Texturing of later projects in this book will use a combination of all methods.

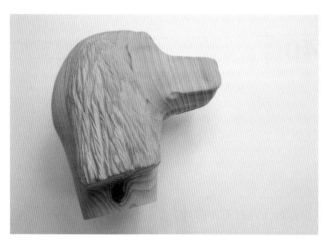

44 Use an inverted-cone, blue ceramic stone to add finer texture to the ears and a light touch to the dewlaps. Lightly sand with 240-grit in the split-mandrel sander to knock off any sharp edges. Finish with a nylon brush in the rotary tool to remove any tiny particles of wood.

FINISH SHAPING THE NECK & SPACERS

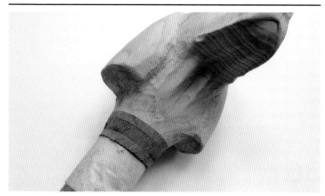

42 Place the head back onto the shank. With the coarse cylinder bit, shape the bottom of the neck and spacers as shown. Use a medium, flamed burr to remove the deep marks if necessary and then sand with 120- and 240-grit sandpaper. Wind a couple of wraps of masking tape around the shank for protection.

43 Remove the head. Draw the flow of the hair on the ears. Use a cylinder carbide cutter to add deep texture.

> **Tip** 🖉
>
> Always keep a couple of scrap pieces of wood after you have band-sawn the blank. They can be used for patching up any split, knot, etc. Also, before texturing the ears, make a few practice cuts with the carbide cutter on a piece with the same orientation of grain as the ears. Invariably, you will find that cutting in one direction will give a smoother cut.

FINISHING

45 Finish sanding the entire head and spacers, working through 240-, 320-, and 400-grit sandpaper. I went further with this project by using 600- and 800-grit, as the finish of cedar of Lebanon will improve with these finer grits. Give everything a final brush and wipe clean with mineral spirits on a lint-free cloth.

46 Apply four coats of your choice of finishing oil to the head, shank, and spacers. I have used a satin finish. Lightly de-nib the surface with 400-grit sandpaper after each coat has dried.

FITTING THE EYES

Fit the eyes with epoxy putty. The eyes are set fairly deep. Make sure to pack the hole with the right amount to stop the eye being pushed too far back into the socket. If this happens you are not likely to be able to do anything about it. However, you don't want to use too much putty, or else it will squeeze out to the front of the eye.

JOINING HEAD TO SHANK

47 Cut the eye from the wire, if it has one, then carefully slip the eye into the bottom half of the socket and push in the top of the eye. Before pushing in the top of the eye, you will get a feel if you have used enough putty in the socket. Any excess putty behind the eye will be squeezed into the pilot hole that was drilled in step 29.

48 Use epoxy glue to join the head and spacers to the shank and fit the ferrule.

(See page 224 for pattern)

PROJECT 6

Black Swan Derby Walking Stick

Black swans (*Cygnus atratus*) range freely in the estuaries and waterways of Western and Eastern Australia and Tasmania. They do not migrate. Dutch mariner Antounie Caen was the first Western explorer to encounter black swans on the Swan River in Western Australia in 1636. Prior to this, the Western world thought all swans were white in color. In 1697, an explorer attempted to take a pair of swans back to Amsterdam to support the story of their existence. Unfortunately, they died during the journey.

This project introduces the concept that a functional walking stick does not have to be plain. This stick is based on a traditional derby-style handle (that by itself is ordinary), but this handle incorporates a simplified version of a decorative head of a black swan.

This project will introduce the fitting of a collar at the joint between shank and handle. The texturing process of this head will go a few steps further than the previous project. The swan will also be painted with acrylics.

MATERIALS

- Wood: lime (*Tilia europaea*) 5½" (140mm) across the grain x 4⁵⁄₁₆" (110mm) along the grain x 1⁹⁄₁₆" (40mm) thickness
- Cardboard for template
- Epoxy and wood glue
- Epoxy putty
- Brass collar; rolled top, 1" (25mm) in diameter and length

- Brass ferrule
- Hazel shank
- Assorted sandpaper: 120- to 400-grit
- ¼" (6mm) red glass eyes
- Finishing oil
- Mineral spirits
- Acrylic paints

LIME WOOD

When texturing is part of any wood carving project, a close-grained species of wood is preferred, as it will hold fine detail. The most common species are lime (*linden*), tupelo, or jelutong. In North America, lime is also known as basswood. This name originates from the inner fibrous bark of the tree, known as *bast*.

The Ainu people of Japan are known to have made clothes and other accessories from the bark of the

Japanese lime for more than 200 years. After being soaked in water, the inner fibers become soft, easily separated, dried, then woven.

The common lime of the British Isles is a hybrid of *Tilia cordata* (small-leaved lime) and *Tilia platyphyllos* (large-leaved lime).

ROUGHING OUT THE HANDLE

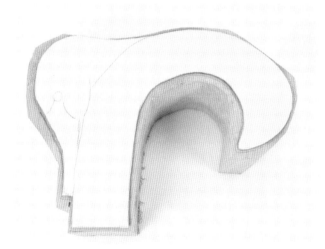

1 Use the drawings to make three templates from cardboard. Bandsaw the blank using the side-view template only. You will need the other two templates for reference later.

2 The drawings are for a shank with a 1" (25mm) diameter plus an extra ⅛" (3mm) to give some leeway for error. Adjust the drawing according to the diameter of your shank. Find the center point on the bottom face of the neck of the head. Draw a 1⅛" (29mm) square around this center point. Drill a hole 1¾" (44mm) deep with a ½" (13mm) wood drill at the center point.

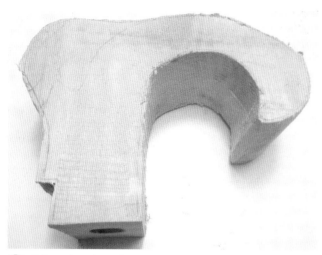

3 Tidy up the side profile, to just outside the line drawn around the template, with a coarse cylinder carbide-point bit.

4 The handle width, not the head of the swan, needs reducing from 1⁹⁄₁₆" (40mm) to 1³⁄₁₆" (30mm). Draw a centerline around the handle, then another line ⅝" (15mm) on each side of the centerline on the handle section. Use the coarse cylinder bit to remove wood from the handle down to these reference lines. Don't go beyond the rearmost position of the swan's neck. Draw the side view of the swan's head. The finished width of the swan's head is approximately 1³⁄₈" (35mm) wide, but keep it at 1⁹⁄₁₆" (40mm) for the time being. Remove the wood below the bottom edge of the head to blend in with the handle as shown in the photo.

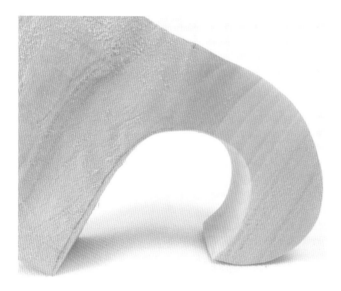

5 Give the handle a rough sand to enable a symmetry and progress check. Adjust if necessary. Redraw the centerline.

SHAPING THE SWAN'S HEAD

6 Draw the rough outline of the swan's head using the two templates. Use a coarse cylinder carbide-point bit to shape this outline.

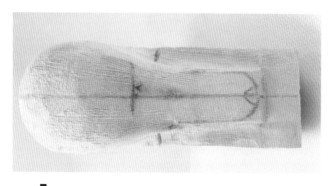

7 Using a coarse bull-nosed bit, start to round over the swan's head. Don't round over the bill.

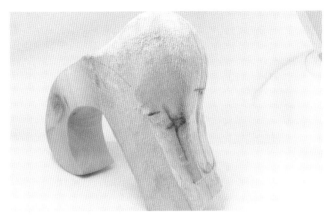

8 This view of the previous step shows that trouble is brewing. This walking stick was a commission for a customer who wanted the handle to have character. The downside of selecting a piece of wood with "character" is you do not know what problems lurk beneath the surface, and which are only revealed as you carve. As will be seen later in this project, some of these knots and splits will need repairing.

PREPARING THE DOWEL ON THE SHANK

9 Prepare the shank to receive the head by carving a 1¾" (44mm) dowel. This stick will feature a brass collar fitted around the joint between the shank and the head. Still aim for a flush joint, but, as it will be hidden by the collar, it is not as critical as if there were no collar. Remember to mark where you achieve the best alignment.

REFINE DIMENSIONS OF THE SWAN'S HEAD

10 Use a carving knife to refine the swan's head to the finished dimensions. You could continue with power for this step if you prefer.

FITTING THE COLLAR TO THE HEAD

11 Place the brass collar centrally over the hole in the bottom of the neck. Draw the inner diameter of the collar onto the head. The collar is 1" (25mm) in diameter and length. It will be fitted ¼" (6mm) on the head and ¾" (19mm) over the shank. Draw a line around the neck of the head ¼" (6mm) from the bottom. Use a knife to place a stop-cut around this line.

12 Pare away wood down to the inner diameter of the collar. Continue until you achieve a tight fit of the collar.

REFINING THE HANDLE

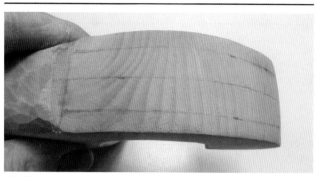

13 Pencil reference lines ⅜" (10mm) on either side of the centerline on the handle.

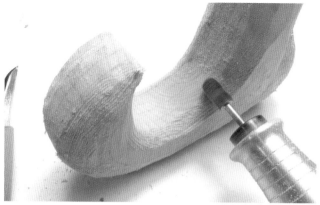

14 With the bull-nosed carbide-point bit, round over the handle down to these lines.

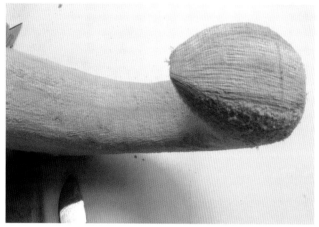

15 Shape the tip of the handle with the coarse cylinder bit. Starting at 1³⁄₁₆" (30mm) from the tip, reduce each side of the handle gradually until it meets the tip at ¼" (6mm) on each side of the centerline.

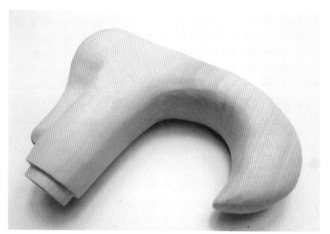

16 Sand the edges just created using the cushioned-drum sander fitted with 120-grit sandpaper.

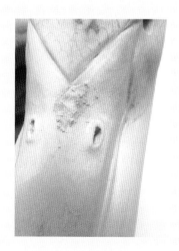

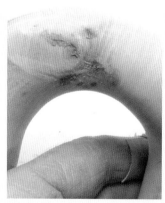

Tip

A small knot on the upper mandible and cracks in the handle needed repair. I drilled out the knot on the bill with a ball carbide cutter, then mixed sawdust from the carving with wood glue to a thick consistency. I then applied it to the two areas, leaving it proud. When dry, I sanded it smooth.

FITTING THE COLLAR TO THE SHANK

Use the following steps to fit the collar to the shank.

17 **(a)** The collar being used is 1" (25mm) in length. In steps 11 and 12, it was fitted ¼" (6mm) from the bottom of the head. Therefore, it will cover approximately ¾" (19mm) of the shank. Measure this down from the shoulder created when shaping the dowel. Secure an edge of magazine paper around this point. Use a carving knife to place a stop-cut around the shank. Carefully cut a groove at this point, working from the top side.

(b) Place the head back onto the shank. Draw a line around the edge at the bottom that was prepared for the collar.

(c) This shows how much wood needs to be removed from the shank.

(d) Start to remove wood using the carving knife.

(e) Continue removing wood down to the circle drawn at (b).

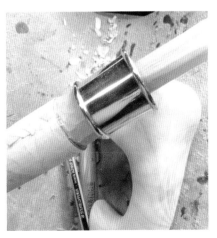

(f) Keep checking the fit of the collar. You want a snug fit.

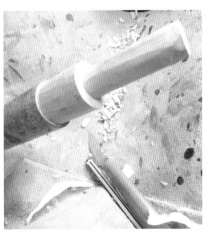

(g) Tidy up when all wood has been removed from the shank.

(h) Place the head back onto the shank and check that the recesses you have carved on both head and shank marry up with the length of the collar.

(i) Fitting of the collar finished. The wood of the head will be reduced at a later stage.

EYES

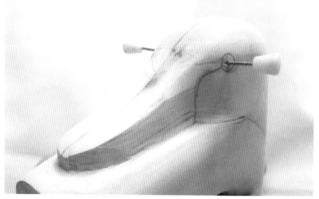

18 Use pins/thumbtacks to locate the position of the eyes. At their center points, drill a pilot hole approximately ⁷⁄₁₆" (11mm) deep using a ⅛" (3mm) drill bit.

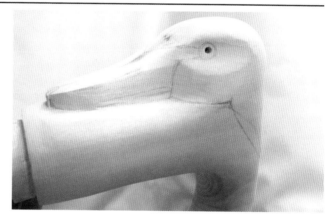

19 With 120-grit paper on the split-mandrel sander, shape the eye depression.

THE BILL & CHEEKS

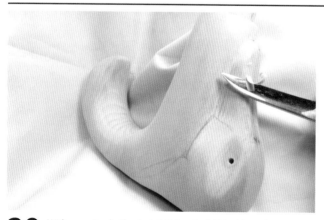

20 With a carving knife, start defining the bill. In this project, only the upper mandible is visible. Reduce it to its final width and slope.

21 Add the shield-shaped nail (unguis) at the tip.

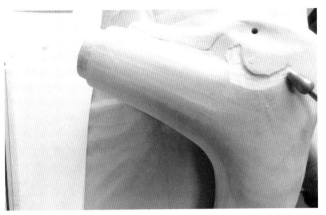

22 Use a bud-shaped diamond bit to outline the cheeks. Round over and blend into the head with the split-mandrel sander and 120-grit paper.

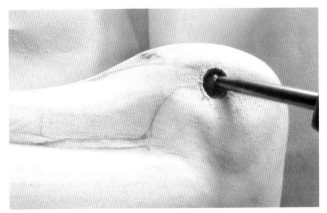

23 Enlarge the eye socket to accommodate ¼" (6mm) red glass eyes. Use a bullet or flamed bit to achieve the correct size. Then use a ⅛" (3mm) ball carbide cutter to enlarge the back of the sockets to allow sufficient epoxy putty to fix the eyes. Lightly round over the edges of the sockets with the mandrel sander.

24 Use the carving knife to separate the bill from the head. This is the "V"-shaped notch on the forehead and the area of the bill adjacent to the feathers of the lores.

Use a stop-cut, then remove a sliver of wood from the bill side of the cut. Drawing sighting lines ¼" (6mm) apart on the head will help you maintain symmetry.

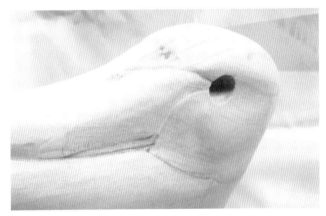

25 Blend the edge into the face with 240-grit paper on the split mandrel.

26 Use the knife to define the upper edge of the lip. Then do the same for the partial section of the lower edge visible, to give a hint of separation. Round over the hard edges with 240-grit sandpaper on the split-mandrel sander.

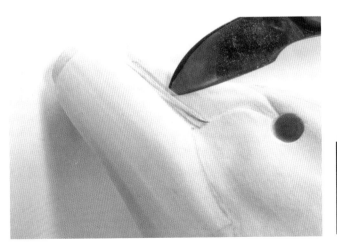

DID YOU KNOW?

On the ground, a group of black swans is called a bank; when flying in a group, they are called a wedge.

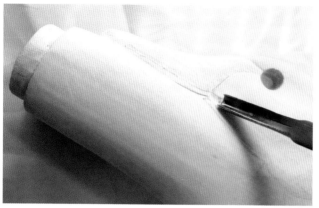

27 Use a small U-gouge to add a small depression behind where the upper and lower bill meet to create the "smile."

NOSTRILS

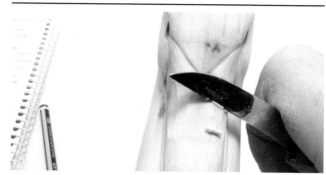

28 Flatten the area of the bill where the nostrils (nares) are located. Use the knife and then the cushioned-drum sander with 240-grit paper. Pencil on the position of the nostrils.

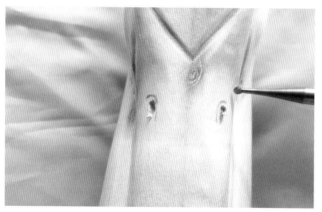

29 Then use a ¹⁄₁₆" (1.5mm) diamond ball to hollow out the nostrils.

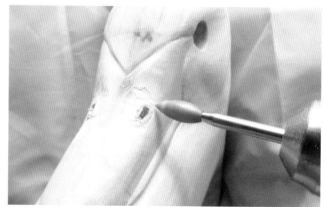

30 Add a lip to the nostrils with a flamed ruby burr and then sand with 240-grit.

LAYING OUT THE FEATHERS

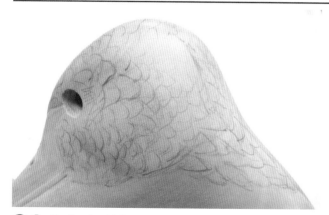

31 The head and bill details are now shaped. Give everything a final sanding by hand with 240-, 320-, and 400-grit sandpaper before texturing. Once done, draw the feather flow, then individual feathers.

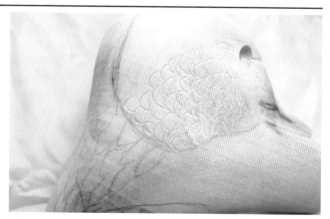

32 The cheek areas and the crown of the head are rows of tiny feathers and rarely need to be outlined on a carving of this size, as the texturing will add the effect needed. It is your choice as to whether you do. I have outlined them using a flamed ruby.

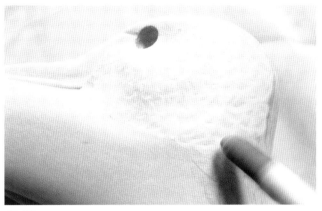

33 Use the mandrel sander and 240-grit paper to soften the edges and remove all tool marks.

34 The small feathers outlined above blend into rows of V-shaped clumps of feathers. The crown merges with the occiput and nape. The cheeks merge with the sides of the neck. Outline the feathers with the flamed ruby bit.

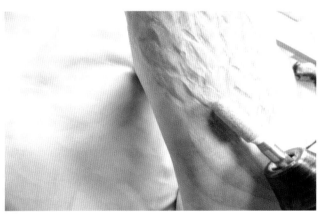

35 Soften the edges of the feathers with a bull-nosed, blue ceramic stone.

36 Sand with 240-grit paper on the mandrel sander. When you have finished sanding, immediately draw back the feathers. If they have been carved and sanded properly, you should hardly be able to see their outline. Therefore, drawing them back will help you when you start their texturing.

TEXTURING

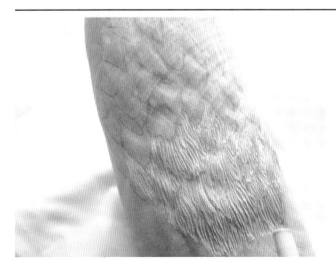

Before texturing, ensure you have removed any tool marks. Whenever possible, start texturing the feathers from the bottom and work upward, as this enables the texturing strokes of the feather above to overlap that below.

37 Start this head by texturing the nape, then work upward. Use a ¹⁄₁₆" (1.5mm) cylinder blue ceramic stone to texture the feathers. Try to create strokes with a degree of randomness and which are neither straight nor regimented.

38 This photo shows the neck feathers finished.

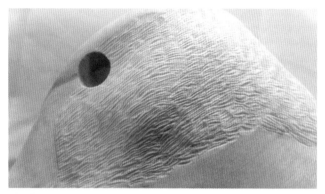

39 Use the same blue ceramic stone to texture the small feathers of the cheeks. If you have not outlined them, just make the texturing strokes mimic the layout and size of the feathers rather than using long strokes.

> Depending on the degree of realism of the project, texturing will involve different sizes and shapes of ceramic stone, and even diamond wheels. Also, there may be two or three different rounds of texturing that will be demonstrated in a later project. For now, all that is needed is some basic texture laid down.

FITTING THE EYES

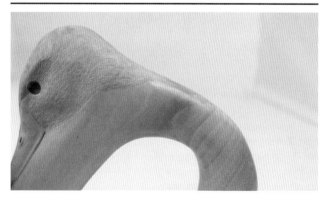

Tip ✏️

There are many opinions as to whether you can use oil over or under acrylic paints. I have finished this carving with several layers of acrylic paint sandwiched between layers of finishing oil. The reason for this is that I wanted the oil to bring out the character of the lime wood of the handle. When trying something different, the key is to test the process before you start on the main carving. It is important that you use an offcut from the same project and use the same oil and paint you intend to use.

I applied three coats of oil to a piece of scrap wood left after band-sawing the blank. I let it dry for seven days. I applied black and red acrylic paint in a couple of layers and let it fully cure over a further seven days. Lastly, I applied two coats of oil over the paint. The most important aspect of this process is to allow each layer to cure fully before attempting the next. A couple of days may suffice, depending on the products you are using; to be on the safe side I allowed seven.

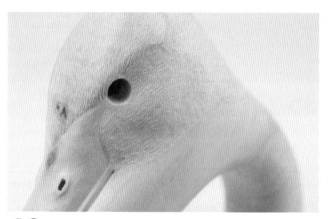

40 Finish the texturing with the crown and forehead. Use a nylon pad in the rotary tool to remove any fuzzy areas left by the texturing.

41 Before fitting the eyes, apply the first three coats of finishing oil and allow to dry for seven days.

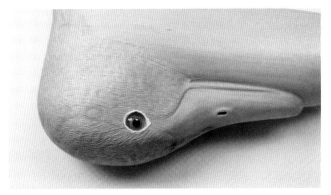

42 Fix the eyes with two-part epoxy putty or wood filler. Make the eye rings by rolling out a thin sausage of putty, placing it around the eye, then pressing into place with a dental tool. Add some fine texture to the eye ring with a scalpel blade.

PAINTING

When painting a textured project, build up the color by applying several coats, the consistency of skim milk. Any thicker and you are liable to spoil the texturing effect.

43 Start on the swan by painting the bill using a mixture of cadmium red (medium) with a hint of golden ochre. Add white for a pink and blend to the tip, including the nail. Add a touch of this pink below the lip of the upper mandible. Use white for the stripe across the bill and a thin application over the nail.

FINISHING

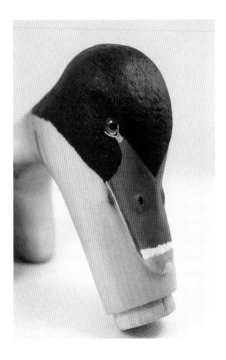

44 Paint the rest of the head with a mixture of ultramarine blue and burnt sienna to create a rich gray-black. With the addition of black and then white to create darker and lighter values, add some random highlights. Paint inside the nostrils with the darker value. Paint the front half of the eye ring with white. Use a weak wash of the dark color to go over the bill and eye ring to tone down the color.

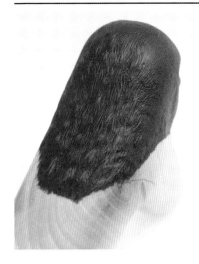

45 After seven days, apply another two coats of finishing oil to the head. Apply three coats of oil to the shank. Fix the ferrule with epoxy glue. Glue the head and collar to the shank with epoxy glue. The finished stick and its rear views should look something like this.

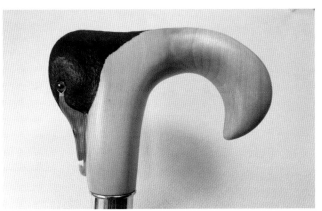

The finished stick.

(See page 225 for pattern)

PROJECT 7
Fox Head Walking Stick

The red fox (*Vulpes vulpes*) belongs to the dog family. It is a resourceful and adaptable animal, which has colonized a wide range of environmental conditions, from sub-tropical to the Arctic tundra.

The pupils of a fox's eyes have vertical slits. These allow the eyes to open very wide and gather extra light. Their eyes are especially adapted for nighttime vision; behind the light-sensitive cells in the eye, another layer, called the *tapetum lucidum*, reflects light back through the eye. This doubles the intensity of images received.

Foxes have whiskers on their wrists that they use as "feelers," much the same as cats do with their facial whiskers. This helps the fox move around more efficiently in the dark.

Thanks to these whiskers and good eyesight, foxes are formidable nighttime predators.

MATERIALS

- Wood for the head: lime (*Tilia europaea*), 4" x 4" (102 x 102mm)
- Wood for spacers: ½" (13mm) spacer or several that approximate this thickness—I have used two African padauk (*Pterocarpus soyauxii*) and two African blackwood (*Dalbergia melanoxylon*), each ⅛" (3mm) thick and approximately 1½" (38mm) square
- Cardboard for template
- ⁹⁄₃₂" (7mm) vertical-slit pupil glass eyes (special fox)
- Shank of your choice and size
- 120- to 400-grit cloth-backed sandpaper
- Brass ferrule
- Epoxy putty
- Epoxy glue
- Sanding sealer
- Finishing oil
- Assorted acrylic paints

PREPARING THE BLANK

As with all projects that aim for a touch of realism, ensure you have plenty of reference material, giving a view from all angles, before you start to carve.

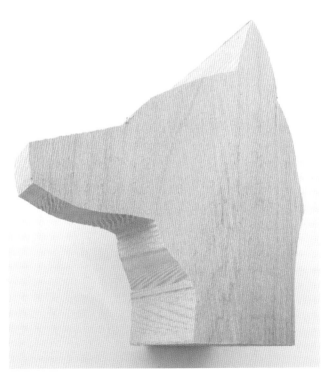

1 Prepare cardboard templates from the sketch on page 225. Use the side template to band-saw the blank.

2 Draw a centerline around the head. Mark the center point at the bottom of the blank. Draw a 1³⁄₁₆" (30mm) square around this point. The diameter of the shank I am using is just over an inch (25mm)—the extra is a safety margin. Remember to alter the drawing for the diameter of the shank you are using. Use a ½" (13mm) wood drill to bore a hole in the bottom of the neck to a depth of 1¾" (44mm). Although there is no danger of the drill breaking through in this project, it is advisable to mark the drill with a piece of masking tape to the depth required.

For this project, I cut on the band saw two padauk and two African blackwood slices of ⅛" (3mm) thickness and 1 ½" (38mm) square. You can use one or more spacers of the material of your choice. Drill the spacer(s).

Fox Head Walking Stick   97

ROUGHING OUT

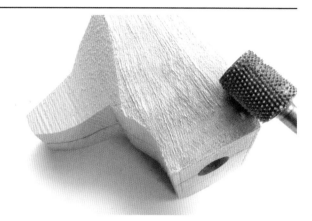

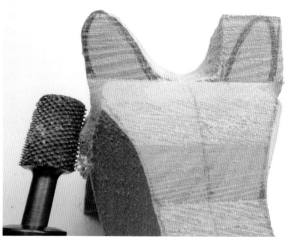

3 Using a cylinder coarse carbide-point bit in the rotary tool, reduce the sides of the neck. Do not remove any material from within the square drawn in the previous step.

4 Follow these steps for roughing out and shaping the ears.
  (a) Draw the rough placement of the ears. Use the same bit to define them by removing material from between and behind. At this stage you are looking to roughly block-in the features, so err on the side of keeping everything on the large side to allow for refinement and sanding.

(b) Round over the back of the ears with the same bit.

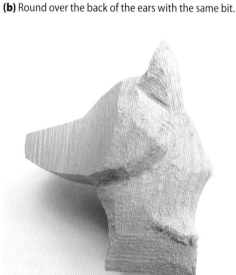

5 Start to shape the top of the neck with the cylinder bit.

6 Draw the cheek line and define by running the cylinder bit beneath.

7 Round over the skull in front of the ears with the cylinder coarse bit.

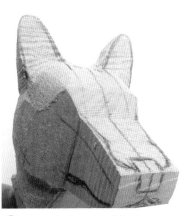

8 Draw the features of the head to help visualize the next steps.

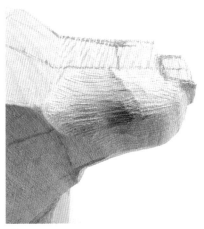

9 Use a safe-ended, cylinder, medium carbide-point bit to define the muzzle. Outline the position of the nose and carve the indentation behind the fleshy pad of the whiskers. Start to round over the top and bottom of the muzzle.

10 Using the same medium carbide-point bit, round over the top of the skull, down the "stop" of the foreface to where it meets the muzzle. Draw reference lines 7/16" (11mm) on either side of the centerline of the skull to help maintain symmetry. Redraw the centerline whenever the carving process erases it.

PREPARING SHANK & SPACERS

11 Prepare the shank for the head using the dowel method. Once you are happy with the fit, mark the positions of all components.

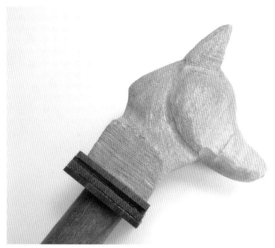

12 Glue the spacer(s) to the shank with two-part epoxy glue—do not glue the head. Allow to cure overnight.

13 Temporarily replace the head on the shank. Use the cylinder coarse bit to carve the bottom of the spacers to fit the profile of the shank. Reduce and shape the top of the spacers and neck to the desired shape. Leave plenty of wood around the neck for the next step.

REFINING FEATURES

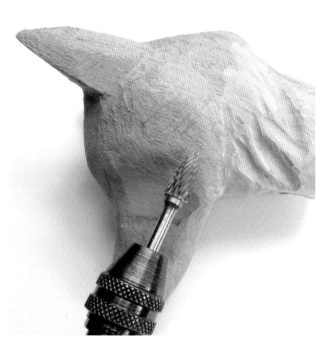

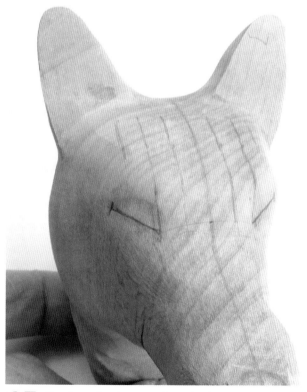

14 Using a flame carbide cutter, take the neck down to its finished dimensions, other than sanding. Then add some large folds around the throat and neck to represent the thicker fur of the ruff. Be careful to not remove any material at the bottom of the head when it is off the shank.

15 Give the entire piece a rough sand with 120-grit paper on a cushioned-drum sander. This is to enable you to check how the carving is looking. At this point, you want the head to be very near to its finished shape. Locate the approximate position and angle of the eyes, and use the sander to lightly flatten the plane where they will sit. Redraw the centerline and the reference lines on the skull. This time draw them at $^{13}/_{64}$" (5mm) to help with locating and carving the eyes.

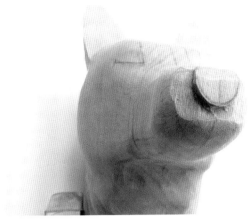

16 Refine the nose shape with a carving knife.

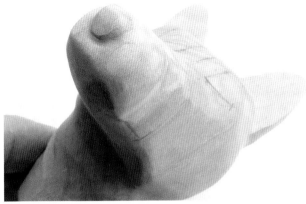

17 Use 240-grit paper on a split-mandrel sander to round over the edges of the nose.

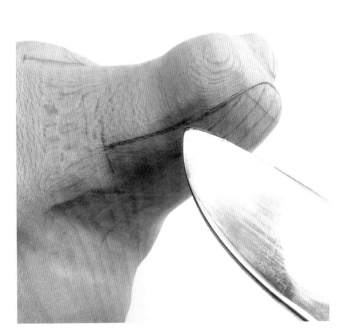

18 Use your reference material to check the shape of the mouth, then draw it on. It runs backward to just short of the inside edge of the eye. The prominent overlap at the commissure of the mouth seen on most dogs is not prominent on the fox. Once again, draw reference lines at ¹³⁄₆₄" (5mm) increments from both sides of the centerline. Using a carving knife, place a stop-cut around the mouth outline.

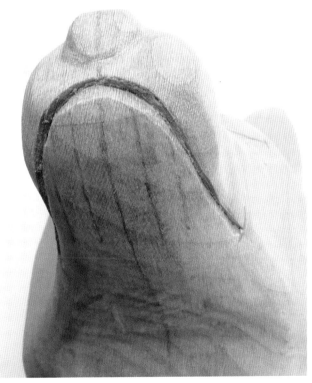

19 Now cut at just under 90 degrees to the first cut and from below. This will relieve the lower jaw and make it sit within the upper jaw.

NOSTRILS

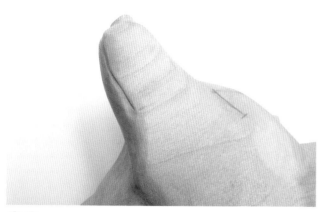

20 Sand the edges with 240-grit paper on the split-mandrel sander. Sand a small dimple at the corners.

21 Return to the nose and shape the nostrils. They are not perfectly round holes but more the shape of a comma. Use a $\frac{1}{50}$" (0.5mm) dental bit to pierce the opening and create the shape.

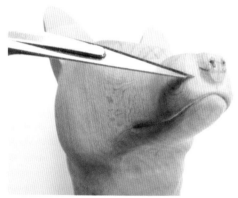

22 The bottom of the nostril openings extends to the outside edges of the nose and then runs up beside it. This creates flaps of tissue on the sides of the nose known as alar flaps. These open when the fox is running and needs to draw in more air, or when scenting. Use a scalpel to define this split that runs from the nostril halfway up the side of the nose.

23 The last part of the nose to carve is the philtrum. This is the line separating the left and right parts of the nostril. Define this with the scalpel or carving knife.

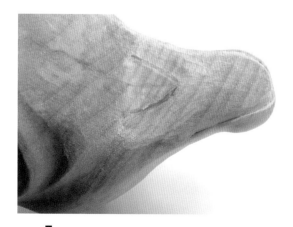

24 Next, define the triangular-shaped bulge caused by the hyoid bone apparatus and muscles at the base of the lower mandible. This bone is attached to the tongue and helps with swallowing food. Use a $\frac{5}{32}$" (4mm) diamond ball to outline, then sand with 240-grit paper on the split-mandrel sander.

EARS

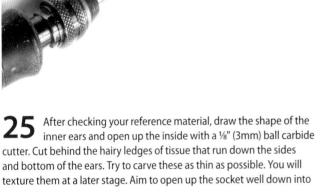

25 After checking your reference material, draw the shape of the inner ears and open up the inside with a ⅛" (3mm) ball carbide cutter. Cut behind the hairy ledges of tissue that run down the sides and bottom of the ears. Try to carve these as thin as possible. You will texture them at a later stage. Aim to open up the socket well down into the head to give the impression of depth.

26 Carefully sand the inside of the ears using the split-mandrel sander, sanding sticks, and by hand. Use 240-grit paper.

EYES

The carving of eyes was first mentioned in the cocker spaniel project. As this project will be painted, there are a couple of options for fitting the eyes. The simplest method is to drill out ⁹⁄₃₂" (7mm) circular holes and use epoxy putty to create their almond shape. Alternatively, you can carve the almond-shaped socket with the opening smaller than ⁹⁄₃₂" (7mm), then carve behind the front of the sockets, as with the cocker spaniel. Insert the eye into the upper part of the socket, then push the bottom of the eye into place.

This is another variation. The eye will be carved almond-shaped and the eyes inserted as above. This is often a tricky procedure, and sometimes it is easier to open up the socket a touch to enable easier fitting. Later on, the almond shape will be remodeled using epoxy putty. Remember this can only be done on a carving that will be painted.

The eyes of the fox have a vertical-split iris. The ⁹⁄₃₂" (7mm) dark-orange glass eyes I am using are specially designed for the fox. Take care when working on the eyes, as they are a major focal point of any carving of a head.

27 On this head, the inner edge of the eye is approximately ⁷⁄₁₆" (11mm) from the centerline. Establish where the eye is placed, then draw a ⁹⁄₃₂" (7mm) line from this inner edge to the outer extremity. Insert a pin into the center point. Use another pin to locate the other eye. Check alignment from both front and top.

28 Pencil on the almond shape of the eyes. The center of the eyes will be approximately ¼" (6mm) high. Drill a ⅛" (3mm) pilot hole at the center point.

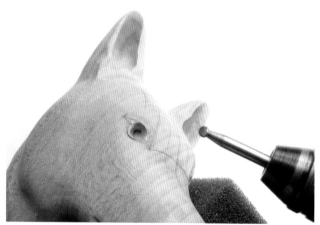

29 Open up and shape the eye socket with the ⅛" (3mm) ball carbide cutter and a ⁵⁄₆₄" (2mm) diamond ball. Carve up behind the outer edges of the sockets to enable the eyes to be fitted.

30 Using a ⁵⁄₃₂" (4mm) diamond ball, create a shallow groove from the inner edge of the eyes running along the bridge of the nose as shown in the photograph. Sand with 240-grit paper.

31 Use a scalpel or knife to remove a triangular pip of wood from the outside edges of the eyes. Shape and sand to give the impression that the lower eyelid fits just inside the top.

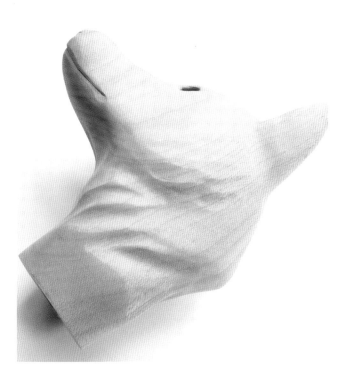

REFINING THE JOINT

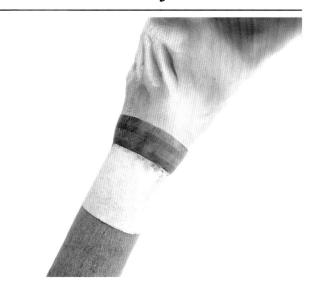

32 Use a ⁵⁄₆₄" (2mm) diamond ball to define the eyebrow ridges. Sand with 240-grit on the split-mandrel sander.

33 Refit the head to the shank. Wrap a couple of turns of masking tape around the shank for protection. Finish the refinement of the joint with 240-grit paper on the cushioned-drum sander.

FURTHER REFINING OF THE HEAD

FIXING THE EYES

34 Remove the head. To give the impression of thick hair, add some folds around the back of the cheek with the ⁵⁄₃₂" (4mm) diamond ball. Use it to add more definition to the neck folds. Sand with 240-grit paper on the split-mandrel sander.

35 Fix the eyes into their sockets with epoxy putty. If you have had to enlarge the socket to insert the eyes (or just need to add a touch more shape), work the putty around the outside of the eye until you are happy with the shape.

TEXTURING

Shine a light at an oblique angle while texturing. This will help you to see where you have worked.

36 The shaping of the head is finished. Sand with 240-, 320-, and 400-grit paper to prepare for texturing. Use a combination of the cushioned drum, split mandrel, and hand sanding.

Use your reference material to draw the flow lines of the hair.

37 With a ⁵⁄₆₄" (2mm) cylinder blue ceramic stone, start texturing the ears. Use small "C"—forward and backward—and "S" strokes. Ensure all of the wood is covered.

Tip ✏️

When texturing the head, leave a small section—around ⁵⁄₈"–¾" (16–19mm)—untouched at the bottom of the neck where it joins the shank. This will differentiate your stick as being a unique carving from wood and not a mass-produced resin copy.

38 Next, texture the distinct hair flow around the eyes.

39 It is advisable to protect the eyes while texturing. I have found a piece of plasticine works well. You could also use modeling clay or you can cut a piece from a self-adhesive, anti-scratch pad used on the bottom of ornaments to protect furniture.

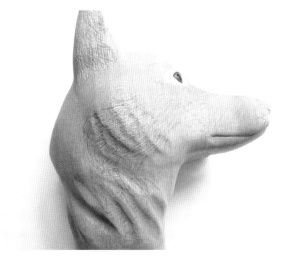

40 Texture the folds at the back of the cheeks.

41 Move on to the muzzle, and texture it to join up with the cheeks and eyes.

42 Now work the top of the head to join up with the texturing of the ears.

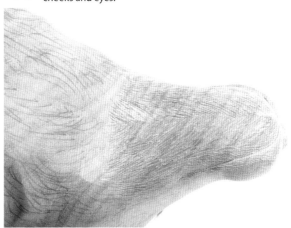

43 Texture underneath the lower jaw . . .

44 . . . and the back of the head.

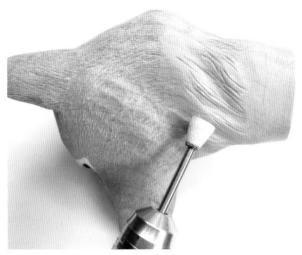

45 Use an inverted-cone, blue ceramic stone to texture the thicker fur around the neck. This stone will add some heavier texture.

46 Now, go over this same area with the ⁵⁄₆₄" (2mm) cylinder to apply another finer layer of texture to the neck. Check over the head to make sure it has all been textured. Finish with a soft nylon brush in the rotary tool to remove any dust or tiny particles.

The texturing is now finished. Wipe the head with mineral spirits on a lint-free cloth to remove any last traces of dust. Apply two coats of sanding sealer to the entire head.

PAINTING

Use acrylics to paint the fox. Always apply each coat thinly to the consistency of skim milk. If you apply the paint in thick coats, it will ruin all your hard work of texturing. Many thin layers will also provide depth to your painting.

47 Start by using titanium white on the underside of the mouth and down the throat to the point where you finished your texturing.

48 Apply the orangey-brown base coat to the remainder of the head. This is a mix of quinacridone gold, raw sienna, and a hint of Payne's gray.

49 Add an additional touch of Payne's gray to this mix and darken the area around the eyes. Add varying amounts of gray to this mix and add random highlights. Add further highlights with titanium white. Use Payne's gray on the nose, the smudge across the muzzle, ears, around the eyes, and for other random highlights.

50 The painting is now complete. Carefully remove the paint from the eyes. This is the finished carving.

FIXING THE HEAD TO THE SHANK

A view from the back.

For this project, I have used a yew shank, as its reddish color complements the coloring of the fox.

51 Apply several coats of your choice of finishing oil to the shank and spacers. Use epoxy glue to join the head to the shank. Make sure there is not an air pocket trapped in the head, as this can cause it to push up before the glue is fully cured. If you keep pressure on the head and shank until the glue has set hard, this shouldn't be a problem. Fit a brass ferrule.

(See page 226 for pattern)

PROJECT 8

Golden Eagle Derby Walking Stick

The majestic golden eagle (*Aquila chrysaetos*) is the most widely distributed eagle in the world, and with its 7' (2m) wingspan, probably the foremost recognized bird of prey in the Northern Hemisphere. In the UK it is confined to Scotland. In North America, it is widespread on the west, from Alaska down to Mexico, but less frequently spotted in the east.

The golden eagle usually preys on small land mammals, such as hares, rabbits, squirrels, prairie dogs, and marmots; however, they are known to take much larger prey, including pronghorn antelope, mountain goats, and bighorn sheep.

MATERIALS

- Wood: lime (*Tilia x europaea*) 6" (152mm) wide (across the grain) x 4" (102mm) high (with the grain) x 1⁹⁄₁₆" (40mm) thick
- Cardboard for template
- ⁹⁄₃₂" (7mm) dark brown glass eyes
- 1" (25mm)–diameter x 1" (25mm)–long copper rolled-top collar
- Epoxy glue
- Epoxy putty
- Brass ferrule
- Hazel shank
- 120- to 400-grit sandpaper
- Satin varnish
- Finishing oil
- Acrylic paints

GETTING STARTED

The first thing I do when carving anything with a degree of realism is collect reference material. You cannot have too many photos of the figure you're carving. After I draw the design, I use it to cut out cardboard templates of the side and plan views.

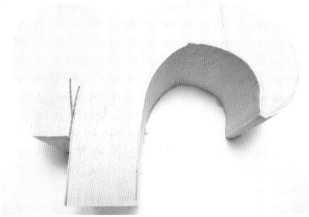

1 This pattern is based on a shank of approximately 1" (25mm) diameter and includes an extra ⅛" (3mm) allowance for error. If the shank you are using is significantly different, adjust the size of the bottom of the neck accordingly. Orient the side template onto your stock so that the grain is running down through the neck of the handle to provide strength at the joint with the shank and along the length of the eagle's beak. Cut out the blank using a band saw.

2 Mark the center point at the bottom of the neck. Draw a square around this center point with sides of 1⅛" (29mm). Clamp the blank in a vice or workbench with the bottom of the neck facing upward. Drill a hole at this center point to a depth of 1¾" (44mm) using a ½" (13mm) wood drill.

Tip

When drilling a deep hole freehand, drill approximately ⅛" (3mm), then turn your body 90 degrees and drill another ⅛" (3mm). Turn another 90 degrees and drill again. Keep doing this until the desired depth is reached. This method will help keep the hole vertical.

ROUGHING OUT THE HANDLE

Draw a centerline around the blank. (Whenever a step removes this line, always redraw.) The finished handle is 1 ³⁄₁₆" (30mm) wide. Draw a line ⅝" (16mm) on each side of the centerline on the top edge. Draw the extremity of the eagle's neck onto the handle.

3 Using a safe-ended, cylinder, coarse carbide-point bit in a rotary tool, carve away the wood from the handle sides to leave it at 1³⁄₁₆" (30mm) wide. Don't touch the eagle's head at present. Taper the end of the handle to approximately ½" (13mm) at the tip. Start to taper around 1½" (38mm), as measured from the tip.

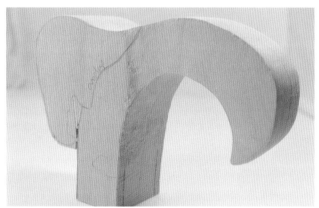

4 Use 120-grit in a cushioned-drum sander to give the handle a rough sanding. Do not round over the handle at this point.

5 Draw the side view, bottom edge of the eagle's head. Use the coarse cylinder bit to reduce the width of the handle under this line and down to the neck of the head. Do not take any material away from inside the square drawn at the bottom of the neck. If anything, err on the safe side and keep well away from the square.

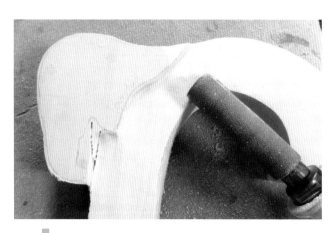

6 Sand with 120-grit paper on the cushioned sander.

ROUGHING OUT THE EAGLE

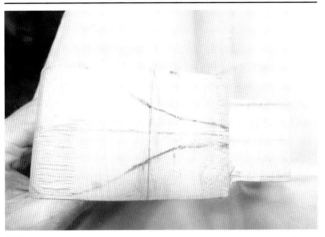

7 Draw the rough plan view of the eagle's head and bill using the template (see page 226).

8 Using the coarse bit, rough out the plan view of the eagle's head. This is the side view and . . .

9 . . . the top view.

DID YOU KNOW?

In the past, the word *beak* was used in reference to the sharp bills of birds of prey. In more modern times, the use of *beak* and *bill* are interchangeable.

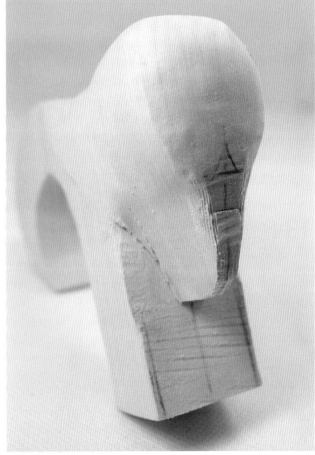

10 With 120-grit paper in the cushioned-drum sander, give the head a rough sand to achieve the shape shown in the photo.

SHAPING THE HANDLE

11 Pencil a line around the top edges of the handle, approximately ⅛" (3mm) in from the edge. Round over the edges of the handle with the coarse cylinder bit.

12 Sand with 120-grit sandpaper on the cushioned-drum sander.

DETAILING THE EAGLE

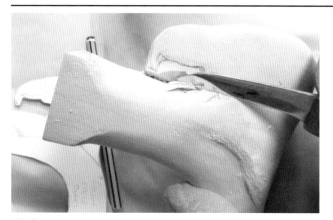

13 Pencil on the features of the eagle's face. Separate the bottom of the bill from the handle with a carving knife and a ⅛" (3mm) cylinder carbide cutter.

14 Use the split-mandrel sander with 120-grit abrasive to clean up under the lower mandible and throat.

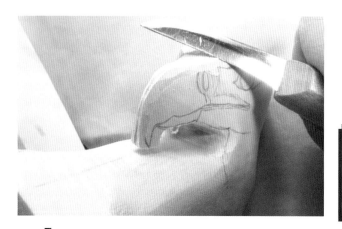

15 Shape the top of the bill using the carving knife and sand with 120-grit abrasive.

DID YOU KNOW?

In Mongolia, golden eagles are used when hunting wolves.

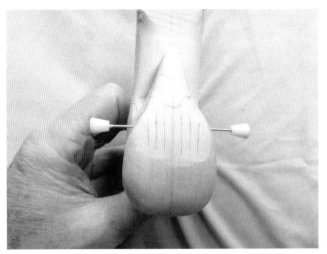

16 Locate the positions of the eyes. Finding the position of one eye is straightforward; the difficulty is matching the second eye's position to that of the first. Once you are happy with the first eye's position, insert a pin in its center, then use another pin to line up the second eye. View from above and the front to ensure accuracy. Drill a ⅛" (3mm) pilot hole in the center of each.

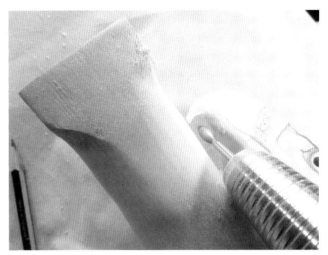

17 Shape the hook part of the bill, the premaxilla, using a ruby flame.

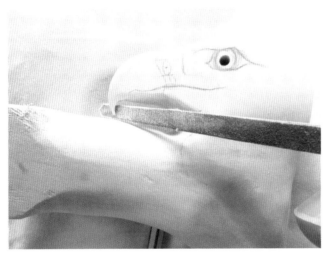

18 Sand the tip carefully using sanding sticks and 240-grit sandpaper.

19 Once you have the bill to its final size, add some superglue to the tip for extra strength.

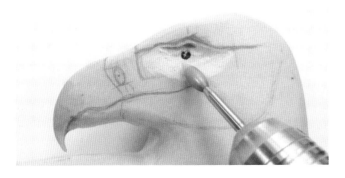

20 Use the ruby flame to create the eye depression as shown.

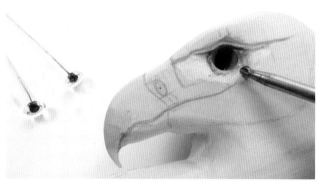

21 With the ruby flame, enlarge the eye orbits for the ⁹⁄₃₂" (7mm) glass eyes. Once you have the outer measurement, enlarge the inside with a ⅛" (3mm) carbide cutter. Cut up into the orbits behind the eye ridges to enable the eyes to be fitted later. Ensure that the orbits are deep enough to receive the eyes and the epoxy putty used to secure them.

> If you enlarge the eye opening gradually, you will be able to check for symmetry and adjust accordingly. You will not be able to do this if you drill the orbits in one go with a wood drill the size of the eyes.

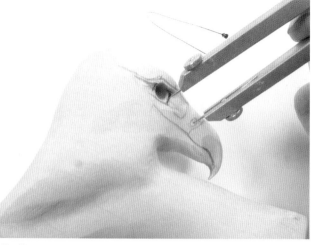

22 Establish the position of the nostrils, the nares, by using the two pins as you did for the eyes. Do not hollow the nostrils, as their position will be used as reference points for measurements with the dividers.

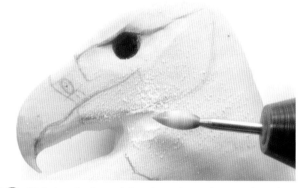

23 With the ruby flame, define the eyebrow. There is a thin ridge above the eyes, the supra ridge, that runs from just in front of the eye to a touch over halfway. Refer to your reference material for the shape. Create the lower extremity of the cheeks with the same bit, as shown in the photo.

DID YOU KNOW?

The cutting edge of the mandible is called the *tomium* (plural *tomia*). Most raptors have the upper mandible near the tip shaped with a "tooth" that corresponds to a notch in the lower mandible. Together, they give a slicing action that is believed to sever the neck of its prey.

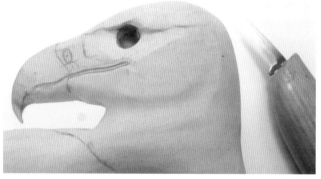

24 Draw the position of the fleshy edges along both the upper and lower mandibles and around the commissure. When you are happy that both sides align, use the carving knife to outline, then soften the edges with 240-grit paper on the split-mandrel sander.

Use the knife to separate the upper and lower mandible. Adjust the distal end of the lower mandible so that if fits just inside the upper.

> The diamond bits do not always have to be used in a rotary tool. Using them by hand will give more control and a delicate touch. I used the ruby flame between the upper and lower lip to round over the inside edges before sanding.

25 Locate the front and back edges of the *cere* (fleshy part) of the upper mandible. Use the carving knife to outline, then soften the edges with the split-mandrel sander and 240-grit paper. Leave the area around the nostril sitting proud by using a ⁵⁄₆₄" (2mm) diamond ball bit. All of the facial features should now be defined.

PREPARE HEAD & SHANK FOR THE COLLAR

For this project I have used a roll-top collar that is 1" (25mm) in diameter and 1" (25mm) in length. The shank and bottom of the neck now need to be prepared to receive this collar. The collar will be fitted ⅜" (10mm) up from the bottom of the handle and ⅝" (16mm) down from the top of the shank.

26 Start by carving a dowel of 1¾" (44mm) length from the end of the shank. Once you have a good fit of this dowel into the hole of the neck, mark the dowel, shank, and head for later reference when fitting. As this joint will be covered by the collar, it does not have to be as exact as when joining the head directly to the shank or when using spacers.

27 Draw a line around the neck of the handle, ⅜" (10mm) from the bottom. Center the collar around the previously drilled hole and draw around the inside diameter. This is the thickness to which the neck needs to be reduced for the collar to fit. Use the carving knife to place a stop-cut around the circumference at the ⅜" (10mm) mark, then cut away the material to enable the collar to fit.

28 Prepare the shank by marking a line ⅝" (16mm) down from the shoulder of the dowel. Place a stop-cut around the circumference of the shank at this mark. (An edge from a magazine wrapped around the shank is an ideal way to place an accurate line.) Shave wood from the shank with the carving knife until the collar slides over. Do this gradually and keep checking the fit. You want to achieve a snug fit. Do not glue anything at this stage.

29 Once you have the head and shank prepared for the collar, reduce the handle to the size of the collar. You should be able to achieve this with 120-grit on the cushioned-drum sander. If not, remove most of the wood with a medium carbide-point bit and then sand.

OUTLINING OF THE FEATHERS

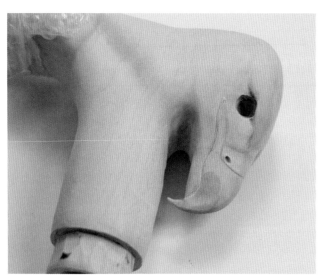

30 Before the next step of feathering and texturing, sand the head and handle with 240-, 320-, and 400-grit paper. Do this final sanding by hand.

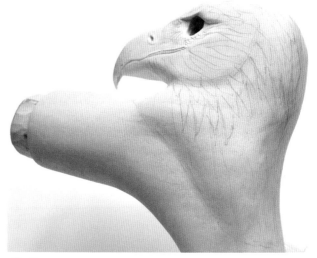

31 Draw the feather flow and lay out the position of the feathers on the top and back of the head. The feathers of the lores and cheeks are so small that it is not necessary to outline them.

DID YOU KNOW?

Golden eagles (*Aquila chrysaetos*) can swoop on their quarry at speeds up to 150 miles per hour (67 meters per second). The force of impact is comparable to the force of a bullet.

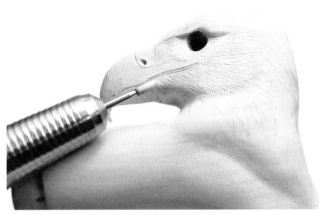

32 Use a ¹⁄₁₆" (1.5mm) cylinder blue ceramic stone in a rotary tool to texture the lores and auriculars (cheek area), as shown in the photo.

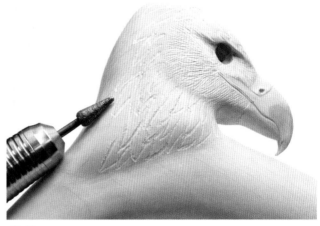

33 The feathers of the back of the head of the eagle are narrow and pointed. Use a round-ended, tapered diamond bit to outline each of these feathers.

34 Deepen the area around the feathers to provide good definition. Use the ruby flame to reduce the shoulders of a feather where it disappears beneath the one above.

DID YOU KNOW?

During courtship, the male eagle is a real show-off. He will pick up a piece of rock or a stick, drop it, then fall into a steep dive and catch the item before it hits the ground.

35 Use 240- and 320-grit sandpaper in the split-mandrel sander to round over and smooth out the edges and remove any burr marks. Any stubborn marks can be removed with a bull-nosed blue ceramic stone.

36 Finally, soften the edges of the feathers with a gray (400-grit) nylon buffing wheel.

Tip

A good, cheap alternative to the buffing wheel is to make your own from a fine-grade Scotch-Brite® scouring pad. Cut the pad into ¾" (19mm) squares and use in layers of two or three on a mandrel with a screw-down head.

37 Redraw the feather outlines. If you have sanded the feathers well, you should barely be able to make out the feather positions. Redrawing them now will help when you come to add texture.

38 Now take the ⅛" (3mm) inverted-cone, blue ceramic stone to lightly run a line down each feather to give the impression of the quill.

39 Use a scalpel to add a few splits to a few feathers—not too many, as this will spoil the carving.

DID YOU KNOW?

The Bald and Golden Eagle Protection Act 1940 makes it a criminal offense in the United States, punishable by one year's imprisonment or $5,000 US fine, to possess a single feather of these birds.

TEXTURING

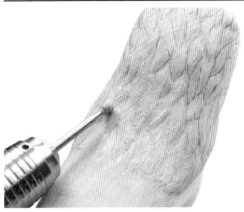

40 With the inverted-cone, blue ceramic stone, texture the feathers starting at the bottom of the neck of the eagle.

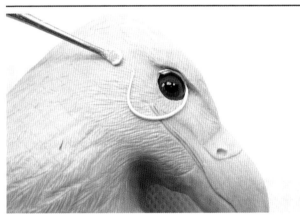

41 Work upward and ensure that the texturing overlaps the feather below.

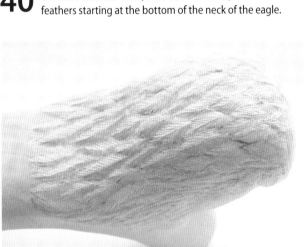

42 The texturing of the head is now complete.

FITTING THE EYES

43 Before painting and fitting the eyes, wipe down the head with mineral spirits to remove any dust. Apply two coats of sanding sealer. Fit the eyes with two-part epoxy putty.

44 Create the eye rings by rolling out a thin worm of putty and applying to the outside of the eye with dental tools. Texture the eye rings with a scalpel blade.

PAINTING

For this project, I used the following Windsor & Newton™ acrylic paints: titanium white; raw umber; Payne's gray; yellow ochre; medium yellow; medium red; yellow oxide; and quinacridone gold.

Apply paint in several thin layers—the consistency of skim milk—to avoid clogging up the texturing.

> **DID YOU KNOW?**
>
> Golden eagles mate for life and use the same nest each year. One has been recorded at being 20' (6m) high.

45 Start the painting with the lores by applying titanium white with the merest hint of Payne's gray.

46 Paint the cere and mouth with a medium yellow plus a hint of yellow ochre.

47 Paint the beak with Payne's gray plus a hint of white. Blend to a darker value at the tip. Apply yellow ochre to the eye ring.

48 Apply a base coat to the head using a mixture of raw umber, yellow oxide, and a hint of medium red. This will take at least four thin coats.

49 Once a base coat is established, apply additional coats with differing values of this mix to add subtle variety to the color. The crown and throat are a darker blend of these colors and are achieved by adding a touch of Payne's gray and burnt umber.

Mix a blend of raw umber, a hint of red, and a hint of yellow ochre for the golden feathers on the back of the neck. Add more yellow ochre for a lighter value to highlight the supra ridge over the eye.

Use a mix of raw umber and a hint of Payne's gray for the tiny feathers of the lores in front of the eyes.

Apply a thin wash of quinacridone gold over the back of the neck.

Finally, apply a very thin wash of raw umber over the lighter-colored areas to tone them down.

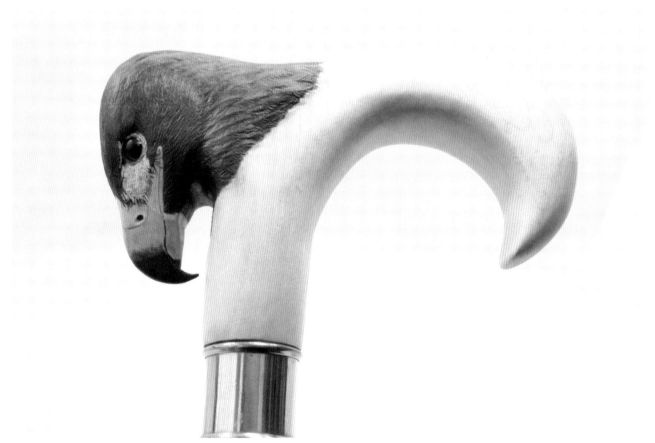

50 Finish the head with a product of your choice. This stick was finished with two coats of satin varnish. You could add a finishing medium to your paint if you wish. Allow the paint to dry fully before finishing.

Apply several coats of finishing oil to the shank, then fit a brass ferrule to the end. Join the handle, shank, and collar with epoxy glue. This is the finished stick.

(See page 227 for pattern)

PROJECT 9

Common Pipistrelle Bat Walking Stick

Near to where I live is the beautiful redbrick Tudor castle of Tattershall, located in Lincolnshire, England. When the castle was built in the 15th century, a huge church was also built beyond the castle moat. A colony of common pipistrelle bats (*Pipistrellus pipistrellus*, the most frequently seen bat in the UK) has long since taken up residence. The inspiration for this walking stick head is from an exhausted bat that took refuge in the church and perched on top of a knob-shaped arm of a pew. By chance, the gentleman who has looked after the church and its bats for decades happened to be present and took a picture of the moment. The walking stick was made for him.

The common pipistrelle is approximately 2½"–3½" (64–89mm) long, including its tail. It weighs (on average) 0.14–0.25 oz. (4–7g). Its wingspan measures between 7" and 9" (178 and 229mm). Its upper surface is dark brown and blends to a blackish brown toward its tail. Its lower surface is slightly lighter than the upper. It has a black nose.

MATERIALS

- Wood for bat: lime/basswood 3¼" (83mm) wide x 2¾" (70mm) deep x 3½" (89mm) long (follow the grain)
- Wood for spacers: two of American black walnut ⅛" (3mm) thick and 1½" (38mm) square; one piece of purpleheart ¼" (6mm) thick and 1½" (38mm) square
- Cardboard for template
- Hot glue and hot glue gun

- 3½" (89mm) long x ⅜" (10mm) thick metal screwed rod
- Buffalo horn for eyes
- Hazel shank
- Two-part epoxy glue and superglue
- 120- to 400-grit sandpaper
- Mineral spirits
- Finishing oil

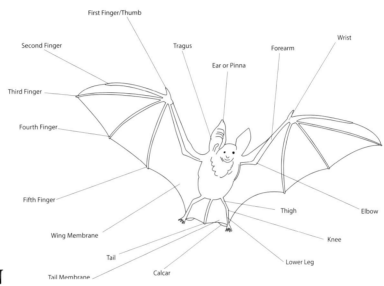

First Finger/Thumb
Second Finger
Third Finger
Fourth Finger
Fifth Finger
Wing Membrane
Tail
Tail Membrane
Calcar
Tragus
Ear or Pinna
Forearm
Wrist
Elbow
Thigh
Knee
Lower Leg

PREPARATION

The block of lime for this project needs to be square, as the blank is double-cut on the band saw in both the front and top views.

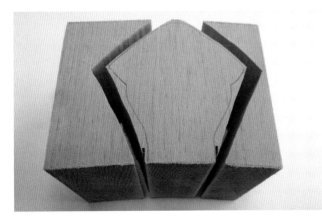

1 Cut cardboard templates from the plan and draw both views on the block of wood. Cut the front view first.

2 When this method was used on the Fox Head Walking Stick (see page 96), the cut pieces were fixed with masking tape. This time the pieces removed from the first step are hot-glued back on.

3 Cut the top view and remove all the unwanted pieces of wood, leaving a blank shape as in the photo.

4 Clamp the blank upside down in a workbench or vice. Find the center point at the bottom and draw a 1⅛" (29mm) square around it. Use a ⅜" (10mm) wood drill to bore a hole at the center to a depth of 1½" (38mm). This head will be placed on a tall shank and will not be used to bear any weight. If you intend to use this head on a short shank and as a walking aide, the hole needs to be deeper—a minimum of 2" (51mm).

I have used three spacers with a total depth of ½" (13mm). Use one or more of your choice. Drill a ⅜" (10mm) hole through the center of each spacer.

DID YOU KNOW?

There are two pipistrelles genera in North America: the Western pipistrelle (*Pipistrellus hesperus*) and the Eastern pipistrelle (*Pipistrellus subflavus*). The western variety is the smallest bat of North America and prefers the rocky canyons and cliffs from the southern border of Washington down the west coast to Southern Mexico. The Eastern pipistrelle is found on the eastern side of North America, from the border between the US and Canada down to Central America.

ROUGHING OUT

5 Use the ⅜" (10mm) wood drill to bore a hole of 2" (51mm) into the center of the top of the shank. Place the metal rod into the shank, then add the spacers and head. Where you achieve the best fit, pencil a line on all components.

6 Wrap a few turns of masking tape around the top of the shank for protection. Use a cylinder, coarse carbide-point bit to shape the neck of the head.

7 Draw the outline of the bat and rough out the position of the wings and the ears with the cylinder coarse bit.

8 Use a carving knife to block in the outer extremities of the front of the bat—the head, ears, and wings.

9 Block in the back view with the knife.

10 Use a flamed medium carbide-point bit to round over the body. Be mindful of where the upper part of the arms and legs join the body and don't go below these positions for the time being.

11 Draw a centerline and then the arms, legs, and wings. Refer to your reference material for the positions of the membrane of the wings and the tail and how and where these attach to the body.

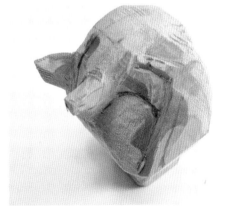

12 Use the knife to cut the shape of the arms and the outer edge of the membrane that stretches between the body and the first finger, or thumb, which is the small hook at the junction (wrist) of the fingers. On this design the membrane disappears beneath the forearm. Cut the bottom of the folded wing (which is the second finger).

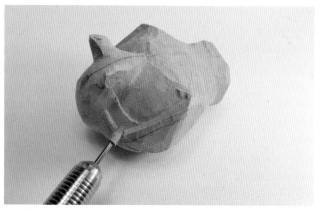

13 Tidy the front legs with a truncated-cone diamond bit. The grain of the wood is likely to be fragile around this area and why I chose to use a diamond bit as opposed to a knife.

14 Cut the rear of the wing membrane with the carving knife and tidy with the same diamond bit.

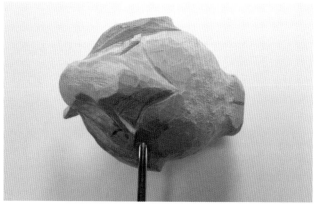

15 Shape the legs, the tail membrane, and the part of the bat's body that connects with the tail. Use a combination of the carving knife and a V-tool.

When I planned this project, the legs were in full view; however, the grain of the lime I was using was too fragile to take the fine detail of the toes. I cheated by raising the lower leg and tucking the toes beneath the wing. This is another reason why I prefer to err on the safe side by leaving plenty of wood to work and taking small amounts away each time, just in case something like this occurs. Carvings can evolve as you carve, and tinkering with them is part of the fun of the process.

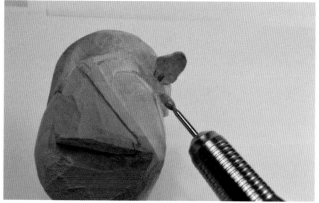

16 Use the knife to outline the forearms. Remember to leave material at the base of the forearm for the "hook," which is the thumb or first finger. Start to add shape to the face and outside of the ears with the ruby flame bit.

17 Still with the knife, put more definition into the face and clean up the base under the bat. As you carve the features of this bat, always take the opportunity to shape the membrane or the base that the bat is resting on.

DID YOU KNOW?

The name for the pipistrelle genus is derived from the Italian for bat: *pipistrello*, which comes from the Latin *vespertilio*, meaning "bird of the evening."

18 Do a rough sand of the head and immediate area with 120- and 240-grit on the split-mandrel sander.

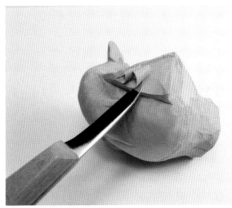

19 Lower the area between the forearm and the second finger with the knife. This is the wing membrane interspersed with the third, fourth, and fifth fingers. Leave the edges sitting proud to enable the forearm and second finger to be shaped. Also, when lowering this area, be mindful that the remaining fingers will be carved in relief during the next step, so leave sufficient wood. Outline the forearm. Sand with 120- and 240-grit on the split mandrel.

20 Use the V-tool to outline the third, fourth, and fifth fingers in between the forearm and second finger. These fingers join at a bone on the end of the forearm at what is the bat's wrist. Lightly concave the sections of membrane between each finger with the split-mandrel sander. This will give a scalloped edge to the bottom of the wing membrane when folded.

21 Shape the second finger and the thumb/first finger with the V-tool and sand with 240-grit sandpaper. The thumb on my piece of wood was cross-grain and very fragile. As soon as I had the shape, I added a touch of superglue. Continue to work on the base around the wings.

Tip ✏️

Everybody carves with a different style. Carving may not necessarily be a matter of following sequential steps, as with these projects. It is likely that your brain will be considering the carving as a whole. As you start to carve a particular feature, you may notice something else that needs attention and jump to that before finishing what you started. (No doubt you will have noticed that I do this on occasions with some of the projects in this book.) In this way, you accomplish better balance and symmetry.

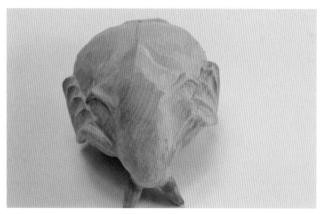

22 Both wings are shaped, other than some finer detailing and undercutting.

23 Before refining the delicate details of the bat, temporarily place the head on the shank and finish shaping the spacers and neck with the cushioned-drum sander and 120- and 240-grit abrasive.

THE FACE

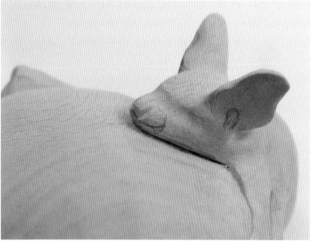

24 Use the knife to cut the nose, which is only a tiny pip. Cut back under the nose to relieve the chin, and undercut around the head where it sits on the base. Define the eye channels with 240-grit paper on the split-mandrel sander.

25 Shape the cheeks with the ruby carver. Add the nostrils with a (1⁄50" [0.5mm]) ball carbide cutter. The nostrils of the pipistrelle sit more on the sides of the nose rather than the front. Outline the mouth line with a scalpel or carving knife.

Tip ✏️

The only issue with adding superglue to a project that will be left as natural wood and then oiled is that the oil will not soak in over the glue. This is a judgment call on your part. Ideally, the superglue should be added after the oil has been applied to provide extra strength; however, if the feature is so fragile that it may break beyond repair, you may need to add a touch of superglue before finishing. If you do this, be mindful of the situation and, instead of smothering an area with glue, apply sparingly to the tips or edges. This can be achieved by adding some glue to a fine piece of wire and then using the wire to add the glue so it will not be noticed when the oil is applied. I save the thin wires that glass eyes are attached to; they are ideal for this precise task.

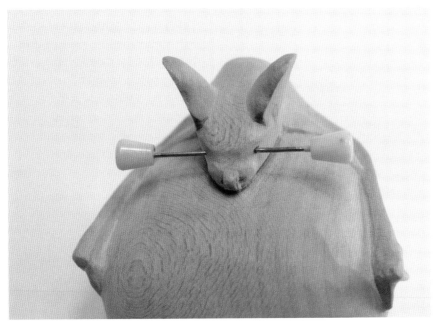

27 I was unable to obtain ⁵⁄₆₄" (2mm) glass eyes. Therefore, I made my own from buffalo horn. Take a small piece and shape into a rod that is a touch over ⁵⁄₆₄" (2mm) in diameter and about ½" (13mm) long to cater for both eyes.

26 Locate the position of the eyes. Use two pins to assist. The eyes are black and ⁵⁄₆₄" (2mm) in diameter. Drill the eye sockets with a diamond point bit. As this project is not painted, the eyes will need to be positioned and drilled out accurately.

DID YOU KNOW?

Bats use echolocation to navigate and pinpoint their prey. They emit short ultrasonic signals and listen for reflected echoes. A study has shown that bats also use echolocation to communicate with other bats up to 50mi. (80km) away. The two major parts of a bat's external ears are the pinna and tragus. Research has shown that the tragus is important for determining vertical sound position.

28 Finish the ears by hollowing the inside with the ruby flame and a ³⁄₆₄" (1mm) diamond ball. Carve the tragus at the front of the ear opening. Don't carve behind the tragus, as it will become too delicate.

29 Clean the inner ear with 240-grit and the split-mandrel sander and sanding sticks. Carve in the indentations of the inner ear with the ³⁄₆₄" (1mm) diamond ball. Apply superglue to the fragile tips of the ears. Undercut the edges of the wings, body, and legs with the knife.

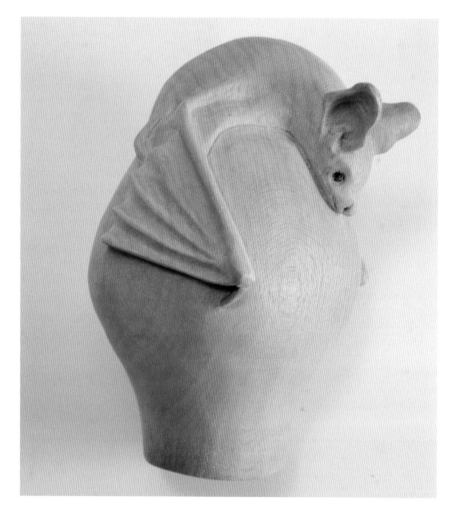

30 Returning to the eyes, take the rod of buffalo horn and lightly chamfer one end with some sandpaper until it fits snuggly inside the eye socket. Keep shaping until you have sufficient material inside the socket, then remove the rod. With a piece of wire, add a touch of superglue to the inside of the eye socket, insert the rod back in, and push in tight. Let the glue dry, then use a diamond disc to cut the rod about ⅛" (3mm) proud of the socket. Use diamond bits to shape and round over this piece of horn to form the eyeball. Repeat the process for the other eye.

TEXTURING

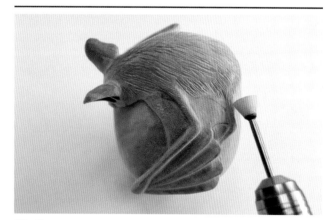

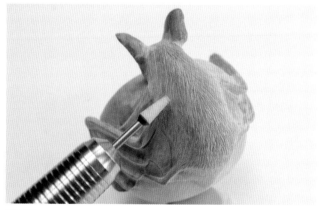

31 Before adding texture to the bat, go over the entire piece and clean up where necessary, sand with 400-grit, and make sure you are happy that everything is finished. Pencil on the flow of the fur on the bat's body. Start the texturing with some deeper strokes, using an inverted-cone, white ceramic stone. Start from the bottom of the body. This texture is only on the body and head of the bat.

32 Repeat the process with a ⁵⁄₆₄" (2mm) truncated-cone, white ceramic stone to add another layer of texture.

33 Texture the wings with a ⅛" (3mm) diamond disc bit. The texture on the wings is a series of short, unconnected dashes, as shown.

34 The wing and tail membranes are textured by using a ³⁄₆₄" and ⁵⁄₆₄" (1 and 2mm) diamond ball to lightly add an indentation. These are the bits that I used for this texturing, but many other implements and bits will do the same job. Clean everything carefully with a fine nylon pad in the rotary tool. Remember the delicate cross-grain features when doing this.

The bat is now finished. Wipe the head and shank with mineral spirits to remove any last traces of dust. Fix the head to the shank with epoxy glue. When dry, apply three coats of a finishing oil of your choice to the head and shank. I used a satin finish. Fit a brass ferrule.

(See page 228 for pattern)

PROJECT **10**

Eurasian Woodcock Walking Stick

There are five main species of woodcock. All are solitary, squat-bodied, long-billed birds. Although their preferred habitat is mature woodland, they are part of the water bird family (*Scolopacidae*).

The American woodcock (*Scolopax minor*) is found primarily in the eastern half of North America. The Eurasian woodcock (*Scolopax rusticola*) breeds in the northern hemisphere from Great Britain across to Japan. There is a small breeding population in the UK that migrate in winter to other parts of Europe and the Indian Subcontinent.

Their mottled-brown plumage provides excellent camouflage when crouched among dead leaves. If disturbed, they remain completely still until almost trodden upon, at which point they explode from the ground.

The woodcock is a solitary bird that is mostly active at dusk. They live chiefly on earthworms, which they attract to the surface by drumming their feet.

MATERIALS

- Wood: lime (*Tilia x europaea*) or basswood (*Tilia Americana*), 4¾" (121mm) along the grain by 3⁹⁄₁₆" (90mm) wide x 1¾" (44mm) deep
- Wood spacers: 2 American black walnut (*Juglans nigra*), 1⅜" (35mm) x 1⅜" (35mm) square x ⅜" (10mm) thick and 1⅜" x 1⅜" x ¹³⁄₆₄" (35 x 35 x 5mm); one of purpleheart (*Peltogyne pubescens*), 1⅜" x 1⅜" x ⅛" (35 x 35 x 3mm) thick
- Cardboard for template
- Hazel shank
- Brass ferrule

- Glass eyes ¹¹⁄₃₂" (9mm) black or dark brown
- 120- to 400-grit cloth sandpaper
- Epoxy glue
- Epoxy putty
- Mineral spirits
- Finishing oil
- Acrylic paints: raw umber, raw sienna, burnt sienna, Payne's gray, provincial beige, titanium white, titanium buff, cadmium red (medium), and quinacridone gold

ROUGHING OUT

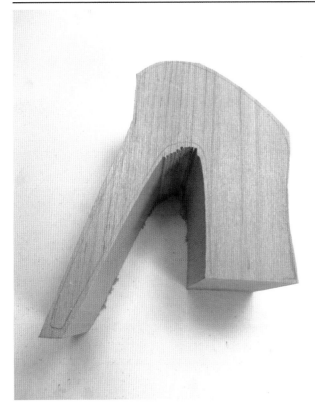

1 Make a cardboard template of the side view of the bird from the drawings. Transfer to your wood and cut out the blank on the band saw. Only the side view needs to be cut. The measurement at the neck on the drawing will accommodate a shank around 1⁷⁄₁₆" (37mm). If the shank you intend to use is significantly different, adjust accordingly.

2 Around the center point at the bottom of the neck, draw a 1³⁄₁₆" (30mm) square. Drill a ½" (13mm) hole with a wood drill at the center of the square to a depth of 1 ³⁷⁄₆₄" (40mm). Use a sharp drill to prevent wander, as it is important to have this hole in the center for later alignment with the shank.

I have used three spacers on this project, but you can replace with one spacer to the same thickness as the combination of the three—⁴⁵⁄₆₄" (18mm). Drill a ½" (13mm) hole through the center of the spacers. If you are using any thin spacers, as in this case, or using a brittle wood (e.g., purpleheart), place a scrap of wood beneath the spacer when drilling to prevent splitting.

3 Using the drawing as a guide, draw the rough profile of the back of the neck and head. At its widest the head is 1½" (38mm), tapering to 1³⁄₁₆" (30mm) where it joins the shank. Use a coarse carbide-point bit to remove wood to just over these dimensions to leave sufficient material for several rounds of sanding.

4 Use the plan and template to draw the outline of the bill on the blank. Use a diamond wheel to remove the majority of the excess wood.

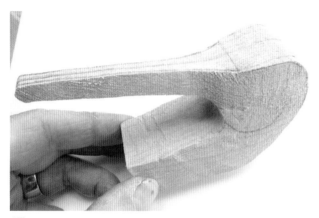

5 With the coarse bit, refine the width of the bill and the area in front of the eyes down to the base of the bill.

6 Still using the coarse bit, define the lower edge of the cheek from the chin/throat up to just under the eye as shown. This is the area of auricular feathers.

7 Prepare the shank to fit the head using the dowel method.

DID YOU KNOW?

Alternative names for the American woodcock: timberdoodle, mudbat, bogsucker, Labrador twister, whistler, bog snipe, bumblebee chicken, hokumpoke, and many other fabulous names.

8 Mark the alignment of shank, spacers, and head where you achieve the best fit.

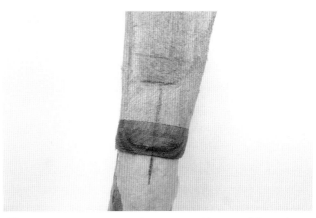

9 Use a coarse bit to shape the spacers and bottom of the neck to the profile of the shank.

10 Remove the head from the shank. Round over the head and top of the neck with the coarse bit. Do not work on the bottom of the neck at this stage.

Tip

Never try to shape or sand the bottom of the neck of this type of project without the spacers and shank being attached, otherwise there is a danger of rounding over the extreme bottom edge and spoiling the joint with the shank.

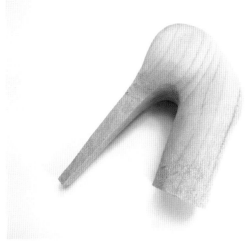

11 Give the head and neck a rough sanding with 120-grit paper on a cushioned-drum sander. As with the previous stage, do not sand the bottom of the neck or bill.

12 Reattach the shank temporarily. Sand the head—not the bill—and neck with 120- and 240-grit paper.

Eurasian Woodcock Walking Stick | 137

THE BILL

On this carving, the bill is the defining feature. Ensure you have good reference material—ideally a real or cast bill. Your local gun shop will happily oblige with a woodcock if you ask. The male's bill is 2¾"–3" (70–76mm) long, approximately ¼" (6mm) wide at the base and ⅛" (3mm) at the tip.

When probing in soft ground, the end of the upper mandible of the woodcock can hinge upward, acting like a pair of forceps and enabling them to grab a worm and pull it out. There is also some hinging at the base. This dual hinging is known as rynchokinesis.

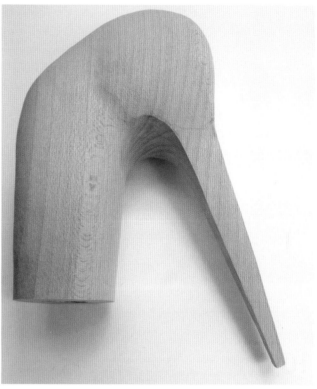

13 Draw the top profile of the bill. Refine to its final dimensions with 120- and 240-grit paper on a small sanding block to achieve crisp, straight edges.

14 Now do the same for the side profile. The bill is not perfectly straight; it slopes down toward the tip in the bottom third of its length.

Ensure you have the bill carved to its final size before refining. The sides of the bill on both the top and bottom surfaces are concave in shape. These grooves do not meet exactly in the middle of the bill nor at the separation between the upper and lower mandibles. They also taper out toward the tip and stop about ⅝" (16mm) from it.

15 Draw reference lines (as shown on the photograph) along the top, bottom, and sides. Use a ruby flame bit to commence the shaping of the edges of the upper mandible. At this initial stage, concentrate on getting straight edges and flat surfaces. The grooves will be defined later.

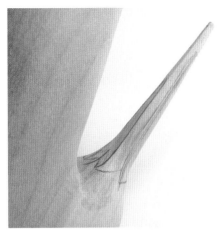

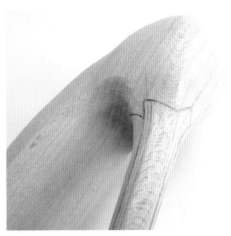

16 Use the ruby flame to do the same as above for the lower mandible. You need to allow approximately ¹⁄₁₆" (1.5mm) on both mandibles for the ridges on either side of the bill opening. Refer to the photo.

17 Shape the head where it meets the bill with the ruby flame, and sand with 240-grit paper on the split-mandrel sander.

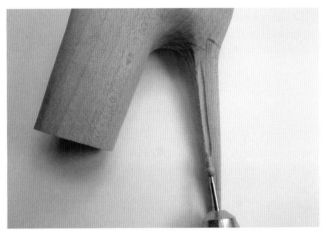

18 Now start to create the grooves in the sides of the lower mandible with the ruby flame.

19 The grooves of the top bill are deeper than the lower. Use a ⁵⁄₃₂" (4mm) diamond ball to define them. Be careful not to drift into the straight edges at the bill opening achieved above.

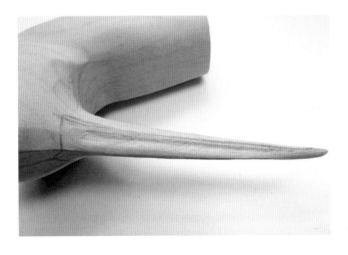

20 Using a ¹⁄₁₆" (1.5mm) diamond ball, deepen the grooves further and refine the ridge along the center. Lightly round over the ridge by hand, sanding with 240-grit paper.

21 Repeat the previous step for the grooves on the lower mandible.

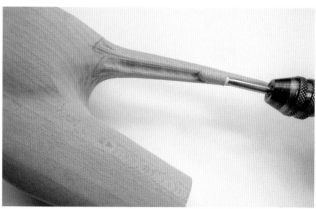

22 Use a blue bull-nosed ceramic stone to smooth the surfaces of the grooves. Then sand the grooves carefully to obtain crisp edges. Check that you are happy with the shape and symmetry of the bill. Draw back the bill opening if it has been erased.

A variety of sanding implements can be homemade so that you have one that fits the task in hand. For example, you can glue pieces of different grades of sandpaper to pieces of thin dowel, cocktail sticks, chopsticks, and coffee stirrers. Slivers of bamboo are especially good, as they are flexible but robust.

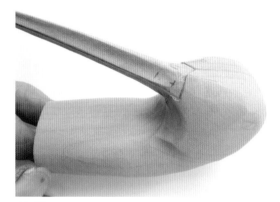

23 Draw the shape of the transition between bill and head. Define with a carving knife. Use a stop-cut at first, then take out a sliver of wood from the bill side of the cut.

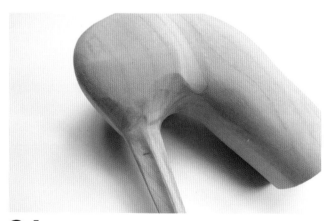

24 With the ruby flame bit, feather the joint from the head into the bill. Sand edges with 240-grit paper on the split-mandrel sander to achieve a smooth transition.

25 Use the bull-nosed stone to slightly undercut the grooves of the upper mandible in the direction of its central ridge.

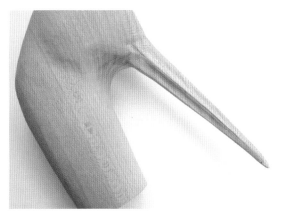

26 Use your sanding sticks to ensure the correct dimensions and the straightness of the surfaces above and below the bill opening. Sand by hand with 240-grit paper.

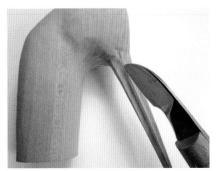

27 Use the following method to separate the upper and lower mandibles.

(a) Draw the bill separation line. With a carving knife, place a stop-cut along this line. Using a carving knife or scalpel, remove a sliver of wood from the lower edge of this line. Remember, this will slope down slightly toward the tip. Using your reference material and the photograph, define the shape of the top mandible at its tip. Remove the sharp edges with 240-grit paper.

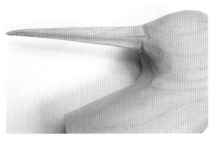

(b) Note where the lower mandible finishes in relation to the upper.

28 The lower mandible has a triangular-shaped indentation at its base. Carve this with the ruby flame and a ¹⁄₁₆" (1.5mm) diamond ball. Sand with 240-grit paper on the split-mandrel sander. Other than the nostrils, that is the bill finished.

Before doing anything else, soak some super glue along the bill to give extra strength—both against accidental knocks while carving and later for the finished head.

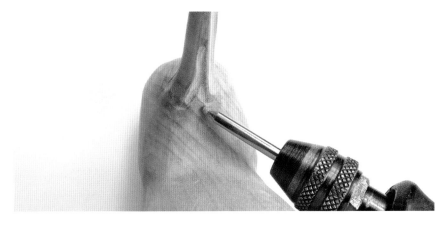

THE HEAD & EYES

The next step is to carve the woodcock's head in preparation for the eyes to be fitted. Evolution has pushed the woodcock's eyes higher and farther back on its head than any other bird. This has resulted in the brain dropping in position and pushing the ear opening below and to the right of the eyes. The normal position of the brain of most birds is behind the eye socket. It is this evolution that has enabled its near 360-degree vision.

29 Use the drawings to locate where the eyes sit on the head. Pencil on their rough position. They sit approximately ⁵⁄₁₆" (8mm) from the centerline of the crown and ¹⁵⁄₁₆" (24mm) from the proximal edge of the upper mandible. Draw some reference lines on the crown ¼" (6mm) apart to help when carving. Use a flame carbide cutter to carve the eye channel. Round over the edges to the crown and the cheek. Sand with 240-grit paper on the cushioned-drum sander.

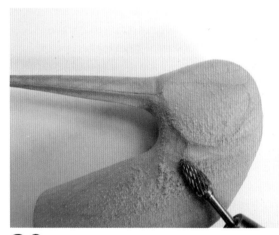

30 Deepen the extremities of the cheek with the same carbide bit. Round over the back of the head. Sand with 240-grit paper on the cushioned-drum sander.

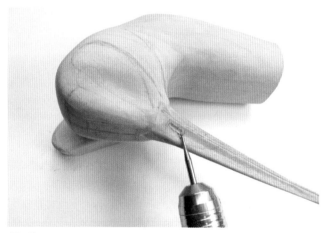

31 Using a ³⁄₆₄" (1mm) diamond ball, outline the nostrils. They start approximately ⅛" (3mm) from the face and are ¼" (6mm) long.

Tip ✎

If you drill the ⅛" (3mm) pilot hole so they meet in the middle of the head, when it comes to checking the eye fit you can afford to push each eye, one at a time, into the socket fully, as it can be pushed out from the other side.

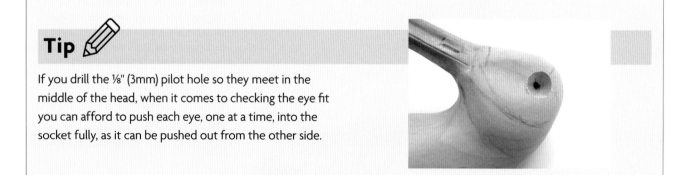

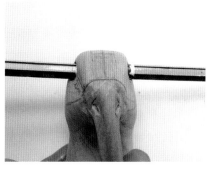

32 **(a)** Now find the exact position of the eyes. For this carving, use 11/32" (9mm) black or very dark brown glass eyes. There are various methods to establish the eye positions. Using two pins to check alignment from top and front is an easy and efficient method. Drill a 1/8" (3mm) pilot hole.

(b) Use a coarse 1/4" (6mm) bit to enlarge the eye sockets.

(c) Keep checking alignment as you carve. A pencil in each socket is one way to keep this on track.

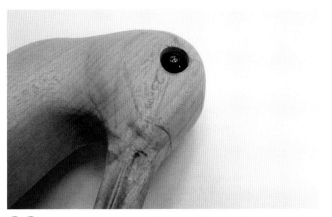

33 This shows the socket drilled out sufficiently for the eye to fit.

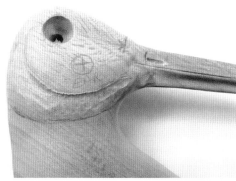

34 Use the ruby flame to outline the lower edge of the auricular feathers (ear coverts) up to the eye line. Round over the edge with 240-grit paper on the split-mandrel sander. The ear is approximately 1/2" (13mm) below the center of the eye and 5/8" (16mm) from the edge of the bill.

35 With the same bit, outline the bottom edge of the head, running from the nape, throat, to the chin. Sand with 240-grit on the split-mandrel sander.

FEATHERING & ADDING TEXTURE

The carving of the head is finished. Before moving on to the detailing, ensure that you are happy with the shape and symmetry and that the surface is smooth to 240-grit and free of any blemishes.

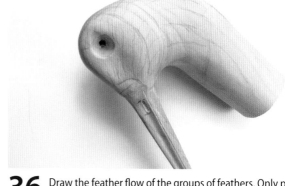

36 Draw the feather flow of the groups of feathers. Only part of the head will be textured. This will leave natural wood showing and distinguish your carving as being handmade and not a resin copy.

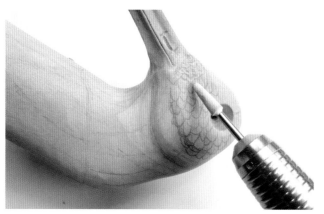

37 Outline the auricular feathers with a rounded-end, blue ceramic stone. This stone was originally a taper, and I rounded it over for this task. The advantage of the blue stone is that it keeps the amount of tool marks to a minimum.

Tip ✎

When you start to texture a project, do small areas that correspond on each side at one sitting rather than doing one side one day and the other side another. If you have a break when texturing, on your return your technique is likely to vary slightly, and this can stand out.

38 Lightly sand the feathers from the last step with 240-grit paper in the split-mandrel sander.

39 With the same ceramic stone, outline the feathers of the forehead, crown, nape, and throat as shown.

40 Draw the feathers of the throat, chin, and neck.

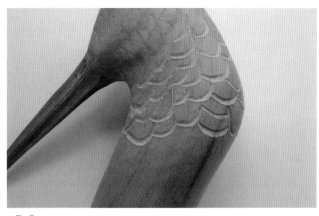

41 Outline with the ruby flame bit.

42 Knock off the shoulders at the base of the feathers and round over the bottom edges with the same bit.

43 Sand the feathers with 240-grit paper in the split-mandrel sander to create soft, undulating bumps.

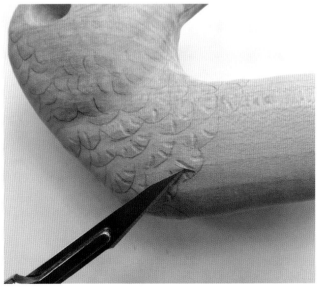

44 Add a few splits to the larger feathers using the scalpel.

45 Use the round-ended stone to add some random waves to the neck feathers.

46 **(a)** Using a blue, inverted-cone ceramic stone, start the texturing of the feathers. First, lay out some strokes that follow the feather flow.

(b) Start from the neck and work upward. Use forward and backward "C" strokes—not straight or regimented. Start from the base of the feather and work to the tip where the stone should be lifted to lighten the strokes. Allow random strokes to carry over to the feather below as a way of joining together the feathers. Reduce the pressure of the strokes as you reach the delicate feathers of the face and forehead.

(c) To add interest, texture the odd feather in different directions so that it looks out of place.

(d) Lay down a second layer of texturing and ensure that there are no gaps remaining. When the texturing is finished, use a nylon brush in the rotary tool to remove any tiny particles of wood and dust. Remember to brush with the flow of the feathers.

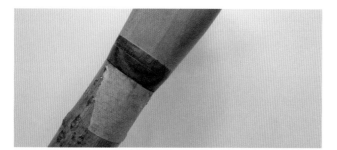

47 Temporarily place the head on the shank with the spacers, and finish sanding the joint with 240-grit paper on the cushioned-drum sander. You may find it easier to glue the spacers to the shank with epoxy glue before sanding. Do not glue the head to the shank.

48 Using epoxy putty, fit the eyes and create the eye rings. You will see from your reference material that the lower part of the eye ring of the woodcock is thickened.

This now completes the carving and detailing of the woodcock head. Ensure it is dust free by wiping with mineral spirits on a lint-free cloth. When fully dry, apply two coats of sanding sealer.

PAINTING THE HEAD

49 Mix titanium buff with a hint of raw umber and raw sienna. Apply as a base coat. Mix paint until it has the consistency of skim milk. Do not put on one thick coat, as this will obliterate the texturing.

Colors to Add for Each Detail of the Head

Add some burnt sienna to the first mix and apply highlights to the back of the head, bottom of the neck, above and to the rear of the eye, and the eye stripe.

With a mix of raw umber and Payne's gray, paint the four bars on the crown and back of the head. Also, use it to add the eye stripe from mid eye to the start of the bill, and for the dark bar mid cheek.

Use this mix to add random wisps and to define the pattern on the tips and mid-point of the feathers of the neck.

Mix some provincial beige with a touch of raw umber and white. Use to lighten the forehead, throat, and lore feathers. Add a touch more white and use around the bottom of the eye and for random highlights.

Add some Payne's gray to the mix of titanium buff, raw umber, and raw sienna used above. Use to darken the crown of the head. Make a darker value of this mix by adding additional gray and paint patches over the forehead, crown, and throat.

Paint the bill with a mix of raw umber, burnt sienna, white, and a hint of cadmium red (medium). Add extra Payne's gray and raw umber to this mix, and use to darken the lower half of the bill. Also, use this darker mix for the nostrils. Use a light value of this mix from mid-forehead to the bill.

Use a mix of quinacridone gold and burnt sienna for the reddish highlights, mainly around the edges of the bars on the head.

Lastly, give the head a couple of weak washes of raw umber to tone down the colors.

50 This is the finished painted head.

Back view.

51 Glue the head and spacers (if you haven't already glued them) to the shank using epoxy glue. Use your choice of finishing oil on the shank. I used a satin finish. Fix a brass ferrule to the tip.

DID YOU KNOW?

In the breeding season, the male woodcock will perform a spiral dance high in the sky, and when competing for airspace it repeats a two-part call. This high nasal whistle, interspersed with low grunts, is called "roding."

(See page 230 for pattern)

PROJECT 11

One-Piece Northern Shoveler Hen Walking Stick

Finding a straight shank that can be cut from a tree with a block of wood at one end is always special. It affords the opportunity to carve a walking stick with a one-piece decorative head. Accordingly, it is reserved for the right project, and the iconic head of a shoveler, or a "spoony" as it is more commonly known, seemed to fit the *bill*. The breeding male, with its iridescent dark green head, is always a favorite, but on this occasion I decided to carve the hen.

Carving a one-piece block-stick is more challenging than carving a head from a separate piece of wood. Access of tools can be awkward, but the main challenge is that you have around four feet (122cm) of shank that you need to manipulate—it will undoubtedly home in on any fluorescent light strip or mug of coffee within range!

The Northern Shoveler (*Spatula clypeata*), is widespread across the northern reaches of North America, Europe, Indian subcontinent, Africa, and Asia. Its name derives from the Latin word for a spoon, *spatula*, and for a shield, *clypeat*.

The unique shape of its bill is longer than its head and longer than any other North American duck.

MATERIALS

- Wood: hazel shank with attached block of wood sufficient to accommodate the pattern: length of the head and bill is 5½" (140mm), the width of the head on the plan view is 2" (51mm), and the head across the side view is 3" (76mm). (This carving is a touch under full size. Alternately, the head can be carved from a separate piece of lime or basswood and attached.)
- Cardboard for template
- Two-part epoxy glue; cyanoacrylate (e.g., superglue)
- Two-part epoxy putty
- Brass ferrule

- Sanding sealer
- 120- to 400-grit sandpaper
- ⁵⁄₁₆" (8mm) olive-yellow or brown glass eyes
- Varnish: matte and satin
- Acrylic paints: gesso, titanium white, raw umber, medium yellow, yellow ochre, buff titanium, cadmium orange, cadmium yellow (light), phthalo blue, and mars black (Sap green will be needed if you paint your own eyes.)

GETTING STARTED

A study cast of a duck's bill is the most helpful reference you can have when carving wildfowl. In its absence, gather as much material you can lay your hands on to ensure that your finished carving has an excellent degree of realism.

Naming and locating the topography of a duck's head can be confusing, as the parts are referred to by different names. Also, their position varies from species to species. Examples: the auricular feathers may also be referred to as the cheek or the ear coverts; the gape is also referred to as the commissure.

Please refer to the diagrammatic drawing of the shoveler's head (page 230) and the glossary for the positions of the parts (as I understand them) that I refer to during this carving.

1 This is the hazel block-stick I am using for this project. I measured the block and the angle of the shank to the block and drew a plan. I ascertained that it could accommodate the shoveler head to just under life-size.

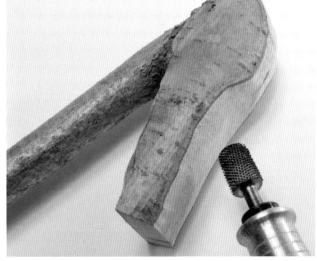

2 Follow the instructions in the following steps (a) and (b) for blocking out the rough shape.

At this stage, the idea is to achieve a rough shape and to leave plenty of wood for any later adjustments and refinement. Leave the bill oversize at this stage, especially on the bottom, to give yourself some wriggle room, if needed, when defining the features later.

(a) From the plan, cut out a cardboard template for the side and top views. You may have to adjust the scale and angle to fit your piece of wood. Draw a good distance beyond the outer extremities of the side view on the block and cut away excess wood using a band saw. Draw a centerline around the head and use the side template to pencil on the outline. Then, using a cylinder-shaped, coarse carbide-point bit, remove wood from outside this outline.

(b) Next, repeat for the top, or plan, view.

SHAPING THE HEAD

Give the head a general sand using a cushioned-drum sander with 120-grit sandpaper. Redraw the centerline and both side and top profiles. It will help with symmetry if you draw reference lines on the top of the head at every ¼" (6mm) from each side of the centerline.

Draw the triangular-shaped notch at the base of the upper mandible and the crown lines that extend from it over the head. The crown on most ducks is about 50–60 percent of the widest measurement of the head. The width of the notch across the bill of this project is about ½" (13mm).

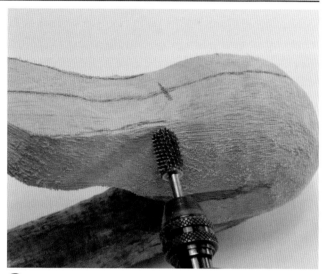

3 Redraw the centerline and the side and top views. Using a bull-nosed, coarse carbide-point bit, shape the head to somewhere near its finished size but allow plenty for sanding. Round over the head but not the bill.

Tip

When you have a blank cut from a block of wood with square sides, it is easy to place the templates against the sides to marry up the features each time they are erased. However, during these initial steps when working with a block-stick, it is not as straightforward. It will help if you mark your side template in at least two places, then match these up on the block. This will give you reference points when drawing back the side view each time it is carved or sanded away.

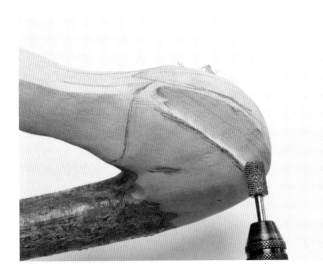

4 Locate the approximate position of the eye. This can be done by piercing through the side template or using your reference material. Draw a line to represent the position of the eye channel. This runs from behind the auriculars, through the center of the eye, and if extended it will go to the tip of the bill. Use a cylinder-shaped, medium carbide-point bit to take the material from above the eye channel reference line up to the crown line. Carve at 90 degrees to the face.

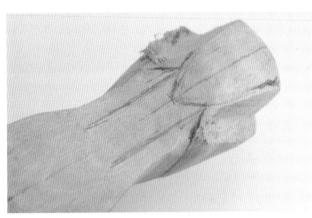

5 Front view of eye channel carved.

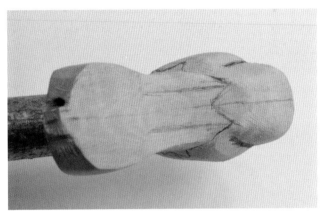

6 Use the same bit to round over the top of the crown and the ledge at the bottom of the eye channel that will form the top of the auriculars, or cheeks.

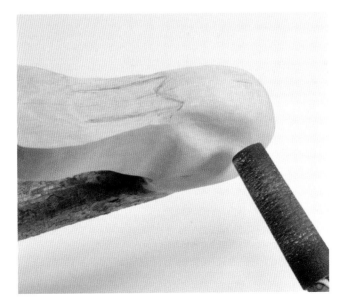

Tip

A pencil line drawn through each eye channel will quickly show up any irregularity of symmetry and accuracy when viewed from the front of the bill.

7 When you are happy with the symmetry and width of the head, use the cushioned-drum sander with 120-grit sandpaper to give the head, but not the bill, another rough sand.

THE BILL

8 **(a)** Refer to your study cast or reference for the unusual shape of the bill. Draw a centerline along the bill. Then draw the notch and the flat area that extends from the notch down to just past the nares, or nostrils. Take the cylinder coarse bit and remove material on either side of the centerline and the flat area, down to the lower margin of the upper mandible. Leave plenty of material over the nares for carving later.

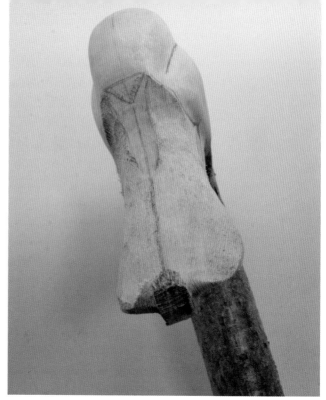

(b) Rough-out the position of the nail. The lower mandible slants upward at the tip. Shape this with the same bit, but don't touch anything else of the lower mandible. Sand with 120-grit paper on the cushioned-drum sander.

Tip

The spatulate, or spoon-shaped, bill of the shoveler is readily identifiable and unique among North American wildfowl. Its length along the culmen, measured from the base of the nail to the start of the feathers in the midline of the notch, ranges from 2⅜"–2⅝" (60–67mm) in the US and up to 2¾" (70mm) in the UK. The width ranges from ⅝"–¾" (16–19mm), measured where the exposed section between the mandibles begins.

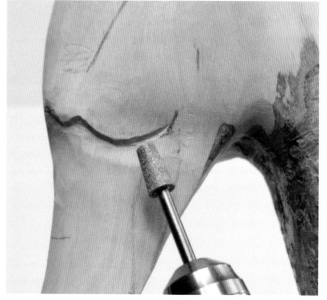

9 Shape the sides of the upper mandible at the point where it meets the feathers of the head, using a diamond, safe-ended, truncated-cone bit. Blend the feather edge into the bill. Work down to the lower margin of the top mandible only.

Using a ruby flame bit, depress the area of the notch and the flat area that runs down the center between the nares, as shown in the photo.

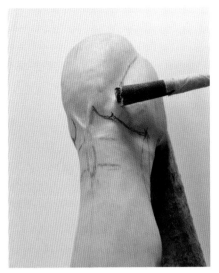

10 Use 240-grit paper on the split-mandrel sander to tidy up both areas.

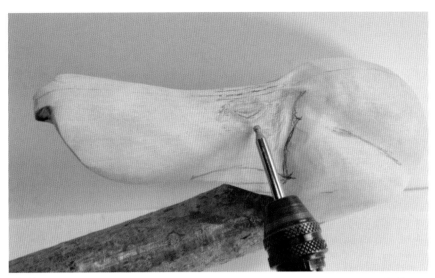

11 Draw the elliptical shape and position of the nares. Use a ⅟₁₆" (1.5mm) diamond ball to shape the outer extremities of the nares. Once this has been done, pierce the inner shape of the nostril with a ⅟₁₆" (1.5mm) wood drill. Enlarge to the shape and dimensions you have drawn with a ⅛" (3mm) diamond-point bit and diamond balls of ³⁄₆₄" (1mm) and ⁵⁄₆₄" (2mm) diameter.

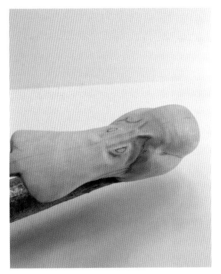

12 Tidy the area around the nares with a circular-end diamond file and 240-grit sandpaper on the split-mandrel sander.

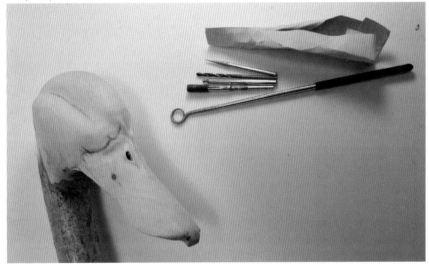

13 Sand the distal section of the upper mandible with 240-grit paper on the cushioned-drum sander. Leave a flat ridge about ¼" (6mm) in width along the center from the nares to the nail. Refine the width of the nail with a carving knife, then sand by hand with 240-grit paper.

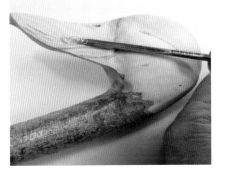

14 Draw the shape of the "lip" of the upper mandible. The shoveler has a double ridge along the edge of the upper mandible. First, use your carving knife to run a stop-cut along the bottom margin of the upper mandible at the proximal end of the bill, over the area where the lamellae are exposed. Then relieve by taking a sliver of wood from beneath the stop-cut.

Define both ridges that start from the proximal end with a ⅟₁₆" (1.5mm) V-tool. Lay the tool on its side so that the side blade pares away wood from the mandible surface as well as defining the ridge. Cut the lowest one first. Tidy with a carving knife if necessary.

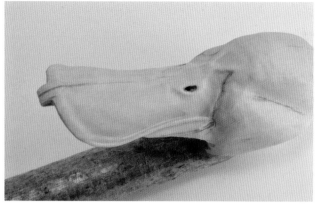

15 Use the V-tool to define the upper mandible ridge/rim. This is the indentation that runs from the sides of the nail, around the front edge of the mandible, and at the other end almost meets with the upper ridge of the lip defined in the previous step. It does not join with it. Refer to the above photo.

Tidy everything with the circular-end diamond file and 240-grit sandpaper in the split-mandrel sander. All of these features can be tidied later on with the pyrograph, if necessary.

16 Before detailing the lower mandible, reduce its thickness to its final size.

Initially, use a flamed, medium carbide-point to reduce the width and depth of the mandible so that it tucks inside, and well up into, the upper mandible. Use the same bit to carve out the recess between the gonys and the inside of the front edge of the upper mandible as shown.

> Carving the underside of the lower mandible is awkward on this one-piece project due to the angle of the head to the shank. Your block-stick may be different and afford you more room to work with.

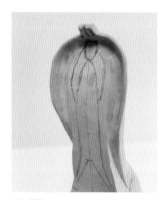

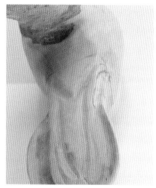

17 Sand the underside of the mandible with 120-grit sandpaper on the split-mandrel sander. Draw the remaining features.

18 Define the cuneate, which is the wedge-shape of head feathers that encroach onto the lower mandible, with a ¹⁄₁₆" (1.5mm) V-tool. The central ridge from the cuneate to the tip is called the gonys and is created using the V-tool. Use the carving knife to outline the lower surface of the nail. At the distal end of the gonys are other small ridges that radiate out. Define these with the V-tool and knife.

19 Sand when finished with 120-grit sandpaper on the split mandrel and the circular-end diamond file.

DID YOU KNOW?

The Northern Shoveler feeds mainly by drawing water into its bill, then pumping it out through the sides with its tongue, filtering out tiny food particles with the long comblike lamellae that line the edges of the mandibles. The diet of the shoveler is varied and includes crustaceans, molluscs, insects and their larvae, small fish, spiders, and even seeds of aquatic plants.

20 Define the "lip" of the lower mandible with the small V-tool. It has another short ridge on the inside edge of the first one carved starting from the gape, or commissure, and is also defined with the knife.

Depending on the shape of your block of wood, you may need to improvise, so use any tool that will help gain access if you also have this awkward angle. These features can be cleaned later with the pyrograph. Make sure that you have sanded the bottom of the lower mandible to its final size before defining the lip and opening the void between the two mandibles that will reveal the lamellae.

21 Use a ruby flame to open the gap between the mandibles and sand with 240-grit paper. The lamellae of the shoveler are plentiful and crowded. The upper mandible lamellae project over those of the lower. They will be defined later with the pyrograph. This photo shows the bill finished except for the lamellae.

THE CHEEKS & EYES

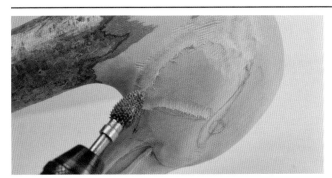

22 Using the medium flame carbide bit, define the two areas that will roughly encompass the cheeks (or auriculars), lores, malar region, and chin.

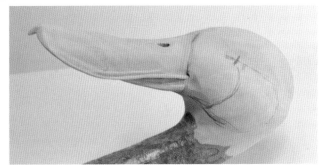

23 Sand this area and the rest of the head with 120- and 240-grit sandpaper.

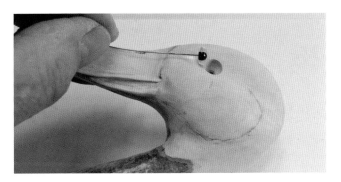

24 The eyes of the shoveler are ⁵⁄₁₆" (8mm), and for this project they will have an olive shade of yellow. Dark brown is probably the more usual color. (Please see the side bar regarding the coloration of a shoveler's eyes on the next page.) Align the position of the eyes using a couple of pins/thumbtacks. View from the top and front. Drill a pilot hole, then use a ¼" (6mm) ball carbide-point bit to open up the eye socket to a touch over ⁵⁄₁₆" (8mm). Check that each eye fits, as they can vary in size slightly. (I have used plain glass eyes that will be painted using a mixture of medium yellow, raw umber, and sap green.)

TEXTURING

Draw the feather flow of the head and neck. Leave some of the wood unpainted around the bottom of the neck to show your project is a hand-carved duck and not a resin copy. Individual feathers of the face could be outlined before texturing, but as they are so small, it is not necessary. They can be simulated by the texturing of curved strokes.

Tip 🖊

From July through to December, the identification of the sex of a Northern Shoveler is challenging. Immature males have the same color plumage as an adult female. The male shoveler has bright yellow eyes, but the eye color of a female ranges from dark brown, dark brownish-olive (in juveniles), hazel, dull olive yellow, and almost amber (in a small percentage of adults). The yellows and ambers are thought to be those of older birds due to a decline of estrogen.

25 Lay out the texturing along the flow lines using a ¹⁄₁₆" (1.5mm) cylinder, blue ceramic stone. The feathers will get gradually bigger as they proceed from the front to the back of the head.

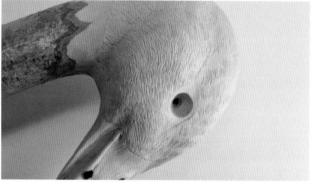

26 Next, go over the whole piece again with the same stone to fill in all the gaps.

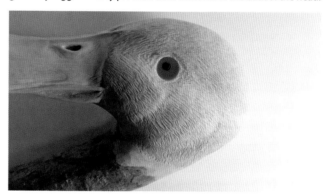

27 Texture the small feather pattern around the eyes.

28 Fix the eyes with two-part epoxy resin before the final round of texturing. There are many brands to use for this task. I have used Milliput. Apply the eye ring and lightly texture with off-set lines using the blade of the scalpel. Add some creases to the bill where it joins the head and around the nares. I used the rounded bottom of a bit with a ⁵⁄₆₄" (2mm) shaft. You can use anything with a similar-sized blunt end. Apply a layer of superglue to the bill and nail. This will protect the nail and give a leathery look to the bill when painted. When the glue is dry, give the bill a light hand-sand with 400-grit paper.

29 Lastly, apply a third layer of texture with the pyrograph and a rounded skew tip. Follow the feather flow laid down in the previous steps.

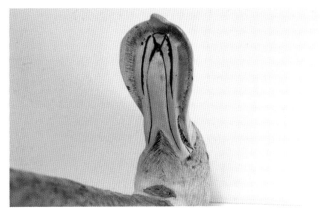

30 With a pointed skew tip, add the lamellae in the opening between the mandibles and on the inside, outer edge of the upper mandible. Clean up features of the lower mandible if necessary. The excessive burning from the pyrograph, and the marks on the lower mandible ridge accidentally made when burning the lamellae, will be sanded before painting.

PAINTING

For this project I have used Windsor & Newton Series 7 Kolinsky sable brushes of sizes 3, 1, 0, and 00. Start the painting with three very thin coats of white gesso. Only cover the area of the head to be painted. Mix to the consistency of skim milk.

The color of each duck will be different. I have painted my duck in accordance with my reference material as a guide only.

31 The pyrographing is finished. Use a nylon brush in the rotary tool to remove any dust and small particles of wood. Wipe down with mineral spirits to remove any remaining dust before painting. Seal with two coats of sanding sealer.

THE HEAD

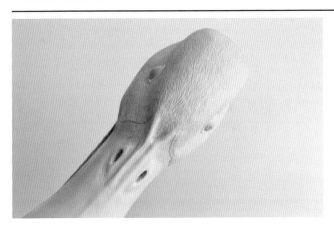

32 Apply three thin coats of a mixture of buff titanium, medium yellow, white, and a hint of raw umber.

> ### DID YOU KNOW?
>
> Northern Shovelers often gather in groups when feeding, when they spin together to disturb the mud and water to extract a greater quantity of food.

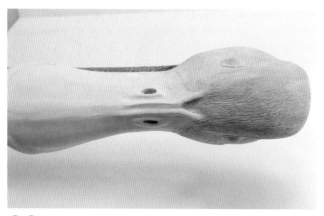

33 Use a mixture of buff titanium and raw umber to apply a couple of washes to build up the darker area on the crown.

34 Using a darker value of this mixture of buff titanium and raw umber, start laying down some flecks on the cheeks. There is a rough row alignment of these flecks. Also, build up some color to the rest of the head, except the lores, malar region, and chin.

35 Following the feather flow, paint additional flecks using a mixture of raw umber with a hint of Mars black.

36 This darker value becomes denser on the crown and back of the head. Add a few random flecks with Mars black to the top and back of the head.

THE BILL

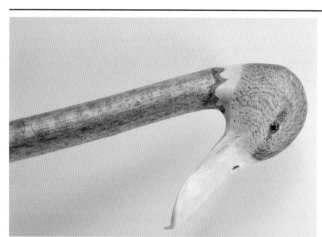

37 Add a touch of white titanium to the mixture of buff titanium and raw umber and use it to paint the edge of the lores, chin, and malar region. Also use it over and under the central section of the eye. Where these areas are painted, the light color touches the eye ring. The rest of the eye ring remains dark. Add a couple of random flecks to the head with this mix and also with straight titanium white.

DID YOU KNOW?

When a female Northern Shoveler is flushed from her nest, she often defecates on her eggs, apparently to deter predators.

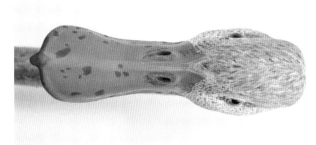

38 Undercoat the whole bill with a mixture of cadmium orange, cadmium yellow (light), and phthalo blue.

39 Add additional phthalo blue to this mixture until you achieve an olive green. Paint the central areas of the upper mandible. Use raw umber to add the blotches and darken the nares and the nail.

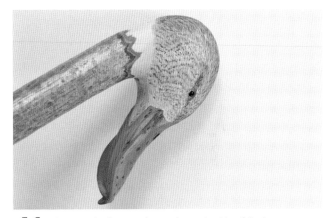

40 Add some white to cadmium orange to use as a wash over the lamellae to make them stand out.

41 Use a wash of raw umber to the underside of the lower mandible to dull the color.

All that is left is to add a brass ferrule to the tip and apply a finish of your choice. I have used three coats of Liquitex matte varnish on the head and a Liquitex satin varnish on the bill.

The finished head.

View of the back of the head.

Tip

There was a small knot along the lip of the upper mandible and a tiny pith hole at the top of the head. I drilled these out with a ³⁄₆₄" (1mm) ball carbide cutter, filled them with two-part epoxy putty, then sanded. I textured the hole on the top of the head.

(See page 232 for pattern)

PROJECT 12

Yellow Labrador & Mallard Walking Stick

For decades, the Labrador retriever (*Canis familiaris*) has consistently topped the charts as the preferred companion and family pet throughout the world.

The original Labrador retriever heralds from Canada's Newfoundland, where its ancestors, the St. John's Dog, helped fishermen pull fishing nets from the Labrador Sea and retrieve game and wildfowl for hunters.

It seems Labradors can be trained to accomplish almost anything. They are widely known as excellent guide dogs for the blind (around 70 percent of guide dogs in North America are Labradors) and working dogs for game and wildfowl hunters. In addition, their intelligence, good work attitude, and sense of smell make them suited to a variety of other roles. They work with the military, police, and other government agencies, tracking smugglers, terrorists, and thieves and detecting drugs and explosives. They also assist in search and rescue, assistance for the disabled, therapy (especially for diabetic and autistic children), and hospital visits.

People often refer to Labradors as two breeds: the American and the English. However, there is only one breed of Labrador retriever. The confusion is due to the body styles. In North America, the breed is slimmer with finer bones, is slightly taller, and bred for hunting and field trials. The English type is stockier, barrel-chested, and bred around the Kennel Club specifications for showing.

MATERIALS

- Wood for head: 3½" (89mm) long; 3¼" (83mm) high and with the grain; 3" (76mm) width measured across the top of the head
- Wood for spacers: all 1¾" (44mm) square—two pieces of purpleheart ⁵⁄₃₂" (4mm) thick; one piece of African blackwood ⁵⁄₆₄" (2mm) thick. Alternatively, one spacer of ⁷⁄₁₆" (11mm)
- Wood for feet: two pieces of boxwood 1" x ¼" x ¼" (25 x 6 x 6mm)
- Cardboard for template
- Hazel shank
- Two-part epoxy glue and cyanoacrylate (e.g., superglue)
- ⅛" (0.12mm) thick, ¹³⁄₆₄" x ³⁄₆₄" (5mm x 1mm) sheet brass
- Two-part epoxy putty
- Brass ferrule
- Sanding sealer
- 120- to 400-grit sandpaper
- ¼" (6mm) dark brown glass eyes
- Varnish (if required)
- Finishing oil
- Acrylic paints: gesso, titanium white, buff titanium, burnt umber, raw umber, cadmium yellow (light), yellow ochre, burnt sienna, ultramarine blue, dioxazine purple, cadmium red (medium), leaf green, phthalo green, and lamp black
- Green and blue pearlescent powder

ROUGHING OUT

Use the side template to cut out the blank on a band saw, ensuring the grain runs downward through the neck. With an intricate carving such as this, it is best not to attempt the two-cut process with the band saw. Just use the side template. This will also leave plenty of material for any slight changes you wish to make to the duck's attitude.

1 Draw the centerline around the entire piece.

2 At the bottom of the neck, find the center point. Draw a square around this point with sides of 1³⁄₁₆" (30mm). With a ½" (13mm) wood drill, drill a hole 1¾" (44mm) deep. This plan is for a shank with an approximate diameter of just over one inch (25mm), plus extra for safety. Adjust according to the size of the shank you are using.

3 Drill a 1½" (38mm)–wide hole through the center of the spacers. Make sure they are clamped and you have a piece of scrap wood behind the spacers when you drill to prevent any cracking.

> I have used three spacers, but you can replace these with one of ⁷⁄₁₆" (11mm) if you wish. The spacers I have are two purpleheart at ⁵⁄₃₂" (4mm) thick and one African blackwood ⁵⁄₆₄" (2mm) thick. The spacers are 1 ¾" (44mm) square to match the square drawn at the bottom of the neck in step 2.

4 Use a cylinder, coarse carbide-point bit in the rotary tool to roughly shape the top profile. Block in the shape of the ears. Do not round over. Block in the top surface of the duck around the Labrador's muzzle. Reduce the neck to just outside the 1³⁄₁₆" (30mm) square marked out previously.

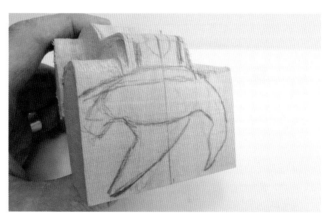

5 This is how the carving should look now.

6 Draw the shape of the duck. You have the opportunity at this stage to alter the duck's attitude if you wish.

7 Using a cylinder bit, rough out the top shape of the duck, leaving plenty of wood for errors or changes at a later stage.

8 Use a bull-nose coarse bit to carve into the smaller spaces.

9 Use the cylinder and the bull-nose bits to rough out the side views of the duck.

10 Now that the head has been roughly blocked in, you can start adding the details. Use a carving knife to define the dimensions of the nose. It is approximately ⁷⁄₁₆" (11mm) in width and in depth.

Tip ✏️

Pencil sighting lines at ¼" (6mm) intervals across the top view of the dog. Redraw these lines at all times when they become erased. These will help with placement of features and symmetry.

11 Use the knife to lightly round over the nose.

12 Locate where the top of the duck's body and wing is, then use the knife to pare away wood from the duck until it sits correctly in relation to the dog's mouth.

13 Use a medium flamed bit to shape the top of the muzzle. Leave enough material for the flews, or the bulge of the upper lip at the bottom of the mouth.

14 Round over the top and back of the dog's head using the cylinder bit.

15 Use a ⁵⁄₃₂" (4mm) diamond ball to create the "stop." This is the furrow in the forehead travelling up from the muzzle to a point between the eyebrows. Sometimes the stop is referred to as the degree of angle change between these points, or as a single point where the muzzle meets the skull.

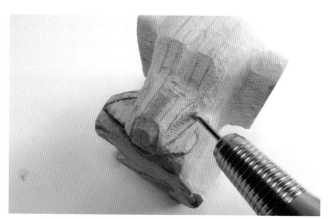

16 The duck will accentuate the flews of the Labrador. With the same diamond ball, create this bulge by removing material from above where the mouth flares over the duck, as shown by the hatched area in the photo.

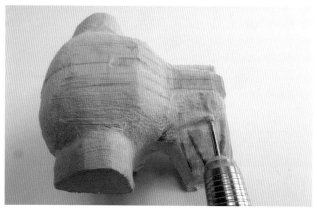

17 Still using the diamond ball, define the fleshy mound of the whiskers at the front of the muzzle.

18 Sand the muzzle with 120-grit sandpaper in the split-mandrel sander.

JOINING THE HEAD TO THE SHANK

Join the head to the shank using the dowel method.

19 **(a)** Ascertain the length of the dowel needed by measuring the depth of the drilled hole in the neck of the Labrador plus spacers.

(b) Concentrate on fitting the tip of the dowel first.

(c) Then continue to remove wood until you achieve a squeaky-tight fit.

(d) Chamfer the hole of the side of the spacer that will sit against the shank. This will help it to seat better. Use a knife or medium bit.

(e) Where you achieve the best fit, mark all components for future alignment.

20 Wrap a couple of turns of masking tape around the top of the shank for protection, then use the cylinder, coarse carbide-point bit to shape the spacers to the same dimensions of the square of the neck of the dog.

21 Then start to shape the spacers and neck with the cylinder bit to the shape of the shank. Ensure you leave enough material for sanding.

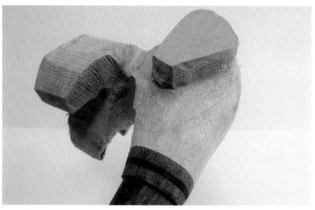

22 This is the neck and spacers roughly shaped.

DOG'S EARS

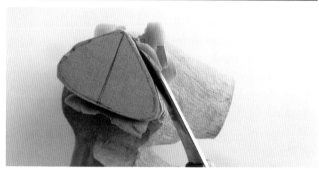

23 Remove the head from the shank. Use the carving knife to shape the ears to their final size, but do not round over at this stage.

24 Ears blocked in, ready for refining.

25 Follow the instructions below for shaping the ears.
(a) The back view of the dog's ears can be confusing. Ideally, you need to have a look at a Labrador's ears to see how they fold at the back against the head. Start by rounding over the top of the ears to the head with the carving knife.

(b) With the carving knife, remove wood from near the bottom of the front face to create a depression that will give a slight curl to the ear.

(c) Use a diamond bud bit to indent the top of the back portion of the ears as shown in the photo.

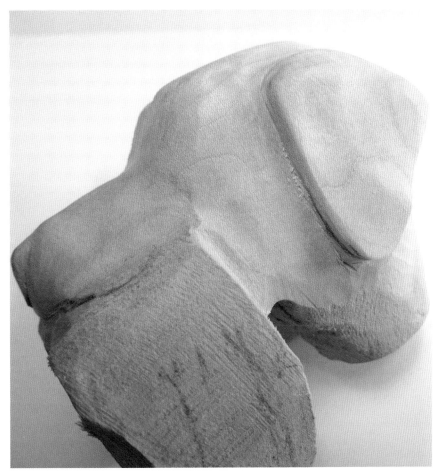

(e) Both ears completed.

(d) Sand the ears with 120-grit in the cushioned-drum sander. The underneath of the ear will be refined at a later stage to prevent any breakage.

DID YOU KNOW?

All chocolate Labradors can trace their origins to eight bloodlines.

EYES

Ensure you have your reference lines drawn on the head. Draw the shape and position of the eye sockets for ¼" (6mm) brown glass eyes. Map out the eyebrow arches and the zygomatic arch that runs from the side of the eyes to the ear, as shown by the hatching on the photo. The inner edges of the socket are about ¹³⁄₆₄" (5mm) from the centerline.

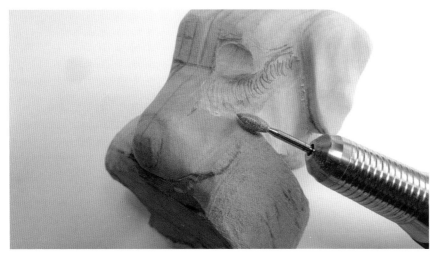

26 **(a)** Use the ruby flame to shape the socket and carve underneath the eye and along the bottom of the zygomatic arch as shown.

(b) Both eyes with the above features completed and eyes roughly positioned.

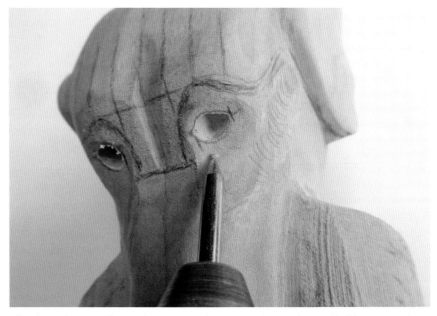

(c) Locate the center of the eyes, which are approximately ⁷⁄₁₆" (11mm) from the centerline. Bore a pilot hole with a ⁵⁄₆₄" (2mm) wood drill.

(d) Enlarge the eye sockets with ³⁄₆₄", ⁵⁄₆₄", and ⅛" (1, 2, and 3mm) diamond ball bits. Create the eyes' oval shape. Slip the eyes into the socket, sliding upward for the lower edge of the eye to fit in and then sliding the eye down into place.

> Another way to create the oval eyes is to drill out round holes and create the oval shape with epoxy putty once the eyes are fitted.

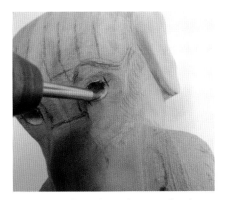

(e) Once you have the socket carved to the required shape, take a ⁵⁄₆₄" (2mm) diamond ball and carve up behind and below the front edges of the socket. Use the glass eyes, by inserting them backward, to test whether they can slide up into this cavity.

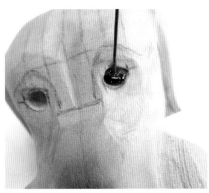

(f) You will only have one chance to place the eyes in their correct position once they are inserted, so ensure you are happy with the socket and the method required to manipulate the eyes to insert them. Ensure the pilot hole is deeper than the socket. This will allow excess putty to be squeezed away when the eyes are pressed in.

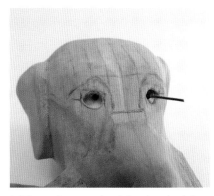

(g) Eye socket carved and showing that it is the correct shape to allow the eye to be fitted. Also showing the deep pilot hole.

(h) Draw the shape of the eyebrow ridges.

(i) Shape the eyebrow ridges with a ⁵⁄₃₂" (4mm) diamond ball.

(j) Sand all of the work around the eye with 240-grit paper on the split-mandrel sander.

Tip ✏️

When purchasing eyes, aim to buy the best quality you can afford—these will come from reputed taxidermist materials suppliers. If you buy cheap eyes from the Internet, you will probably end up receiving eyes that are not the correct size, pairs of eyes where the sizes do not match, and eyes with the pupils in strange places. However, even good quality can throw up the odd blip. I measure all my eyes with a set of digital calipers, and if the tolerance is too great, or there is some other problem, I return them and obtain replacements. I keep the unsuitable eyes and use these for testing the eye fit. This way, you won't damage the good set, and if they become stuck you can drill them out and not waste a pair of eyes.

(k) Round over the inside edges of the sockets with the sander.

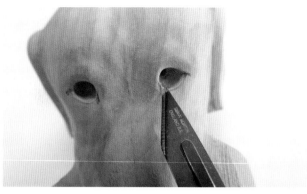

(l) Define with a scalpel the tear ducts at the inside edge of the eyes, then sand with 240-grit on the mandrel sander. The eye sockets are now finished.

REFINE HEAD & SHANK JOINT

27 Place the head back on the shank and use a cylinder, medium carbide-point bit to refine the spacers and neck to conform to the shape of the shank. Ensure you protect the top of the shank with a couple of wraps of masking tape.

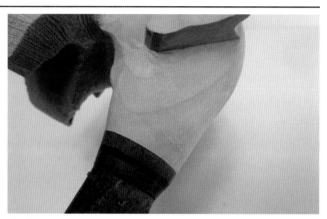

28 Sand the neck and spacers with 120- and 240-grit sandpaper on the cushioned sander.

CARVING THE MALLARD

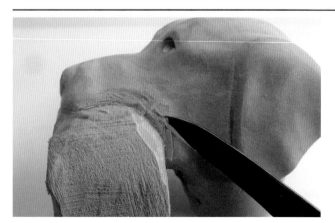

29 Use a carving knife to start shaping the mouth of the dog where it meets the top of the duck.

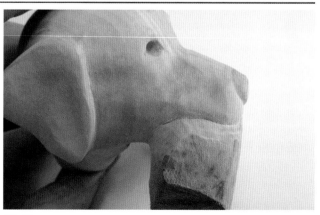

30 Give the area a rough sand with 240-grit sandpaper.

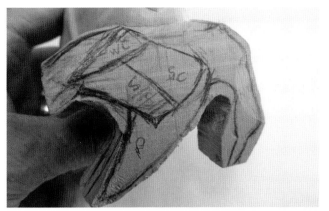

31 Draw the shape of the duck and, most importantly, the position of the wings. You could consider making a model with plasticine of the duck to help visualize the position of the various parts. There will be little room for changes once work begins.

32 Start with using the bull-nose coarse bit to shape the right wing. Leave the wing at least $^{13}/_{64}$" (5mm) thick. For this project the left wing is tucked up on top of the duck and in the mouth of the dog and is largely hidden from view.

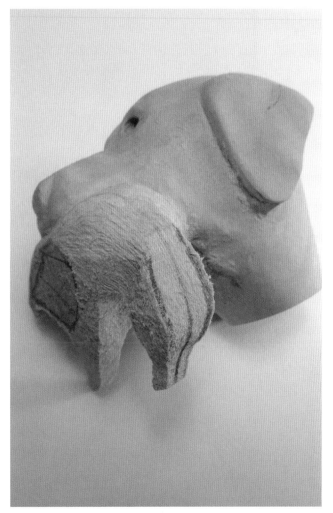

33 Use the same bit to begin shaping the neck and head. The purpose of this initial work on the duck is just to achieve the rough shape. The neck does not hang straight but turns to the right and away from the head of the dog.

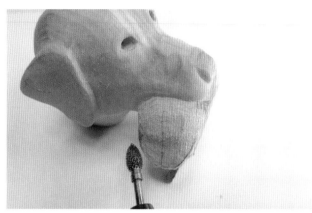

34 Shape the rear of the duck and tail with the medium flame bit. The tertials overlap the tail feathers on the right-hand side, so leave plenty of material.

Using the same bit, shape the part of the left wing that will be seen and under the tail.

Leave features fairly thick at this point for protection.

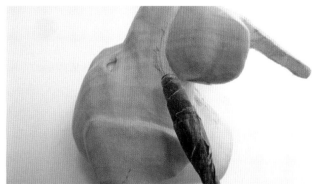

35 Sand the back of the bird and tail with 240-grit sandpaper in the mandrel sander.

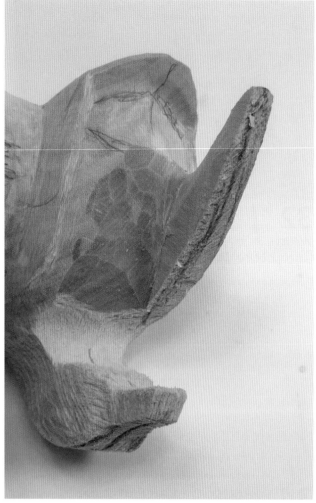

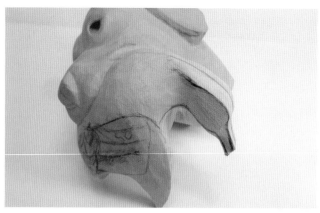

37 Use 120-grit sandpaper to sand the neck, head, and bill.

36 Use a carving knife to reduce the thickness of the right wing and to remove wood from where the breast joins the wing.

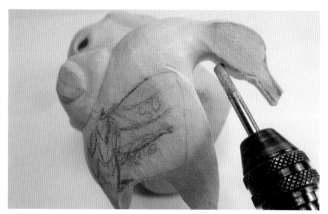

38 Using a cylinder-shaped diamond bit, shape the head to its final size.

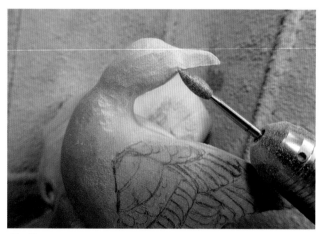

39 Use a ruby flame to finish shaping the head, neck, eye channels, and bill.

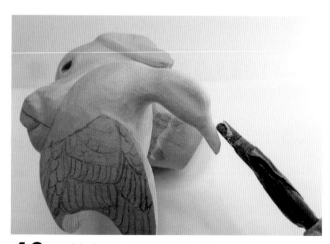

40 Sand the head and bill with 240-grit paper.

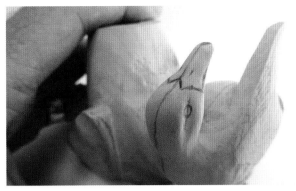

41 Pencil on the position of the eyes and demarcation between bill and head feathers.

42 The duck's eyes in this situation are likely to be closed, or maybe partially open. For this project, I have made the closed eye with epoxy putty. You may insert a glass eye if you wish. Once you are happy with the eye position, use a ⁵⁄₆₄" (2mm) diamond ball to create a shallow hole to give better adherence of the putty later on.

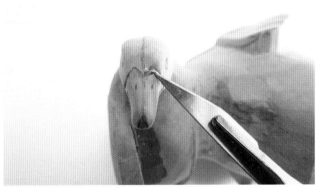

43 Use a scalpel to define where the head feathers meet the bill. Cut the separation of the upper and lower mandibles and define the nail. These details will be tidied later, if necessary, with a pyrograph. Sand with 240-grit paper on the mandrel sander.

44 Add some detail to the underside of the lower mandible with a knife, and sand with 240-grit sandpaper.
Use a ¹⁄₅₀" (0.5mm) ball to define the nostrils. Add superglue to the bill to provide extra strength

At this point, the duck is almost finished. All that's left is the texturing of feathers, making the eye, and reducing the thickness of the right wing, which will be left until later for protection against breakage.

DEWLAPS OF LABRADOR

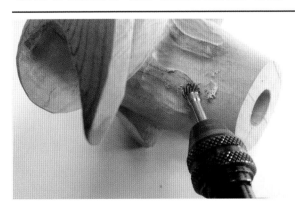

45 Draw the position of the dog's dewlaps and define with a ¹³⁄₆₄" (5mm) carbide cutter.

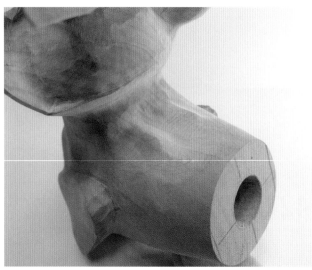

46 Sand the dewlaps with 120- and 240-grit paper in the mandrel sander. Do not go anywhere near the bottom of the neck, as it will likely round over and spoil the alignment with the spacers.

FINISHING THE LABRADOR'S EARS

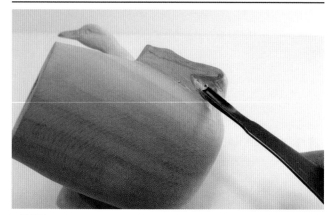

47 Now go back and finish the ears. Draw how the back of the ears will look. Start with the top rear surface where the ear folds under and attaches to the head. Use a ⅛" (3mm) U-tool to hollow out a groove.

48 Sand this area with 240-grit. You need to finish this feature before removing wood from behind the earflap.

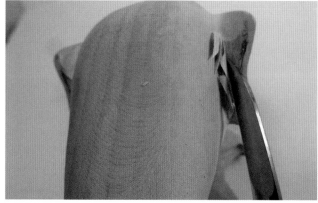

49 With a carving knife, define the area behind the ears. Just take sufficient wood away to give the impression of the gap between head and earflap.

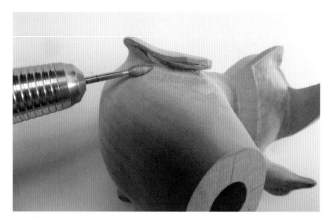

50 Use the ruby flame to tidy up any knife marks. Remember, the bottom of the ears curl up slightly.

51 Use a diamond-point bit to carve deeper behind the earflaps. Run the carving knife down the front edge of the ear, then cut at an angle to remove a sliver of wood to give the impression of a gap.

52 A circular-ended riffler will help to clean up any hard-to-reach areas.

53 The ears are now finished. The intention is to make them look thin, while at the same time keeping them fairly thick for protection.

Rear view of ears.

FINISHING THE NOSE

54 Back to the dog's nose. Draw the shape of the nostrils. Use the 1/50" (0.5mm) carbide ball to define the openings.

55 Use the scalpel to create the alar fold by cutting from the nostril and halfway up the side of the nose.

56 Sand the nose and nostrils. Use a 5/64" (2mm) diamond ball, by hand, to smooth out and round under the edges of the openings.

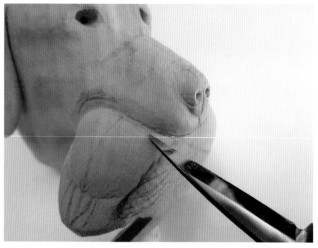

57 Using the scalpel, cut the groove that runs through the middle of the nose down to the top lip of the dog—this is the philtrum. Also, separate the mouth from the top of the duck by carving away a thin sliver of wood.

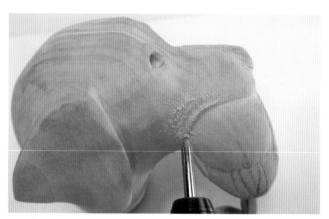

58 Check over your carving. I have used the ⁵⁄₆₄" (2mm) diamond ball to create more definition at the back of the mouth as it folds around the duck. Once happy, sand everything with 240- and 320-grit sandpaper by hand. Ensure that you attach the head temporarily when you sand anywhere near the neck. Finish sanding the spacers with 320-grit sandpaper.

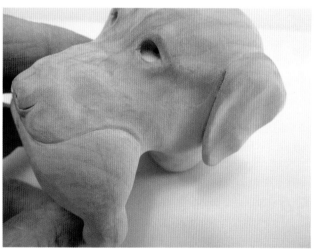

Labrador and mallard ready for texturing.

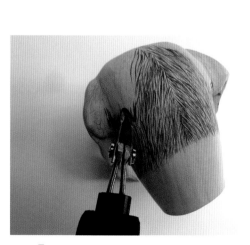

TEXTURING THE LABRADOR

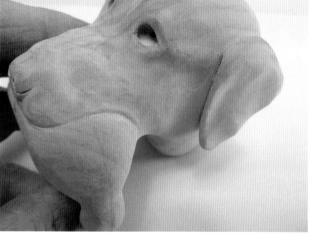

59 First, draw the flow lines of the hair on the head of the dog.

60 With a rounded skew tip in a pyrograph unit, start to texture the back of the dog's head.

Note how the texturing does not start at the joint with the spacers. If, whenever you are detailing a decorative head, you leave some of the wood showing, it will distinguish your head as a carved piece of wood rather than a resin reproduction.

61 Use your reference material to look at the conflicts of hair on the head. There is a conflict at the back of the skull and around the eyes as shown. Texture these areas next.

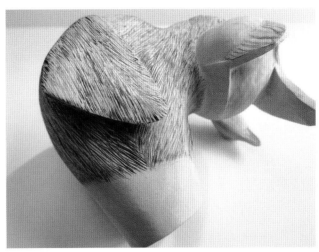

62 Another runs from behind the ears down the side of the neck.

63 Once you have finished all texturing of the head, go over the entire piece again with a fine-pointed skew to add another layer. This will give your texturing better depth.

The texturing of the dog is finished.

DID YOU KNOW?

A study has shown that the Labrador is the most likely dog to be obese.

FEET OF THE MALLARD

Create the legs and feet of the mallard using two pieces of boxwood measuring 1" x ¼" x ¼" (25 x 6 x 6mm).

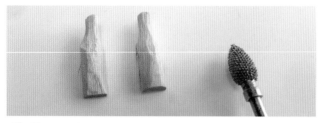

64 Draw the shape of the feet, then rough out using a medium flame bit.

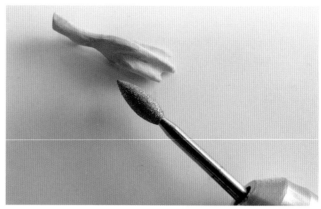

65 Shape the finer details with the ruby flame. Shape underneath the feet with a ⁵⁄₆₄" (2mm) diamond ball.

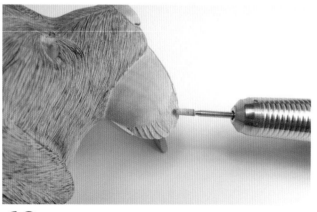

66 Sand the feet with 240-grit and then add the scales and web pattern with a pyrograph.

FEATHERING & TEXTURING THE MALLARD

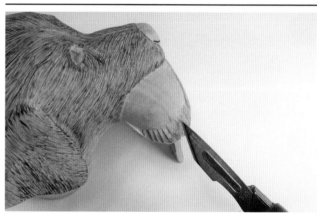

67 Start defining the tail feathers with the scalpel. For this design, the right wing covers the edge of the tail.

68 Sand with 240-grit and clean with a nylon bristle brush. Then add the barbs with a ⁵⁄₆₄" (2mm) blue ceramic stone in a rotary tool.

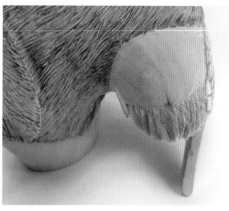

69 The reason for texturing the tail now, before finishing the remainder of the feathering, is so that it can be strengthened with a layer of superglue.

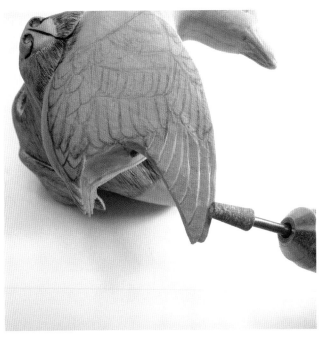

70 Define the primaries of the right wing with the scalpel and a safe-ended, truncated-cone diamond bit.

71 Define the secondaries, coverts, and alula with the same bit. Sand with 240-grit sandpaper on the split-mandrel sander.

72 Next, define the tertial feathers with the knife, or scalpel, and the truncated-cone bit.

73 Add a couple of splits to these feathers with the scalpel. Use the 5⁄64" (2mm) cylinder, blue ceramic stone to add the barbs to the feathers defined in the previous steps.

Reduce the belly of the duck. Texture as best as possible with the 5⁄64" (2mm) blue stone.

Drill 1⁄8" (3mm) holes to accommodate the legs.

> Access to the left wing is difficult, but fine detailing is not necessary as it will be flattened and largely hidden by the lower mandible.

74 With the carving knife, reduce the thickness of the right wing down to its final size. Sand by hand with 240-grit sandpaper. This wing needs to be kept as thick as possible, as it will be fragile, while at the same time giving the impression of thinness.

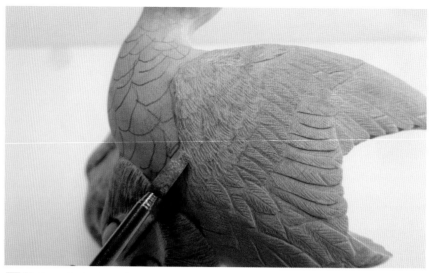

75 Draw the feathers of the lesser and median coverts at the top of the wing. They are so small that they do not need to be outlined with a bit. Texture with the 5/64" (2mm) blue stone. Draw the feathers of the body.

76 Texture the body of the mallard with the blue stone. Start with the head.

77 Then the rump . . .

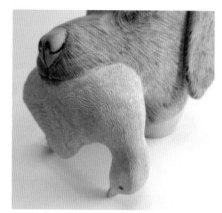

78 . . . the neck . . .

79 . . . and the belly. Outline the feathers on the inside face of the right wing. These are now too delicate to push against with a knife. The pyrograph will be used to outline the feathers and texture the barbs.

Texturing with the blue ceramic stone is now finished.

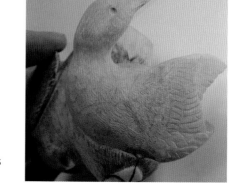

MAKING THE CURLY TAIL FEATHERS

81 Cut two pieces of ⅛" (0.12mm) brass plate for the curly feathers of the tail. Cut approximately ¹³⁄₆₄" x ³⁄₆₄" (5 x 1mm).

80 Use a fine nylon brush in a rotary tool to clean the right wing. Apply superglue to the edges of the feathers of the right wing to give better protection.

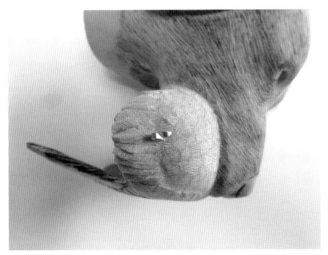

82 Mark on the tail where the two feathers sit—one in front of the other. Open up two slots with the ¹⁄₅₀" (0.5mm) ball cutter.

83 Fix the curly tail feathers and the feet with epoxy glue.

THE LABRADOR'S EYES

Labradors have their eyes set at an angle of about 20 degrees. Although this reduces their field of vision, it increases depth perception and binocular vision, which aids their hunting skills. Dogs with a longer nose have a better field of vision.

Their field-of-view is around 240 degrees compared to a human's 180 degrees. One of the reasons that dogs want to chase after anything that moves is because they have a high level of vision cells concentrated in the retina in something called their visual streak. This enables them to focus sharply on these objects at the extreme ends of their peripheral vision.

Humans have three types of color cones in their eyes. Dogs have only two. This reduces the spectrum of color they can see to blues and yellows. They struggle to see reds and greens.

On the plus side they have more rods, and this gives them superior nighttime vision.

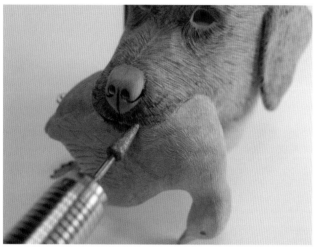

84 Add some whisker dimples with a ⅛" (3mm) round-ended, tapered stone.

85 Seal the carving with three coats of sanding sealer.

86 Round over a small blob of epoxy putty in your hands and place it in the eye position. Create a slit—not a straight line—through the middle with a scalpel. Do the same for the other eye.

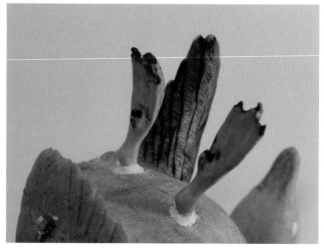

87 Use a small ribbon of epoxy putty to seal around the joint where the legs meet the belly. Texture with the blue ceramic stone when dry.

PAINTING THE LABRADOR

Before painting, use 400-grit sandpaper to very lightly go over the carving, then wipe to ensure it is clean of dust. I used Windsor and Newton Series 7 sable brushes, sizes 3, 1, 0, and 00, and Windsor & Newton acrylic paints for the project.

There are many variations of the coloring of a golden Labrador. I will be painting mine to represent a middle-aged dog. Use your reference material to select the variation of your choice.

88 Attach the ¼" (6mm) dark brown eyes into the Labrador with epoxy putty. Make sure there is enough putty at the back of the eyes to prevent them from being pushed in too far. Any excess should squeeze into the pilot hole. Allow the putty to dry, then fashion small pieces of putty at the sides of the eyes to achieve the finished effect. Don't try to do this until the putty behind the eye has set, as there is a chance that you will change the orientation of the eyes when adding the extra putty at the sides.

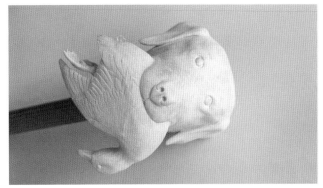

89 Mix some gesso with water to the consistency of skim milk. Apply four coats to the dog and duck.

90 Start with the dog's head by applying several washes of buff titanium mixed with a touch of titanium white.

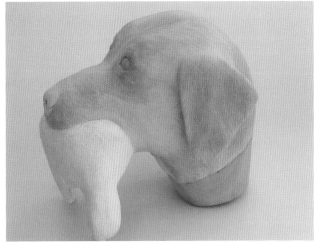

91 Build up a darker value with a mixture of buff titanium and yellow ochre, and apply to the ears and sides of the muzzle. The sun will bleach the top of a Labrador's head, so this can remain a light color.

92 Undercoat the nose pad with a mixture of cadmium red (medium) and white.

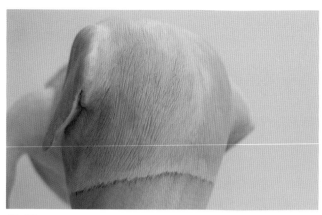

93 Add darker patches to the ears and back of the head with a mixture of buff titanium, golden ochre, and raw umber.

94 Use a mixture of ultramarine blue and raw umber on the nose, sides of the muzzle and around the eyes. This darkened the nose too much and the pink hue did not show through. I added a few washes over the nose with the mixture of cadmium red and white until a hint of pink could be seen.

95 Use the mixture of buff titanium, yellow ochre, and raw umber in the whisker dimples. Soften the eyes and muzzle with a lighter value of this mixture.

THE MALLARD

96 Paint the breast of the duck with a mixture of burnt sienna, burnt umber, and a hint of dioxazine purple. Use four thin coats.

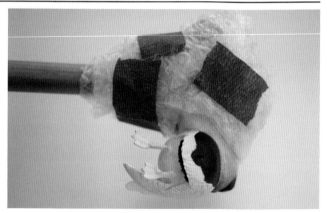

97 Paint the top and bottom of the rump and the curly tail coverts with a mixture of ultramarine blue and burnt sienna. Add raw umber to this mixture and blend from the rump to the edge of the dog's mouth.

98 Paint the cape up to the edge of the dog's mouth with a mixture of raw umber and white. Use pale values at first from the edges and gradually darken as it moves toward the top of the cape.

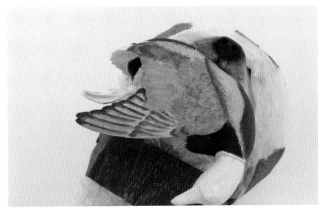

99 Use a pale value of raw umber and white to wash the belly and the wings. Increase to a darker value by adding a touch of burnt umber on tips and inside edges of primaries, edges of the secondaries, secondary coverts, tertials, and edges of the scapulars. Use this mixture on any of the left wing that is visible on your carving.

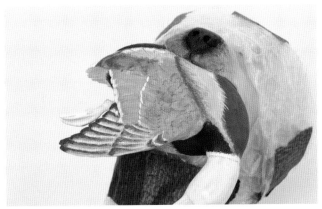

100 Use white to cover the outside edges of the primaries, secondaries, coverts, tail, rump, and ring around the neck.

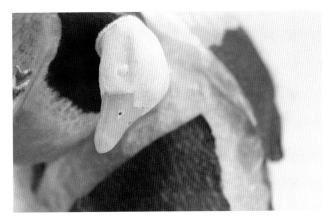

101 For the bill, use a mixture of cadmium yellow, yellow ochre, white, and a hint of raw umber. Lighten the tip with added white to the mixture. As there is no texturing on the bill, the paint does not need to be watered down as much.

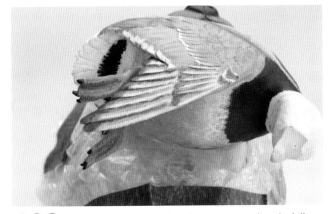

102 Add some cadmium red to the mixture used on the bill, and use to paint the feet and legs. Use raw umber for the claws, and finish with a couple of weak washes of raw umber over feet and legs to pick out the highlights.

DID YOU KNOW?

A Labrador with a flesh-colored nose and eyelids is called a Dudley.

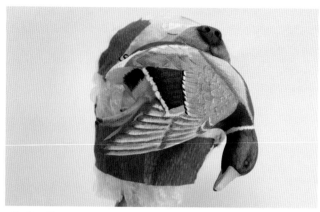

103 Use a mixture of phthalo green, leaf green, and lamp black for the head and top of the rump. Add green pearlescent powder to the final coat. Add blue pearlescent powder to the final layer on the back of the head. Use a wash of black for the eye channel and nail of the bill, and to darken the nares.

104 Mix ultramarine blue with dioxazine purple for the secondary feathers, but not the feather nearest to the front edge of the wing. Add blue pearlescent powder to the final coat. Use lamp black to paint the bar above the white tips of the secondaries and tips of the secondary coverts. Use black and white, as appropriate, to pull some strokes into the opposing color of the neck and rump.

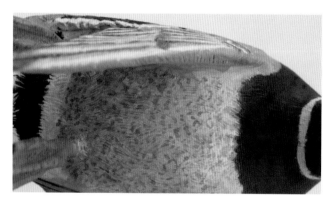

105 Paint the vermiculation of the belly with a mixture of burnt umber, burnt sienna, ultramarine blue, and white. Lastly, use a weak wash of this mix to take the brightness off the white areas of paint of the mallard.

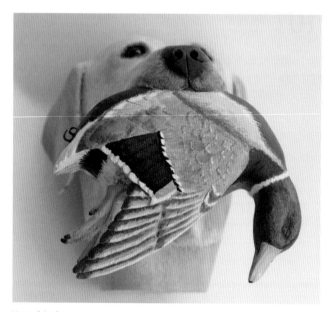

View of the front.

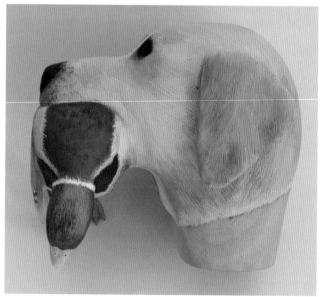

The left side.

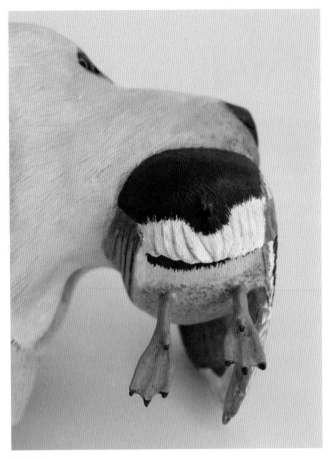

Right side.

Top.

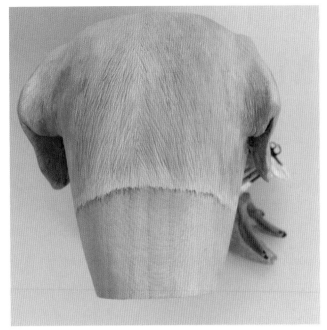

Rear.

106 This is the finished carving of the Labrador and mallard. All that is left is to apply several coats of finishing oil of your choice to the shank and spacers and fit a brass ferrule. Fix the head to the shank with epoxy glue and varnish the head if required.

(See page 233 for pattern)

PROJECT 13
Mantling Barn Owl Walking Stick

The barn owl (*Tyto alba*) can be found on six continents and is only absent from the most northern reaches of North America, north of the Himalayas, most of Indonesia, and extreme northern reaches of Europe. Scotland is the furthest north that it breeds.

There are 28 subspecies, which are typically between 13"–15" (33–38cm) long and with a wingspan of 31"–37" (79–94cm). The largest barn owls are found in North America and the smallest in the Galapagos Islands.

Barn owls are believed to have the most sensitive hearing of any animal tested and are able to hunt and capture prey in complete darkness by sound alone. Their extremely long and sharp talons cut through long grass and snow to reach their prey, which they kill with a nip to the back of the head. They swallow their kill whole, but as they cannot digest everything, they regurgitate bones and fur in the form of the familiar owl pellets.

Their feathers have evolved to enable silent flight, but the downside is they are not completely waterproof. Generally, barn owls do not hunt in wet weather. This vulnerability can lead to a decline in number in any year with particularly inclement weather.

MATERIALS

- Wood for the body: lime/basswood, 6" (152mm) with the grain x 3¼" (83mm) wide x 2" (51mm) thick
- Wood for the wings: 4" (102mm) with the grain running along the primary feathers x 2½" (64mm) x 2" (51mm) thick
- Wood for the spacers: all 1¼" (32mm) square; laburnum—2 pieces, ³⁄₁₆" (4.5mm) thick; sweet chestnut—one piece, ⅛" (3mm) thick; alternatively, you can use one spacer ½" (13mm) thick
- Cardboard for template
- Hazel shank
- Brass ferrule

- 120- to 400-grit sandpaper
- Two-part epoxy glue
- Epoxy putty
- Finishing oil
- Varnish: matte (optional)
- Acrylic paints: titanium white, zinc white, titanium white, buff titanium, yellow ochre, quinacridone gold, dioxazine purple, raw umber, burnt umber, raw sienna, burnt sienna, cadmium red, and cadmium yellow

ROUGHING OUT THE BODY

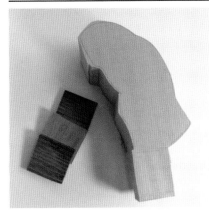

1 Use the drawings to make cardboard templates of the owl's body. Draw on your block of wood using the side template only. Cut out the blank on the band saw. Draw a centerline around the entire surface. Cut your three spacers to size.

2 At the bottom of the blank, find the center point and draw a square around it with 1" (25mm) sides. Drill a 1 ½" (38mm) hole at this point with a ½" (13mm) wood drill. Drill the spacers. Remember to drill the spacers on a piece of scrap to prevent them from splitting.

3 Use a cylinder, coarse carbide-point bit to shape the sides of the body, using the front template for reference.

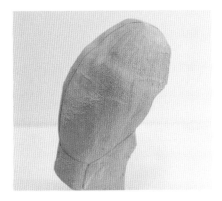

4 Using the same bit, round over the back of the owl's body.

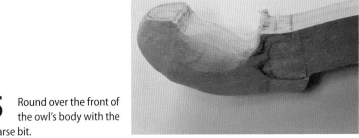

5 Round over the front of the owl's body with the coarse bit.

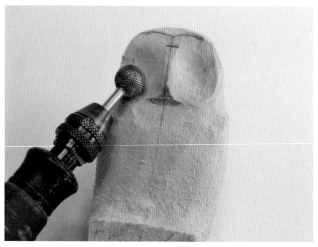

6 Draw the facial disc with the position of the central ridge and bill. Use a medium-grit carbide-point ball and a medium-grit flame to create the rough shape of the face.

SHAPING THE WINGS

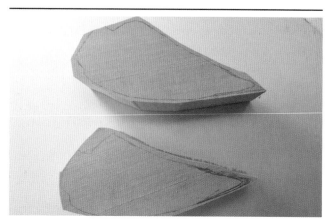

7 Cut a cardboard template for the wings from the drawing on page 235 and use it to cut two blanks.

8 Use the coarse bit to round over the blank of the left wing, making sure to include the fixing tab.

At this stage you are looking to achieve only the approximate dimensions of the wing. It is the rounded surface that needs to be checked against the template. Keep checking the dimensions as you carve by bending the template over the surface, and err on the safe side by having them larger at this step. Do the same for the right wing, but remember to reverse the template.

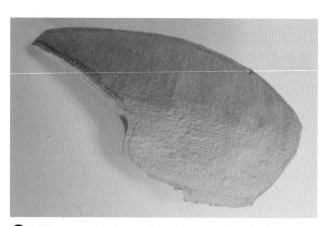

9 When you are happy you have the correct shape for the upper surface of the wing, shape the wing blanks to the exact shape of the template.

10 Hollow out the underside of the wings using the largest rounded coarse bit you have. I used a ¼" (6mm) shank, bull-nose carbide point that made easy work of this process. Ensure you leave around ⅜" (10mm) thickness to allow for detailing and corrections later on.

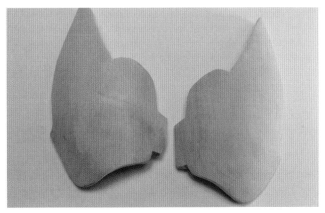

11 Sand only the top surface at this stage with the cushioned-drum sander and 120-grit paper.

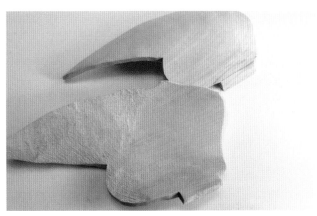

12 Sand underneath the top part of the wings—the coverts—with 120-grit paper. The finished size of the fixing tab is ³⁄₁₆" (4.5mm) thick, at least 1" (25mm) wide, and to fit into the body by about ³⁄₈" (10mm). Shape the tab to just over these dimensions to allow for adjustments during fitting.

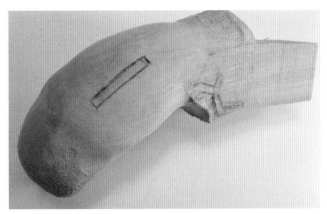

13 With 120-grit paper in the drum sander, shape the back of the owl's body around the area where the wing fixing slot will be cut. Use the left wing to ascertain the exact position it needs to be fitted. Line up the tab of the wing at this position and draw the outline of the slot corresponding to the tab size. Check the angle as well as the alignment with the body, for if it is too steep, the wing may touch the base.

FITTING THE WINGS

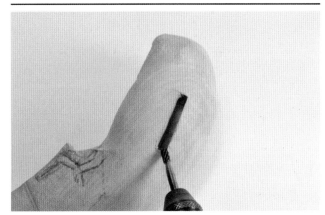

14 Double-check that the alignment of the wing is correct. A small change in position can have a huge effect on the design. Adjust the position of the slot if necessary. Use a carving knife to cut around the inside edges of the slot. Once the outer shape of the slot is achieved, continue to excavate with a ⁵⁄₃₂" (4mm) carbide cutter. Deepen the slot until the wing fits up against the body. It will not fit flush at this point due to the rounded shape of the body. Keep checking as you carve to ensure the slot is being carved at the correct angle.

15 As shown in the photo, you will need to draw the profile of the body on the top and bottom of the wing for it to fit flush. Use the carving knife to gradually remove material from the upper and lower surfaces of the wing until they match the profile of the body. You will need to shape the wing in front of and behind the fixing tab. Due to the angle of the wings, the ventral surface will need to be cut back more than the upper. Do all this fitting gradually until you achieve a snug fit.

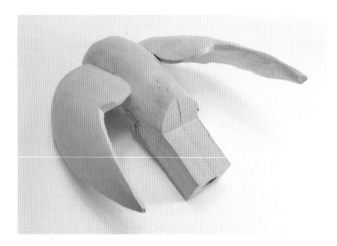

16 Fit the right wing. The only difference in the process is that after you have drawn the position of the slot, and before you cut it, hold the wing up to the body and ensure the leading edge aligns with that of the left wing. If the tab positions vary by a small amount, the leading edges will not coincide and will stand out. Cutting the tab slightly oversized gives the opportunity to reduce the length of tab at either end, if necessary, to achieve this alignment.

The joint between wing and body will be reinforced with epoxy putty at a later stage, which will also cover any small gaps. However, reinforce the tabs by soaking them with superglue.

As long as the leading edges of the wings align, it does not matter that the primary feathers of each wing are set at a different angle. Personally I prefer this, as it adds character and realism.

PREPARING THE SHANK

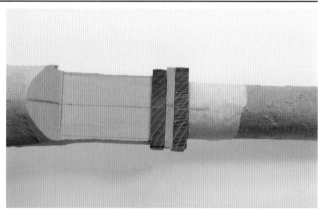

17 Carve and mark the shank as follows:
(a) Carve the top of the shank into a dowel to fit into the hole of the body section.

(b) Mark the shank, spacers, and neck of the body where the best fit is achieved.

FITTING THE EYES

18 Use the coarse cylinder bit to shape the spacers and the neck of the body section to fit the shape of the shank. (I have used a twisty shank, as the bulkiness of the twisty section balances the size of the owl. The top of the shank is egg shaped.) This needs only be rough at this time. Remove the head from the shank.

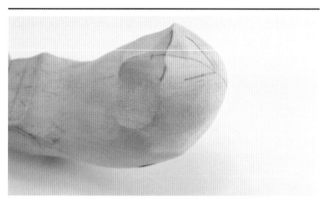

19 The angle between the center of each eye of the barn owl is 82 degrees. Mark this angle on the top of the head as a guide. With the medium, flame carbide point, carve out the face on either side of the central ridge until the correct angle is achieved. Sand with 120-grit abrasive.

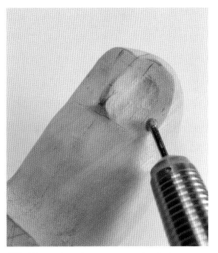

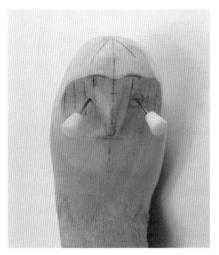

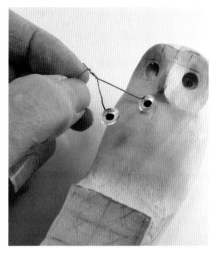

20 Follow these steps to finish fitting the eyes:

(a) Draw reference lines across the face, ¼" (6mm) apart. Use a ⁵⁄₃₂" (4mm) diamond ball to start defining the central nose ridge and bill and to carve the facial disc to the correct depth for the eyes.

(b) Locate the position of the eyes using the reference lines. The eyes are ⁹⁄₃₂" (7mm) glass. Use pins/thumbtacks to line up the eye centers. Drill pilot holes with a ⁵⁄₃₂" (4mm) wood drill.

(c) Open up the eye sockets to a tad over ⁹⁄₃₂" (7mm) with the medium flame. Keep checking that the socket is deep enough to receive the eyes. Ensure that the pilot hole extends beyond the back of the eye socket. This will help when fitting the eyes.

THE TAIL

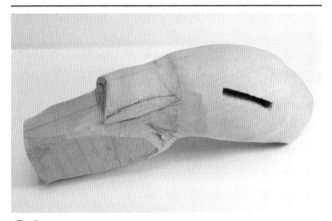

21 Use the carving knife to position the top surface of the tail.

LEGS & TOES

When an owl is in flight, three of its four toes normally face forward and one backward. However, it has a flexible joint that enables it to turn the outer front toe of each foot to face backward when perching or holding onto its prey. This is known as *zygodactyl*.

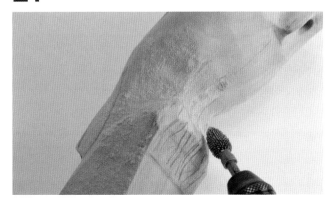

22 Follow these instructions to create realistic legs.
(a) Barn owls have very long legs. Use the medium flame to rough in the position of the legs. Use the U-tool to cut deeper between the legs toward where the undertail coverts would be.

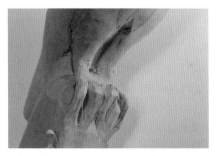

(b) For this carving, two toes are facing forward, the outer toe to the side, and the fourth hidden from view. Start by drawing on your stance, then outline the approximate position of the toes with the carving knife.

(c) Toes blocked in, joints located and ready to be detailed later. When perching, the talons can dig into the base, or often they are turned slightly at an angle to the base. A couple of the talons will be carved in this manner for interest.

(d) Use the ruby flame bit to round over the toes, then give a quick sand with 240-grit in the split-mandrel sander.

MUSCLE GROUPS OF BREAST & SHOULDER TRACT

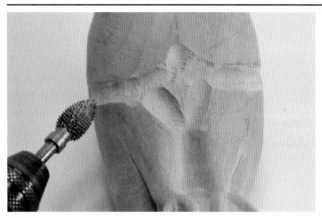

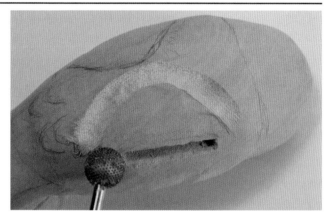

23 Draw the muscle groups of the chest and shape with the medium flame, then sand with 240-grit in the split-mandrel sander.

24 Use a medium, ball carbide-point bit to outline the shoulder tract as shown in the photo. This essentially defines the edges of the wing coverts.

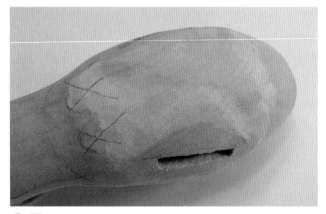

25 Give a quick sand to the back of the body with 120-grit paper in the cushioned-drum sander. Leave the bottom area, as shown by the crosses, with plenty of material, as these feathers will be lifted and undercut.

DID YOU KNOW?

Birds of prey and owls have a locking, ratchetlike mechanism in their foot that keeps the toes locked around a perch or prey without the need for the muscles to remain contracted.

TAIL FEATHERS & FACIAL DISC

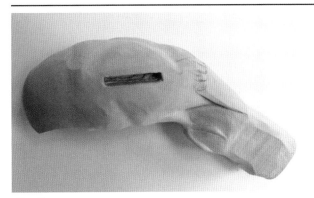

26 Draw the lower tail coverts and use the medium-grit cylinder to lower the tail so that it sits against the base. Sand with 120-grit paper in the cushioned-drum sander.

27 Map out the facial disc. Draw reference lines to assist with symmetry. Use the ruby flame to reduce the nose ridge and the bill.

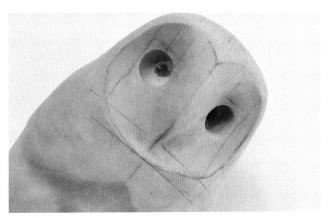

28 Sand with 240-grit abrasive on the split-mandrel sander, then redraw reference lines.

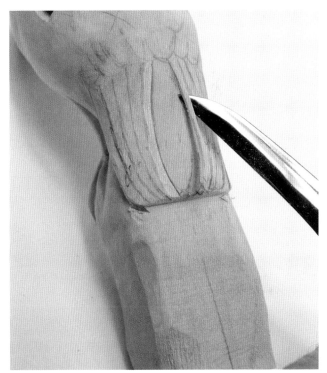

29 Sand the remainder of the body with 240-grit to prepare for shaping the feathers. Start by drawing on the tail feathers, then use a carving knife to define. Place a vertical stop-cut, not too deep, then take a sliver away from the correct side of the line.

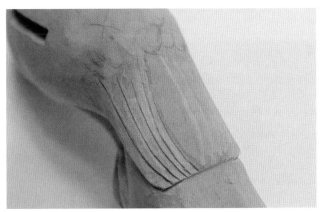

30 Looking at the tail from the back, there are two central feathers (the left overlaps the right), and the tail feathers on their left side overlap the feather to its left. On the right side the feathers overlap the feather to its right.

FEATHERING THE BODY

Before you can start to feather the body, the scapulas (or shoulder tract) and tertials need to be mapped out, as they overlap both body and wing.

31 When temporarily fitting the wings, I double-checked the wing angle and wasn't entirely happy. I thought they needed to come in closer to the body. If you need to do this, chamfer the underside of the wing where it meets the body until you achieve the desired angle.

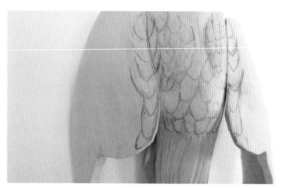

32 Draw the lower tail coverts, the feathers above them that are to be lifted and undercut, both sets of wing coverts, and the first line of the tertials that cover the wing joint. Remove the wings and put them aside.

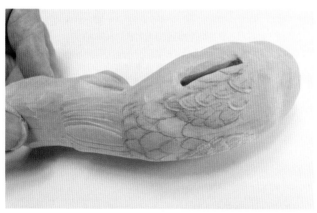

33 Use the ⁵⁄₆₄" (2mm) diamond ball to outline the feathers of the wing coverts on the body. As you do so, knock off the shoulders of the feather below.

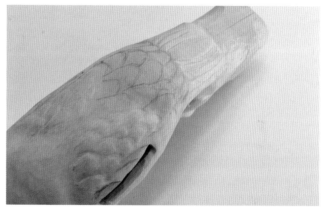

34 Sand with 240-grit paper and the split-mandrel sander until you have some well-defined undulating feathers.

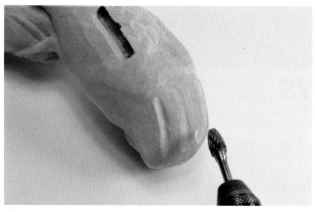

35 With a bullet-shaped carbide cutter, lay down some tracts for the head feathers. Sand with 240-grit paper.

36 Draw the layout of the head feathers and those of the mantle or cape.

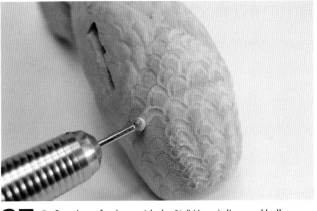

37 Define these feathers with the ⁵⁄₃₂" (4mm) diamond ball.

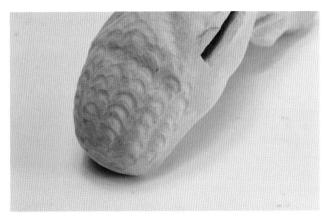

38 Sand with 240-grit in the split-mandrel sander.

39 Lay out the feather flow of the breast and flanks. Define with the ⁵⁄₃₂" (4mm) diamond ball and sand as above. The result should look like rows of gently undulating bumps that blend into each other.

Tip

When creating the undulating rows of feathers, sanding should wipe out virtually every trace of their individual shape. However, you should just be able to still pick out each feather enough to outline it with a pencil to help when texturing.

40 Go back to the feathers of the rump above the upper tail coverts that are to be lifted. Define them with a carving knife, but keep them around ³⁄₁₆" (4.5mm) thick so they can be undercut later.

41 Sand these feathers and the tail feathers with 240-grit sandpaper.

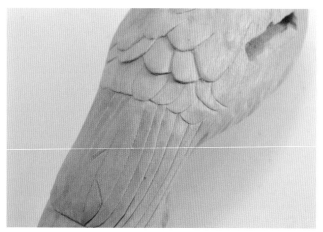

42 Outline the upper tail coverts with the carving knife and sand. These will not be undercut.

FINISHING THE FACE

43 Refine the bill to its final size and shape. Sand with 240-grit sandpaper on some sanding sticks to keep the crisp edges and symmetry.

44 Refine the lower part of the central ridge by lowering it back into the inside corner of the eye. Use the ruby flame. Sand with 240-grit. The bill is too small to separate the upper and lower mandibles. With the split-mandrel sander, lightly round over the bottom and outside edge of the eye sockets.

FEET

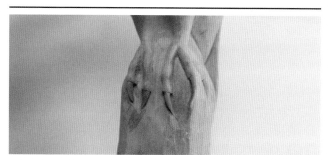

45 Return to the feet and apply more detail. Define the sections of the toes and the talons. Remember, these feet are gripping onto a branch, so you can have the talons buried into the wood, or often they lay to one side, as I have done. You will need several tools to achieve this detail, including a ³⁄₆₄" (1mm) diamond ball, scalpel, diamond files, and sanding sticks—basically anything that will do the job. Soak some superglue on the talons as a precaution against knocks.

JOINT WITH SHANK

46 Place the body back onto the shank and reduce the spacers and the bottom of the head, which will be carved as a branch, with the coarse cylinder. Decide your layout of the branch—maybe a couple of branch collars—as I have done. Wrap a couple of pieces of masking tape around the top of the shank for protection.

47 Sand with 120-grit on the cushioned-drum sander. The joint will be sanded finer later on.

FEATHERING THE DORSAL SURFACE OF THE WINGS

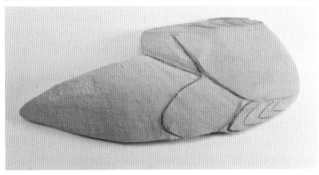

48 Draw the feather groups of the dorsal surface of the right wing and define with the medium-grit cylinder.

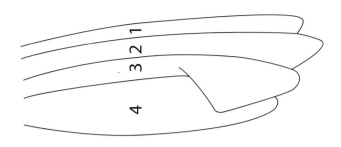

Feather displacement of right wing, dorsal view.

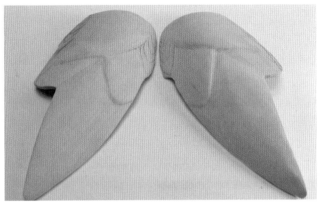

49 Sand with the cushioned-drum sander and 120-grit abrasive. Repeat this shaping and sanding on the left wing.

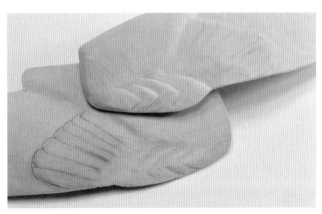

50 Outline and carve with the knife the four alula feathers on both wings. Sand with 240-grit.

51 Draw the primary covert feathers and define with the carving knife. Run the knife along the edge, then lay it almost flat to take out a sliver of wood, leaving the edge proud. The edges will be rounded over, so leave about ¹⁄₁₆" (1.5mm) of wood at the edge. Sand with the split-mandrel sander and 240-grit abrasive.

Tip

The carving knife is my preferred method of relieving the primary, secondary, and some covert feathers as I can cut a straighter edge. You could also use a safe-end, diamond cylinder to do the same task, provided you have a steady hand!

Don't try to create a mirror image of each wing when laying out the feathers. In reality, the feathers will lay differently. Some will have the full shaft in view, others will be tucked under the feather to its side, and others will only have part of the shaft in view. Try to create these differences for interest.

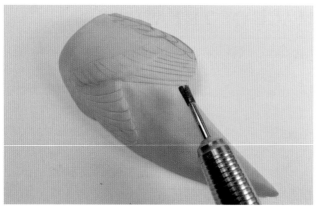

52 Use the knife and same technique to define the secondaries. I have only drawn and carved seven feathers to ensure they will not be too tightly packed.

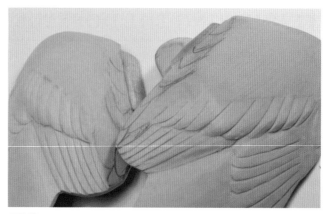

53 Do the same for the secondary coverts.

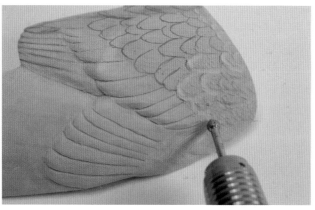

54 The marginal, lesser, and median coverts are less pronounced and can be carved in the same way as the body feathers. Take the 5/32" (4mm) diamond ball, outline their edges, and knock off the shoulders of the feather below.

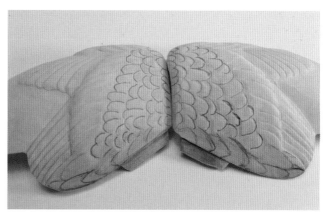

55 Sand with 240-grit on the mandrel sander. As before, the test is to sand smooth but to still be able to redraw each feather ready for texturing. Don't define the scapulars at this stage.

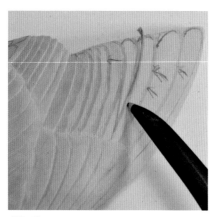

56 Carve the ten primary feathers of both wings with the carving knife.

57 Cut the tips of the feathers with the knife to start the appearance of them overlapping. The corresponding feather will be relieved when the underside of the wing is carved.

Tip

Before defining the feathers with a knife, draw some arrows to indicate which side of the feather needs to be relieved. It is easy to become confused when relieving so many feathers.

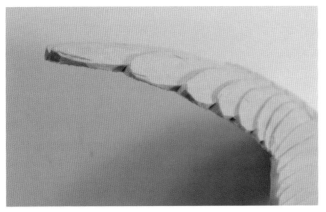

58 The preceding step is the reason why the wing is not sanded on the underside at the same time as the top. This photo shows how much wood has been removed from the tips to create this effect. If both surfaces were sanded at the same time, they invariably end up being sanded too thin at the tips and this would not be possible.

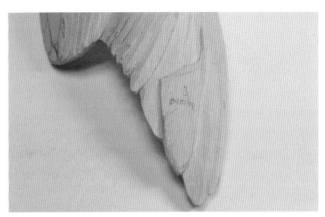

59 For some added interest, I have displaced one of the primary feathers, as shown. When this is painted it will stand out more.

60 Round over and smooth the feathers of the top of both wings by hand with 240-grit sandpaper.

FEATHERING THE VENTRAL SURFACE OF THE WINGS

With the upper surface feathering complete, the ventral surface can now be thinned to its final thickness. Use a combination of the coarse cylinder and the medium flame. There will be some thickness around the coverts that reduces as it moves down toward the primary feathers. The idea at this stage is to give the impression of thin feathers while retaining some degree of thickness for practicality. Once you are happy with the approximate thickness, sand with 120- and 240-grit sandpaper on the cushioned drum.

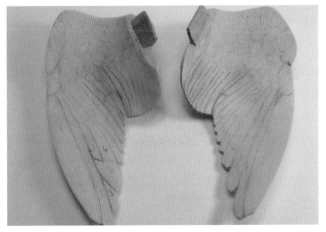

61 Draw the feathers of the lower side. Make sure that you pencil the track of the feather edge from the upper surface.

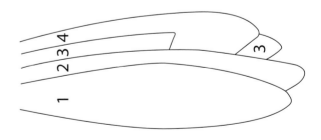

Feather displacement of right wing, ventral view.

Tip 🖉

Remember that if you have overlapped the feather on the upper surface, the pattern has to carry through to the lower surface. This can be confusing, so to avoid errors I cut four primary feathers, roughly the same size as those of the carving, cut the split in feather three, and joined them together to find the pattern on the lower side of the wing.

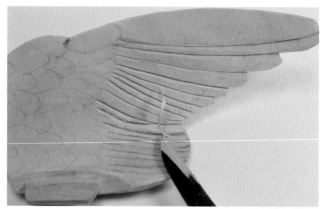

62 Define the primaries and secondaries with the carving knife as you did for the upper surface. Carve the tips of the feathers to make them appear to overlap. The coverts do not need defining with the knife. These are softer feathers and will be defined during the texturing stage.

63 Use 240-grit in the split mandrel to sand and round over the feathers.

64 Repeat so that both wings have feathers defined on ventral and dorsal surfaces.

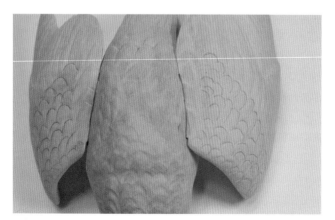

65 Reattach the wings to the body. Do not glue. Ensure their correct alignment, then draw the scapular feathers and shape with the carving knife. This will establish the position of the feathers and will help when it comes to finishing the joints.

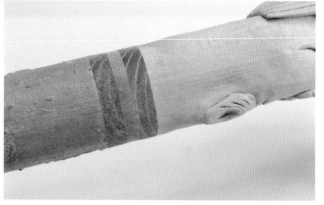

66 Temporarily attach the body to the shank. Do not glue. Finish the joint between body, spacers, and shank with 240-grit sandpaper on the cushioned drum and finally sand by hand with 320-grit abrasive. Remove the body and place the shank to one side.

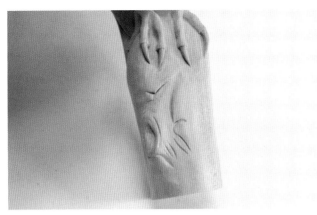

67 Put any detail you wish on what will be the branch. I have carved a couple of branch collars with the knife. Make sure that while doing this you do not touch the bottom of the section that will join the spacers. The branch doesn't have to be sanded smooth.

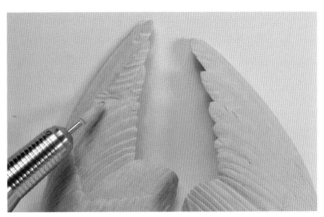

68 Use the scalpel to apply a couple of splits to the primary feathers. Using a round-nose, blue ceramic stone, place a couple of waves in the trailing edge of the displaced feather and the trailing edges of the first couple of primaries. Before doing this, either visualize where the shafts will be placed or pencil them in. The splits and waves will go no further than the edges of the shafts.

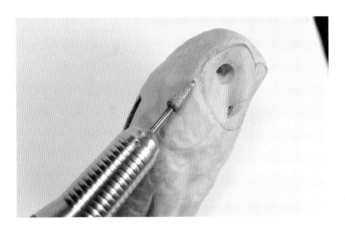

69 Redraw the facial disc if it has rubbed out. Pencil a line approximately ¹⁄₁₆" (1.5mm) on the outside of it. This narrow strip will be feathered and textured later. To make it stand out more, define by lightly running a round-nose taper around the outside of this new line. Sand with the split mandrel and 240-grit sandpaper.

TEXTURING

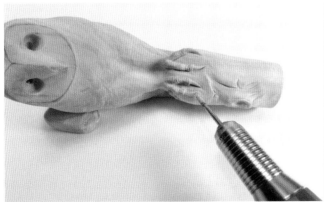

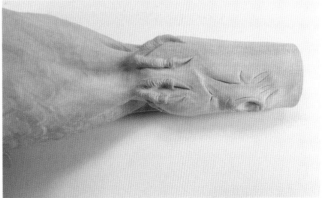

70 Use a ¹⁄₁₆" (1.5mm) cylinder, blue ceramic stone to add scales to the toes.

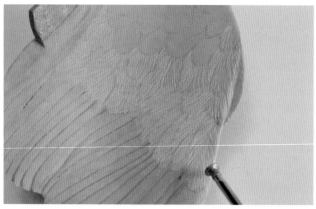

71 Relieve the ventral faces of the alula feathers of both wings with a knife, then sand.

Redraw the covert feathers of the underside of the wings if they have been erased. Define using a ⅛" (3mm) diamond disc. This will create slightly thicker texturing than the blue stones. Just follow the shapes of the feathers. Use forward and backward "C" strokes and change their direction to add interest.

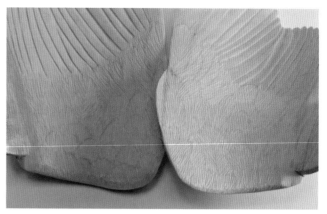

72 Repeat so that both wings have underside coverts textured.

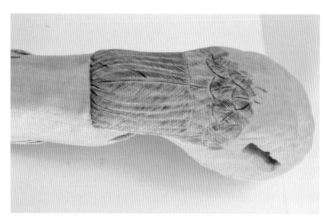

73 Use a pyrograph unit with a rounded skew tip to draw the shafts of the tail feathers, the upper tail coverts, and the lifted feathers of the rump. Undercut the later feathers with the tip, then texture them and the tail with the rounded skew tip.

74 Use the ¹⁄₁₆" (1.5mm) blue cylinder stone to start the texturing of the owl's body. Start adjacent to the lifted feathers of the rump, work toward the head, and overlap the feather below. This photo shows the fuzzing that happens when using a stone on basswood/lime, but most can be removed later. When texturing starts to fuzz, try texturing in a different direction, as this can reduce the effect.

DID YOU KNOW?

The flight of a barn owl is almost silent. The swooshing heard when other owls fly is due to the airflow over their wings. The barn owl has large wings and a small body—its body weight is comparable to that of a pigeon. This creates more lift, resulting in an effortless and graceful flight. There are other factors that are believed to help eliminate any noise during flight. These include hooklike serrations on the leading edge of the 10th primary feather, which breaks up and reduces the air flowing over the owl's wing. The dorsal surface of the feathers has a velvetlike appearance with a fringe at its edge, which allows more air to flow upward and through the wing. Any residue noise is absorbed by the fluffy down on its legs and wings.

75 Texture the front with the same stone, starting with the toes and legs. Don't encroach on the facial disc.

76 Draw the remainder of the feathers around the facial disc and texture.

77 Apply a second layer of texture to the whole of the body. I used the pyrograph with a rounded skew tip, but you can use the blue ceramic stone. Keep the setting of the pyrograph low.

> In addition to the added depth a second layer of texturing gives, it should also be used to cover any gaps remaining from the first layering. A third layer of texturing can be applied if you wish. Remember to texture the underside of the outer tail feathers that can be seen—if you can reach them.

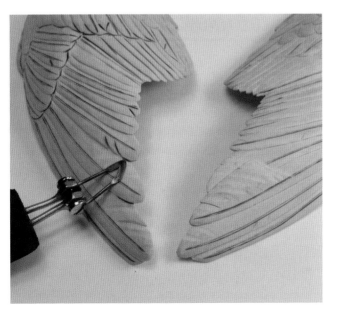

78 Use the same tip on the pyrograph to lay out the shafts of the feathers on the dorsal surface of the wings. Some feathers might be tucked under others and you will not see the full length of the shaft. Where a part of the shaft would ordinarily be seen, add this to break up the pattern. Use the tip to tidy up any feather edges if necessary.

79 Change to a pointed skew tip and detail the barbs of the coverts, secondary feathers, and alula of the dorsal surfaces of the wings. Do not texture the lesser coverts.

80 Finish the upper surfaces of the wings by texturing the primary feathers with the pointed skew tip.

81 Use the ¹⁄₁₆" (1.5mm) cylinder blue stone to texture the lesser coverts of the upper surfaces of the wings. Do not texture the auricular feathers yet.

82 Repeat so that both wings have their upper surface textured.

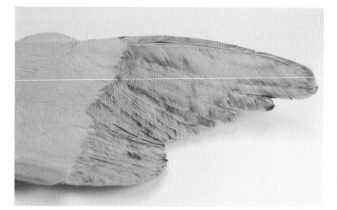

83 Use the pyrograph to detail all of the remaining feathers of the ventral surface of both wings. When finished, add a second layer of texture by lightly texturing with the blue stone to ensure no gaps and to overlap and tie in the pyrographed feathers. Carry out this same procedure for the dorsal surface of both wings. All feathers are now complete, with the exception of the scapulars.

DID YOU KNOW?

Some nocturnal species of owls, such as the barn owl or the boreal owl, have asymmetrically set ear openings. (The left ear opening and the earflap are located higher on the head than those on the right side.) The facial disc of these owls has a feather arrangement that gathers sound waves and funnels them toward the ear openings—similar to how a radar dish works. To further enhance this process, the owl can use its facial muscles to alter the shape of the disc. Even the flaps that cover the ears are oriented differently to accentuate this process. The time difference and intensity of the sound reaching each ear enables the owl to pinpoint the position, elevation, and direction of the noise.

84 Texture edge of facial disc.

85 Use the blue stone to texture the face, following the flow drawn.

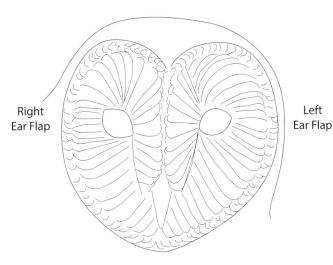

Right
Ear Flap

Left
Ear Flap

Facial feather flow of a mantling barn owl.

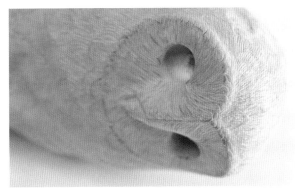

86 This step is optional. The very small feathers on the extremities of the facial disc are in fact the tips of several layers of the feathers that run across the face. An impression of these can be achieved by using the smallest U-tool you have. I am using a ⅛" (3mm). Very carefully, use the tool to cut into the edge of the facial disc to create these feather tips. Try to create the impression of at least a couple of rows.

It may help to practice on a piece of scrap wood first to test how far you can insert the tool before the chip breaks away, as this is something you do not want to happen. When these have been defined, strengthen them by carefully applying superglue with a toothpick. Aim to have a touch of glue fall to the point where it may break away. Obviously, these will be very delicate and the reason they are left to last.

87 Use two-part epoxy putty to set the eyes.

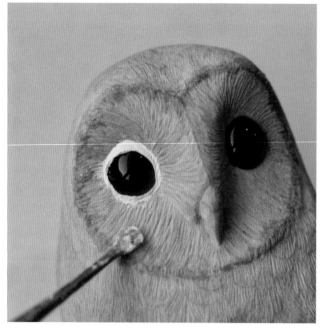

88 Roll a thin worm of putty for the eyelid and eye ring. Press the eye ring into place with a dental tool and remove any excess. Use the excess on the upper part of the eye to create the eyelid. Texture the eye ring and the edge of the eyelid with a scalpel blade.

89 Apply two coats of sanding sealer to all pieces. When dry, use epoxy glue to fix the wings to the body of the owl.

90 Cover the joint between wings and body with a layer of epoxy putty.

91 Sand with 240-grit sandpaper on the split mandrel when the putty has dried, then define the feathers with a safe-end, truncated-cone diamond bit. Sand the edges with 240-grit sandpaper.

92 Use the blue stone to add the shaft and texture. Carving of the owl is finished.

PAINTING

Before starting to paint, ensure that you brush and wipe down the owl with something like mineral spirits on a lint-free cloth to remove any last traces of dust.

The color of the barn owl can vary from almost white to almost black. The male is generally paler than the female. Where I live in Lincolnshire, there are plenty of barn owls and these are pale in color. Consequently, this is how I will be painting this owl. Obviously you will paint yours with regard to the reference material you are using. If you wish to make yours darker, just increase the value of the paints I have used. Remember that you can always increase the intensity of the colors, but it is more troublesome to lighten them if you have started with too dark a value.

93 With a mixture of titanium white and buff titanium, apply three base coats to the whole carving.

94 Add more titanium white to this mixture to make off-white. Apply to the underside of the wings, the abdomen, legs, top of tail, and facial disc, but not the bill. To the original mixture add yellow ochre and apply to the upper surface of the wings, the crown of the head, and the chest.

95 Make a mixture of buff titanium, quinacridone gold, and dioxazine purple. Apply random flecks to the underside of the body. Add a touch of raw umber to this mixture and add the bars on the under surface of the primaries and secondaries. These bars can sometimes be seen on all primaries and secondaries but are often only seen on the first four primaries, as I have painted. Paint the toes with the original mixture plus titanium white.

96 Use zinc white on the facial disc but not the bill; on the upper surface of the tail and what can be seen of the lower surface; and on the toes to tone them down. Apply to the inside vanes of the primaries and secondaries of the upper surface of the wings. Add a touch to the inside vanes of the alula feathers and a touch on the top edge of the wings and the top joint where the wings attach to the body.

97 Use a mixture of buff titanium, quinacridone gold, and dioxazine purple to add random shadows to the back of the head, the tertials, wing coverts, bottom edges of primary coverts, outside vane of the alula feathers, and the back down to the lifted feathers.

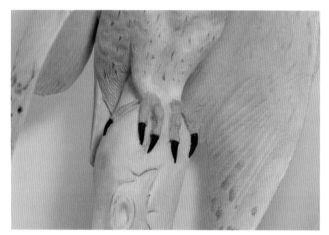

99 Darken the mixture of raw umber and burnt umber with a touch of lamp black to make a rich brown. Use this to go over the markings on the top surface of the primaries, secondaries, and tail. Add a touch more black and paint the talons.

Use a weak wash of zinc white to go over that part of the bar markings of the primaries and secondaries that encroach onto the outside vane. Use this wash to paint over all areas that were previously stippled with brown. Then stipple back over the same parts with the rich brown. This will build up depth to your painting.

Apply some random highlights with a mixture of raw sienna and burnt sienna to the outside vanes of the primaries, secondaries, primary coverts, secondary coverts, lesser coverts, median coverts, and alula. Add random lighter and darker patches by adding either zinc white or quinacridone gold to the original mixture.

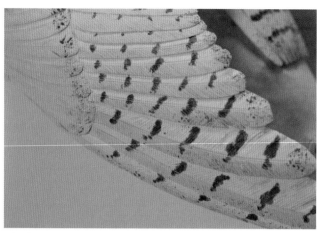

98 Use an undiluted mixture of the brown to stipple the fine pattern of dots onto the tips and outside edges of the primaries, secondaries, the inside vane of the alula, and the bottom section of the tail.

Use a weak wash of buff titanium, quinacridone gold, and dioxazine purple to add a shadow effect in the hollows of the ripples carved on the primary feathers. Add the markings to the upper surface of the primaries, secondaries, and tail using a mixture of raw umber, burnt umber, and zinc white. These markings are mainly on the inside vane but do encroach onto the outer vane. The first primary feathers often have five bars of these markings and the remaining feathers have four.

100 Paint the inside edges of some of the primary coverts, secondary coverts, and some random patches of the median and lesser coverts with zinc white. Use the white to add a few random flecks through the back of the head and the cape. Also, pull brushstrokes of zinc white from the leading edges of the wings onto the marginal coverts along the section from where the wing attaches to the body up to the alula feathers.

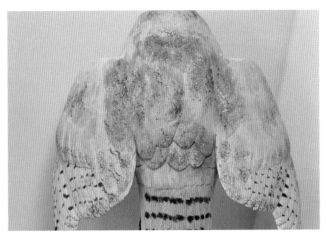

101 Using a mixture of burnt umber, raw umber, and zinc white, stipple over the areas highlighted in the previous step. When dry, stipple over the same areas again with zinc white. This procedure can be applied several times until you achieve the desired effect.

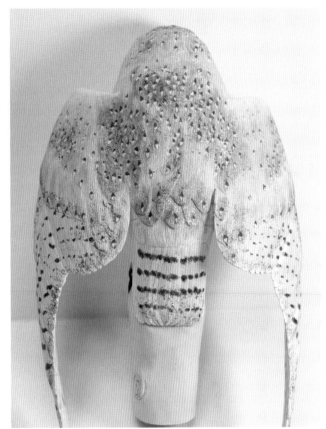

103 For the face, use a combination of both burnt sienna and raw sienna to add color randomly to the ruff. Follow this with other random patches of both buff titanium and titanium white. Paint the bottom row of the bottom edge of the ruff below the bill with burnt umber. If you have cut the feathers with the U-tool, try to pick out the individual feathers with the different colors.

102 The markings on the tips of some feathers are shaped like squashed kites. Paint these over the body and head where the golden patches were applied, as this is where these markings are more concentrated. They also appear on the tips of the primary and secondary coverts, the lesser and median coverts, and the alula feathers. However, as with the color of the owl, it is your choice as to where and how many of these markings you add. For the top half of the kite, use titanium white with a hint of buff titanium. Use raw umber and buff titanium for the lower section. The white half is encased in a thin layer of brown. Add this to some of the prominent markings. You will probably need to go over these markings several times until they stand out.

Paint the facial disc with zinc white and a hint of buff titanium mixed in. Use a touch of buff titanium mixed with yellow ochre to add the smudge around the eyes and in front of the eyes down to the start of the bill. Tone this down with a wash of zinc white.

Add a shadow of brown down through the middle of the nose ridge with a wash of a mixture of raw umber and burnt umber.

Use a mixture of buff titanium, quinacridone gold, dioxazine purple, and zinc white for the bill and eyelids. Add a lighter value on the tip of the bill and edges of the eyelids. Use this to add random highlights to the disc.

Add some stray hairs over the upper end of the bill with a titanium white and hint of buff titanium mixture. When I textured the face, I added some lines at the top of the bill for use as these feathers. I painted these individual lines with a liner brush. They are barely visible on this scale.

Remove paint from the eyes.

Tip

For stippling the feather edges, I used the tip of a fan brush, which I lightly dabbed down at a 90-degree angle. For tighter areas, my favorite brush is an old brush, cut to make the end square and the hairs stiffer.

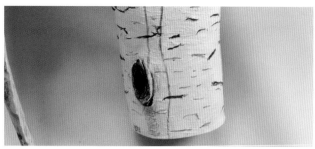

104 Base coat the base with very thick strokes of titanium white. Brush in a horizontal direction. As you do this you will notice that the thick edges that are left are identical to the texture of birch bark.

Next, add some shadows to the upper area of the perch and in between the toes. Use a mixture of cadmium red, cadmium yellow, titanium white, and some black. This should give a rich mossy green color.

Apply a dark gray over the majority of the thick strokes created with the base coat. The bark may also have some vertical lines as if someone has poured something dark down the trunk. Add black to the green mix to add these features. I depressed the wood adjacent to the branch collars, and in nature this would normally be a darkish color. However, when I tried this, I found that the stark blackness dominated the whole carving. For this reason I painted this area with titanium white.

> I painted the branch that the barn owl is perched on as a silver birch. Previously, I have recommended that, when painting a head that is to be added to a shank, leave a section of bare wood to show that it is hand-carved from wood and not a resin copy. Not thinking it would look right for this project, I went against my own recommendation.

Finished owl front view.

Now is the time to check over your painting and tinker with it until satisfied. I added a few shafts using buff titanium, but they are on such a small scale that they were not necessary.

Finally, I used a very weak wash of raw umber to paint over the entire carving. This helps highlight the texturing, especially on the undersides of the wings. I applied several washes to the silver birch perch.

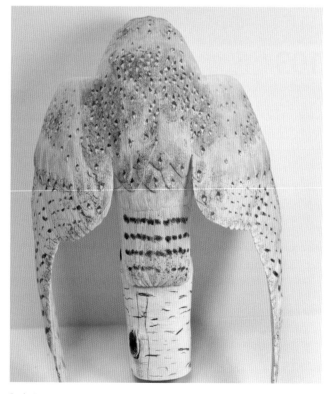

Tip

When painting this owl, it is important that no two feathers are the same in either pattern or color value. This, as equally applies to texturing, would look regimented and unnatural.

Back view.

Right side.

Left side.

Finished walking stick front view.

DID YOU KNOW?

The color of an owl's eyes indicates the time of day they hunt: those with orange eyes are active during twilight (crepuscular); dark brown or black eyes indicate nighttime hunters (nocturnal); and owls with yellow eyes prefer daytime (diurnal).

Back view.

Right side.

Left side.

APPENDIX

Key Fobs from Shank Offcuts

I have mentioned in the sections on seasoning and joining that it is advisable to cut your shanks a couple inches longer than needed as it helps cut away any cracking or splitting at the ends during seasoning.

I never throw away any scrap of wood, for one day it may come in handy. Then I had an idea to put these shank offcuts to good use by turning them into key fobs.

Pick up any spent shotgun cartridges when you are out walking. Alternately, approach the owner of a gun shop or one of your friends and ask them to collect their cartridge cases after a shoot.

Cartridges come in different lengths. In the UK, 2½" (64mm) are common as game cartridges and mainly fit the older guns. Most game and clay cartridges are 2¾" (70mm), and 3" (76mm) cartridges are reserved for high-performance wildfowl shooting. There are also smaller .410-caliber cartridges. Remember that these lengths refer to a cartridge case after it has been fired.

The following steps show how to turn offcuts into key fobs.

1 Use a diamond disc to remove the plastic casing level with the top of the brass case. Then remove the stub of plastic from within the brass case with something like an inverted-cone carbide cutter.

2 Select some of your best-looking shank offcuts.

3 Take your first offcut, cut to the length of a cartridge of your choice, shape, and sand until it fits snuggly inside the brass case.

4 The top can be kept smooth, but it will look better if it is carved to look like the crimping folds of a real cartridge. First, use a carbide cutter to reduce the level of the top by an ⅛" (3mm), but leave a rim around the outside.

5 Then use a combination of diamond bits to cut the five triangular sections of the crimping of the plastic case. Sand with the split-mandrel sander and 240-grit abrasive.

6 Apply a couple coats of finishing oil. Fix the wooden top into the brass case with epoxy glue. When the glue has set, apply some wax. Drill the middle of the top to receive a brass eyelet. Attach a key ring or other clip to the eyelet. This is the finished cartridge key fob.

7 These are some other finished key fobs. They make ideal gifts for friends and family.

PATTERNS

TOP PROFILE

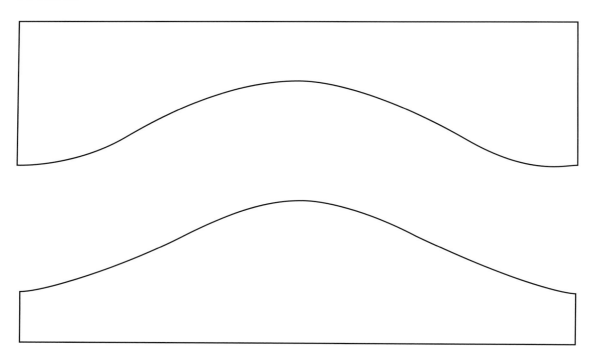

SIDE PROFILE

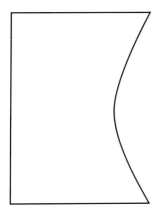

Straightening Jig (page 32)

Carving Creative Walking Sticks and Canes

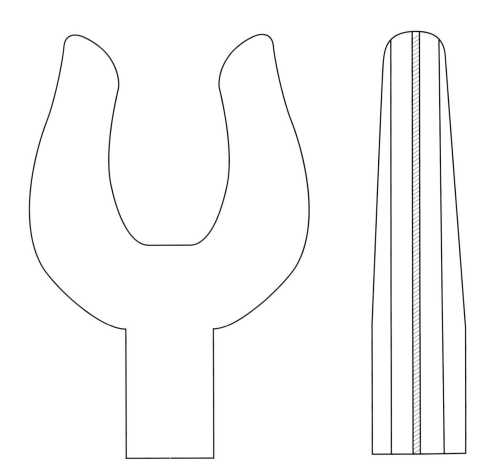

Multi-Wood, Lyre-Shaped Thumb Stick (page 46)

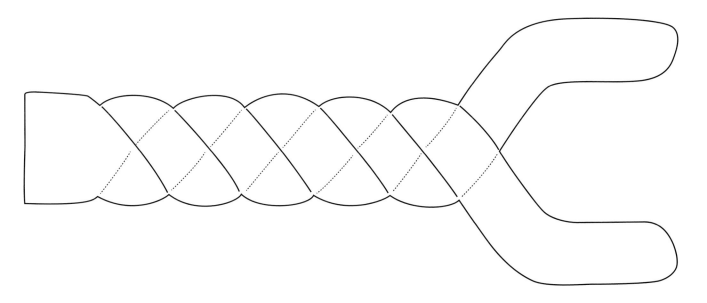

Barley Twist Thumb Stick (page 53)

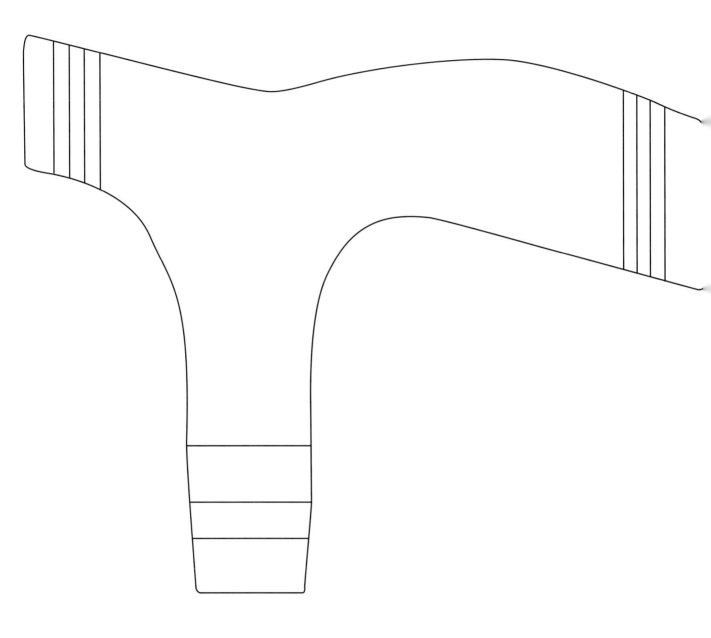

Gentleman's Dress Stick (page 64)

Carving Creative Walking Sticks and Canes

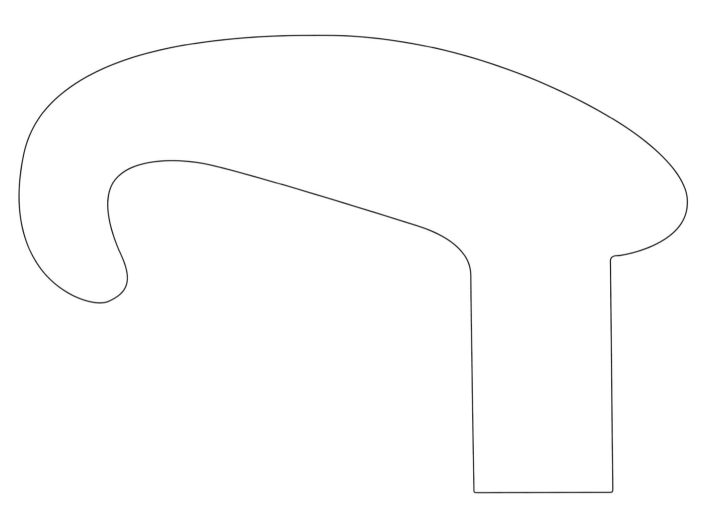

Lady's Half-Crook Walking Stick (page 59)

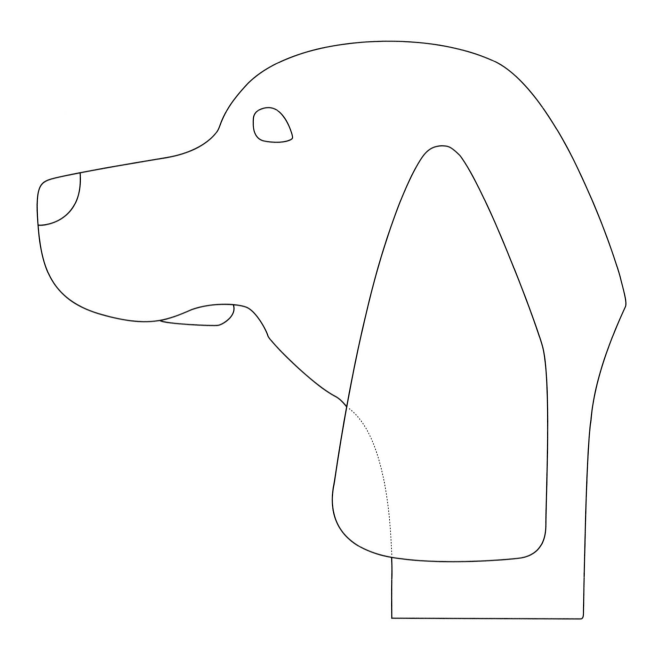

English Cocker Spaniel Head Walking Stick (page 72)

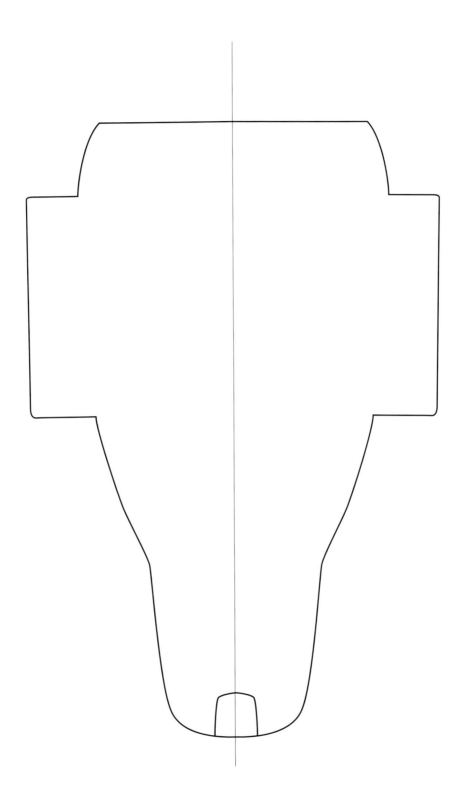

English Cocker Spaniel Head Walking Stick (page 72)

English Cocker Spaniel Head Walking Stick (page 72)

Carving Creative Walking Sticks and Canes

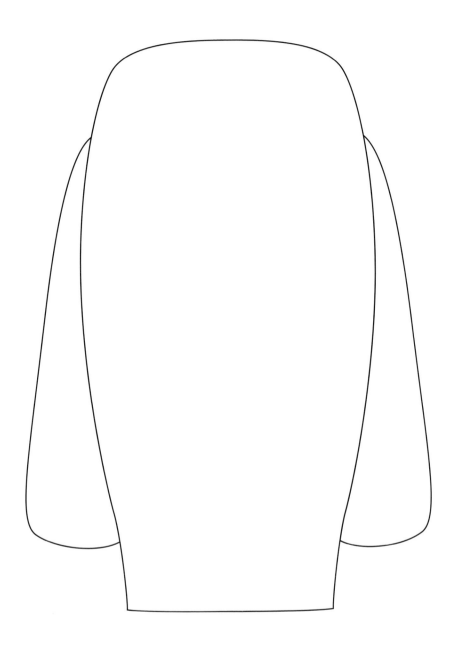

English Cocker Spaniel Head Walking Stick (page 72)

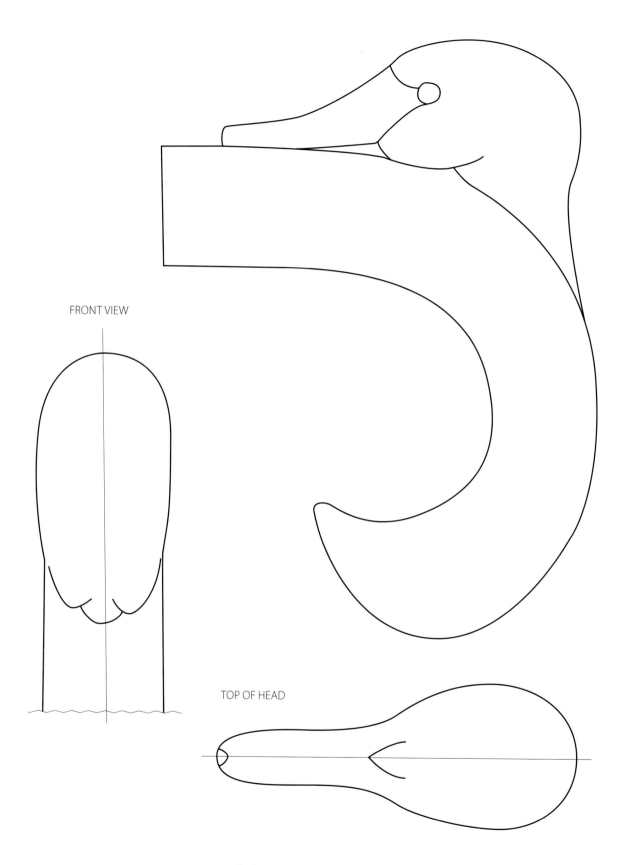

FRONT VIEW

TOP OF HEAD

Black Swan Derby Walking Stick (page 84)

Carving Creative Walking Sticks and Canes

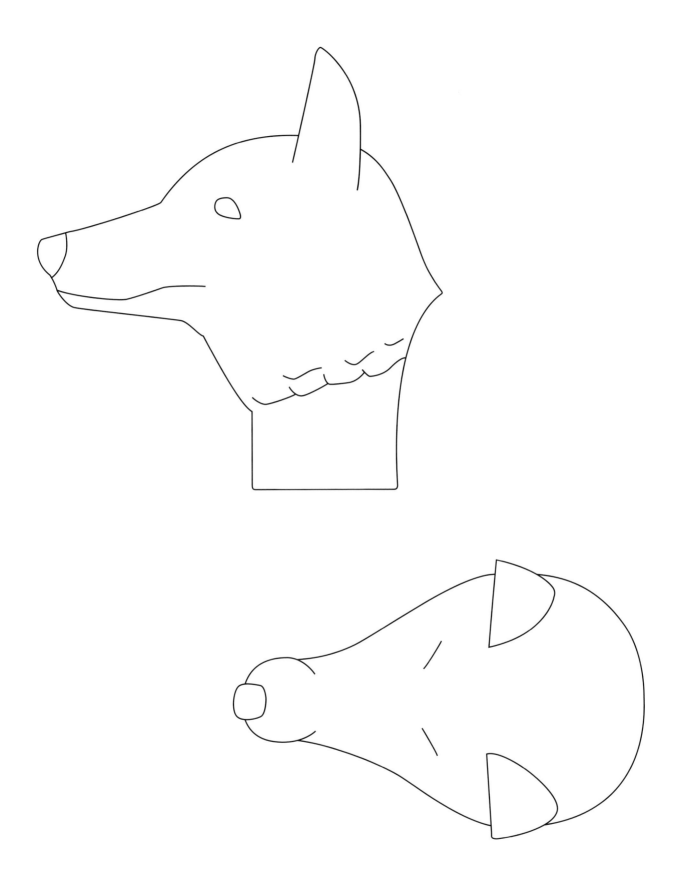

Fox Head Walking Stick (page 96

Golden Eagle Derby Walking Stick (page 110)

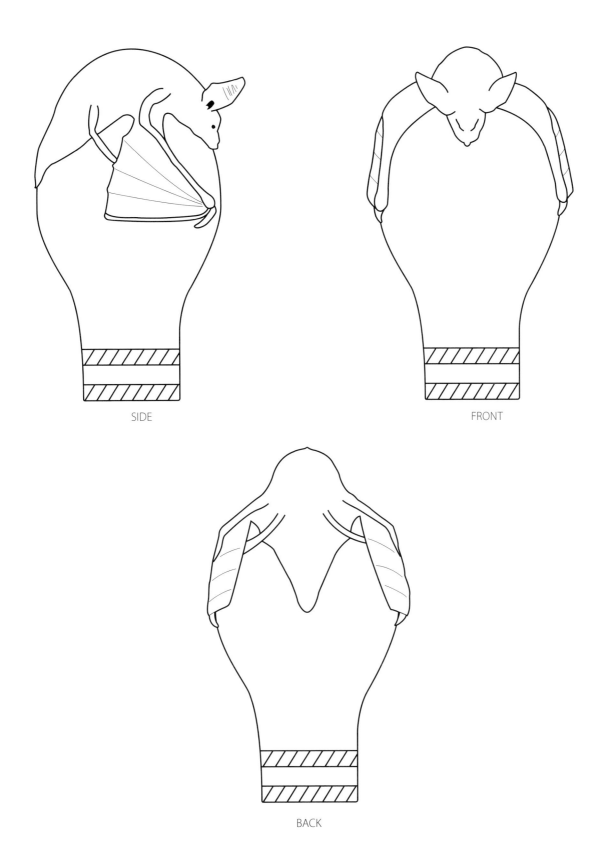

SIDE

FRONT

BACK

Common Pipistrelle Bat Walking Stick (page 124)

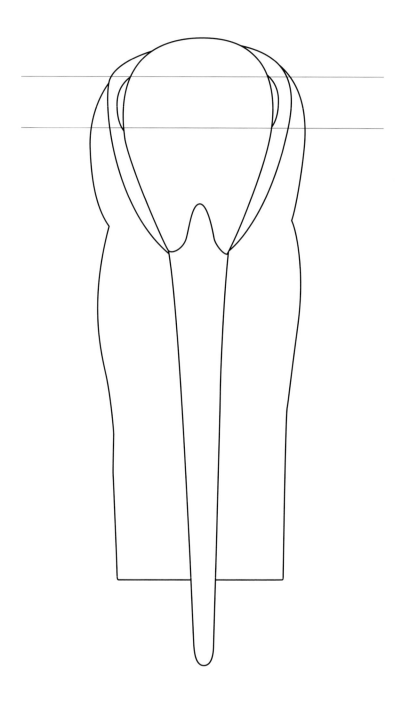

Eurasian Woodcock Walking Stick (page 134)

Carving Creative Walking Sticks and Canes

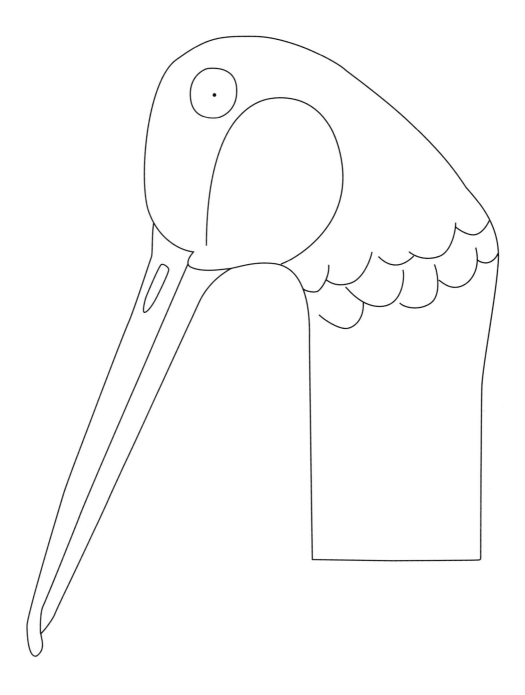

Eurasian Woodcock Walking Stick (page 134)

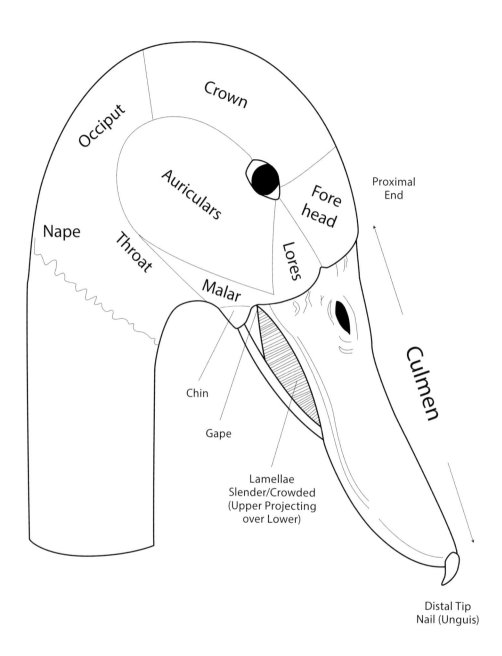

Crown

Occiput

Auriculars

Fore head

Proximal End

Nape

Throat

Lores

Malar

Chin

Gape

Culmen

Lamellae
Slender/Crowded
(Upper Projecting
over Lower)

Distal Tip
Nail (Unguis)

One-Piece Northern Shoveler Hen Walking Stick (page 148)

Carving Creative Walking Sticks and Canes

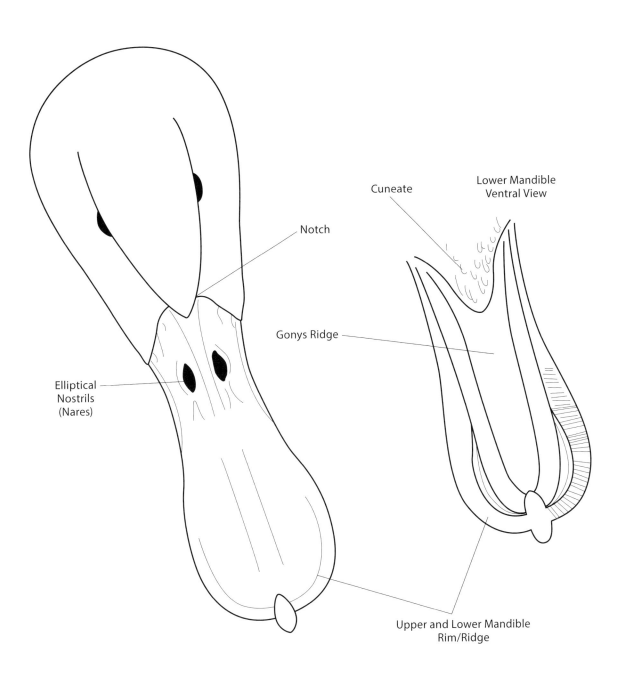

Notch

Cuneate

Lower Mandible
Ventral View

Gonys Ridge

Elliptical
Nostrils
(Nares)

Upper and Lower Mandible
Rim/Ridge

One-Piece Northern Shoveler Hen Walking Stick (page 148)

Yellow Labrador & Mallard Walking Stick (page 160)

Carving Creative Walking Sticks and Canes

Mantling Barn Owl Walking Stick (page 188)

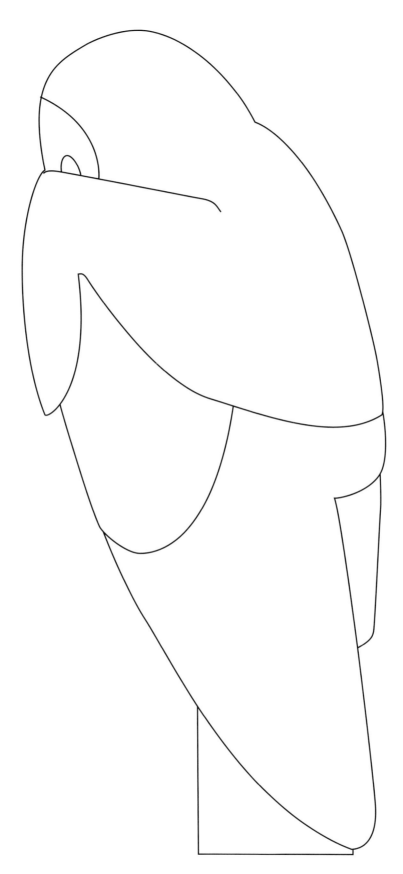

Mantling Barn Owl Walking Stick (page 188)

Carving Creative Walking Sticks and Canes

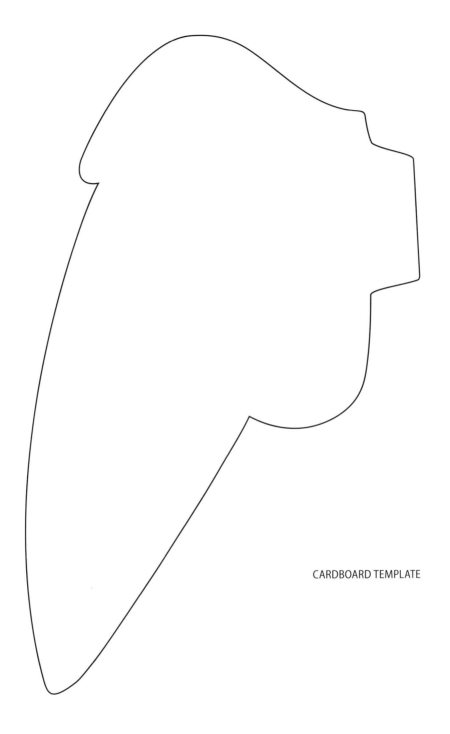

CARDBOARD TEMPLATE

Mantling Barn Owl Walking Stick (page 188)

INDEX

Note: Page numbers in *italics* indicate projects and patterns.

PHOTO CREDITS

All photos are by the author except for the following: page 6 (inset) courtesy Tuff Saws UK; pages 7 (left), 8 (left top, left bottom, middle bottom, right), 10 (Creamcut stones and Ruby-coated bits), and 11 (bottom left) courtesy Foredom; page 9 (top) courtesy Saburrtooth; page 13 (Scale-making tip) courtesy Razertip; page 14 (bottom left) YolLusZam1802/shutterstock; page 14 (bottom middle left) Stock Up/shutterstock; page 14 (bottom middle right) Oleksandr Grechin/shutterstock; page 14 (bottom right) Sergiy1975/shutterstock; page 15 (right) photopia90/shutterstock.

MESSAGE FROM THE AUTHOR

Working long hours as a police detective for thirty years didn't afford me much time for hobbies. I enjoyed DIY projects and making wooden toys and games for my children and grandchildren. One Christmas, I cut the bottom twelve inches from our tree before recycling. With some flat chisels (primarily used for opening paint cans), a cheap rasp, and some sandpaper, I carved a penguin—well, that was my intention. How I ever managed to turn a round piece of pine wood into a square penguin, I'll never know! Nevertheless, I was hooked.

I made a trip to a woodworking supplier intent on buying the largest set of carving gouges for the cheapest price. I was advised by the proprietor not to splash out on a cheap set of gouges, but instead spend all of the money I had on one quality tool. I took his advice and bought my first Ashley Isles gouge. Each month on payday, I returned to the store and bought another gouge until I had a decent set. Whenever possible, I have continued to abide by that invaluable advice when adding to my carving equipment.

When I retired, around fifteen years ago, I started carving on a regular basis—mainly small birds and animals for family and friends. I taught myself by reading books from the master carvers of the United States. I loved the learning process and pushing my own boundaries a little further each time I carved.

I began selling my carvings at county shows in the UK. During one show, I was approached by a committee member of the Royal Society for the Protection of Birds, RSPB, who asked if I wished to join them as their "front man." I had a table of my carvings at the front of their marquee at large shows; when the public stopped to talk with me about my carvings, the RSPB committee would slip a direct debit for membership in their handbag or back pocket!

As a result of continued contact with the RSPB, and having the opportunity to visit their stunning nature reserves in Lincolnshire, I focused on carving birds—especially owls and other birds of prey. Over the years, I have tried many forms of carving, from netsuke through to rocking horses. I discovered that I preferred the detailed aspects of carving, especially feathering and texturing of birds and other wildlife.

At a county show, I was approached by the owner of my local gun shop, who asked if I made walking sticks. I didn't, but the question piqued my interest. I subsequently set about learning another woodworking skill. Essentially, making a walking stick is no more than a small carving attached to a shank.

I now make a range of walking sticks, from the basic—but practical—for game shooters through to those with decorative heads for stick collectors. I sell these at my local gun shop, together with an assortment of other carvings of wildfowl, birds, and animals.

I have contributed projects and other articles to *Wood Carving* and *Woodworking Crafts* magazines in the UK and *Woodcarving Illustrated* in the US.

I live in the beautiful village of Woodhall Spa, Lincolnshire, UK, with my wife and three dogs, who are very obliging for reference material—the dogs, not my wife! Although, I did carve a mermaid once . . .

Since my first involvement with making walking sticks, I have seen it become a very popular hobby. This is no surprise to me, as traipsing around the countryside in search of a good shank—maybe a "twisty" or a block-stick—brings immense enjoyment, as does turning one into a practical or decorative stick of your own design, once seasoned.

You have the choice as to whether your stick will be kept simple or made complex. In its simplest form, the shank, whether it be straight, twisted, or bent, can be cleaned and finished with oil. Its bark could be stripped and the shank possibly decorated with a pyrograph unit, or it could have patterns carved along its length with a knife or basic carving tools.

Once you have mastered the art of joining a head to a shank, the possible combinations of shank and head are limited only by your imagination. These can range from carving a simple "Y" thumb stick with the handle made from wood, antler, or horn or carving and painting decorative heads of animals, birds, etc.

I have intended for the projects in this book to take you on a progression from making a simple thumb stick in wood through to a couple of highly detailed and decorative walking stick heads. Plans are included which you can follow or adapt to your own design.

I hope you enjoyed the journey.

More Great Books from Fox Chapel Publishing

Cane Topper Woodcarving
Projects, Patterns, and Essential Techniques for Custom Canes and Walking Sticks
LORA S. IRISH
Paperback • 176 pages • 8" x 10"
978-1-56523-959-3 • #9593 • $19.99

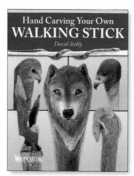

Hand Carving Your Own Walking Stick
An Art Form
DAVID STEHLY
Paperback • 72 pages • 8.5" x 11"
978-1-56523-897-8 • #8978 • $14.99

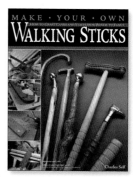

Make Your Own Walking Sticks
How to Craft Canes and Staffs from Rustic to Fancy
CHARLES SELF
Paperback • 152 pages • 8.5" x 11"
978-1-56523-320-1 • #3201 • $19.95

The Complete Book of Woodworking
TOM CARPENTER, MARK JOHANSON
Paperback • 480 pages • 8.25" x 11"
978-0-980068-87-0 • #70C • $29.95

Fantastic Book of Canes, Pipes, and Walking Sticks, 3rd Edition
A Sketchbook of Designs for Collectors, Woodcarvers, and Artists
HARRY AMEREDES
Paperback • 136 pages • 6" x 9"
978-1-56523-515-1 • #5151 • $14.95

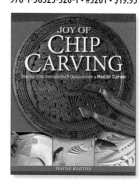

Joy of Chip Carving
Step-by-Step Instructions & Designs from a Master Carver
WAYNE BARTON
Paperback • 152 pages • 8" x 10"
978-1-4971-0056-5 • #00565 • $24.99

Complete Starter Guide to Whittling
24 Easy Projects You Can Make in a Weekend
EDITORS OF WOODCARVING ILLUSTRATED
Paperback • 96 pages • 7.5" x 9"
978-1-56523-842-8 • #8428 • $12.99

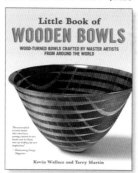

Little Book of Wooden Bowls
Wood-Turned Bowls Crafted by Master Artists from Around the World
KEVIN WALLACE, TERRY MARTIN
Paperback • 192 pages • 5.75" x 7"
978-1-56523-997-5 • #9975 • $12.99

20-Minute Whittling Projects
Fun Things to Carve from Wood
TOM HINDES
Paperback • 96 pages • 6" x 9"
978-1-56523-867-1 • #8671 • $12.99